Contents

C000181651

Preface

This book is born of a desire by the Coastal Communities Alliance (CCA) to maintain and extend the national debate on how to address the complex social and economic problems that are associated with English coastal resorts. As such, it is very much *work in progress*, and the debates that are generated here will be continued on the CCA website to create a resource for organisations concerned about the future of England's seaside resorts.

The publication has been made possible by the financial support of national and regional organisations involved in varying aspects of coastal resort regeneration. These include the Department for Communities and Local Government, the Improvement and Development Agency, the LGA Coastal Special Interest Group, and the South East, East and East Midlands Regional Development Agencies.

The small budget that the CCA garnered, combined with the intrinsic interest and value of the project, was sufficient to secure the services of Professor John K. Walton, formerly of Leeds Metropolitan University and now beginning a new academic life as IKERBASQUE Research Professor in the Department of Contemporary History at the University of the Basque Country in Bilbao. John's contribution has gone way beyond his modest retainer and his four chapters to embrace a co-editing role, which gave practical weight to his love, knowledge and enthusiasm for some of the most evocative settlements in England.

While the organisational generosity provided the financial mortar for the book, the bricks of words were, in the main, provided free of charge by a range of authors from around the country. The CCA wishes to acknowledge our deep gratitude to: Jane Atherton, Newcastle University; Leigh Sear and Jo Lee, WoodHolmeGroup; Fred Gray, Sussex University; Chris Bamber, GONW; Lesa Dryburgh, Clore Fellow, Ivan Annibal, Lincolnshire County Council; Stephen Hayler, Canterbury Christ Church University; David Powell, DPA; Ben Cave Associates Ltd., and the Centre for Tourism and Cultural Change, Leeds Metropolitan University.

We are also indebted to the many local authorities, coastal MPs and coastal networks and organisations that have provided articles and responded to our various questionnaires and requests for follow-up information.

The Coastal Communities Alliance would finally wish to acknowledge the contribution of Lincolnshire County Council, particularly the staff time of Nicola Precious and for housing Jessica Ireland, an admirable graduate intern during 2009.

John Walton would like to conclude this preface by emphasizing the indispensable nature of Patrick Browne's contribution to this project. Without his enthusiasm, commitment and expertise it is hard to imagine it having got off the ground or arriving at this tangible and, we hope, successful birth.

Patrick Browne, John Walton
Lincoln and Lancaster,
11 January 2010

Foreword

Britain's coastline is rightly and widely celebrated as one of our national treasures. From steep cliffs to flat salt marshes; from sandy beaches to rugged rocks; from fishing villages to bracing resorts and bustling ports – the images of our coastal regions are a fundamental part of our identity as an island nation. Yet, as well as distinctive physical features and landscapes (which themselves bring unique problems), Britain's coastal towns and communities also share particular socioeconomic characteristics and concerns, characteristics that are typically quite different from those of inland communities.

In 2007, the Communities and Local Government Select Committee, which I chair, launched an inquiry into coastal towns. We concluded that many coastal towns share common factors including physical isolation, significant levels of deprivation and transience, and low-waged, low-skilled, seasonally dependent economies. As older – and in some cases vulnerable – people move in, young people tend to leave. There is a lack of affordable, suitable housing, with large former hotels and guest houses often converted for multiple occupancy. All these problems are exacerbated by the declining and seasonal nature of the coastal economy. None of these characteristics is unique to coastal towns; but the combination of them, together with the particular environmental challenges, led us to conclude that these communities face significant and specific challenges that warrant government action.

The committee was very disappointed with the government's initial response to our report because it failed to recognise this need for specific measures for coastal communities. I wrote to the Secretary of State, asking for a second, more considered response and that second response in October 2007 was much more positive. It accepted many of our recommendations, including the establishment of a cross-departmental working group and a coastal areas network of Regional Development Agencies.

However, an inadvertent but positive additional outcome of the initial response was that, because of the level of dissatisfaction amongst various concerned organisations and groups, they independently formed the Coastal Communities Alliance, which has published this book. My fellow committee members and I welcome the formation of this Alliance, which is open to all coastal local authorities in the UK and to any public or private sector organisation with an interest in coastal communities. It focuses on socioeconomic and regeneration issues, and works with the government's working group and the RDAs network without duplicating the core services they provide.

This authoritative handbook is just one example of the contributions that the CCA has made, providing as it does a toolkit for coastal regeneration practitioners. It encourages new approaches to address long standing problems of deprivation, shares knowledge and best practice, and outlines who is doing what in coastal regeneration.

I wish the Coastal Communities Alliance and all those working towards coastal regeneration every success in their efforts to revitalise these valuable communities.

Dr Phyllis Starkey, MP
Chair, Communities and Local Government Committee

Introduction by John K. Walton

This Handbook responds to the growing awareness at the beginning of the twenty-first century that British seaside towns, and especially the seaside tourism industry, are in difficulties. Those difficulties, though real, are not as severe as they are often painted, and are far from being terminal.

There is scope for positive intervention by all levels of government in seaside economies, societies and environments; and there is every reason to provide and support such intervention. This will not be easy, because local and regional experiences are many and various (though strong shared themes are apparent, setting the seaside apart as a 'special case'), and because the nature of their geography and of shapes and structures of local government makes it more difficult to 'see' and analyse the nature of the problems. There are

also diverse and sometimes contradictory proposals for solutions, especially where the contested terrain of 'regeneration' is at issue. And there is a continuing need to convince central government of the need to develop a national policy framework for coastal towns, and to recognise the distinctive nature of the problems they present.

What follows is intended as a map to guide practitioners through this minefield, while offering them suggestions about ways forward, best practice and encouraging a broad outlook and joined-up thinking. We need to avoid silo mentalities, whether they are thematic (looking at particular issues in isolated depth) or administrative (looking at one's own district in isolation, or rejecting evidence and experience because it comes from outside an established framework of expectation). We begin by elucidating the issues and laying

out the groundwork.

A new optimism about the state of British seaside resorts was becoming apparent at the start of the school summer holidays in 2009. A full-page feature in the *Guardian* on 18 July captured the tone, referring to a new pattern of 'staycation' holidays and to the British seaside as the 'Costa Fraction'. Good early summer weather, the fall of the pound against the euro, evidence of buoyant seasonal employment in resorts (at least in parts of the south and south-west), and indications that 'towns that have spent cash on making themselves better able to compete with European destinations seem to be thriving', were strung together to produce an optimistic interpretation. It was qualified by suggestions that 'people are downsizing from the middle', creating problems in the upper and middle levels of the holiday industry, while heavy demand for pasties in Cornwall was thought to reflect a preference for cheaper picnics over restaurant meals. But that was a remarkably up-beat presentation of the prospects for the new season, reflecting a widespread perception that the recession marked an opportunity for traditional British holiday locations to compete effectively with Mediterranean and long-haul destinations. An imagined 'Europe', sophisticated and modern, was clearly being used as the key comparator and experience to aspire to. As journalist Helen Carter put it, 'British seaside towns are enjoying a renaissance not seen for decades as the credit crunch bites and staycations become appealing'.[1] By mid-August another full-page feature confirmed a decline in overseas package tours, and especially British visits to North America, as Peter Walker claimed that 'the British tourist industry's fervent hope has come to pass – that a combination of the recession and the feeble pound would see millions of families abandoning their villa on the Algarve for a ... cost-conscious domestic alternative'.[2] Nor were these the first journalistic offerings to detect or anticipate an upturn: in April, Laura Barton found a 'sense of resilience' in Skegness, recently named as 'the country's most traditionally British town, where Britishness is measured in tearooms, cricket clubs, pubs, chip shops, holiday camps, stately homes and theatres' – perhaps this should be Englishness. Admittedly, she spoke of Skegness as one of 'a cluster of fading seaside resorts', and thought it was near Scarborough, while referring to 'regeneration' in

terms of a £140,000 project to provide new flowerbeds and picnic benches: not exactly the stuff of social transformation. She also referred to recession 'forcing' the British 'to return to our seaside resorts'.[3] Already in September 2007, Allan Brodie of English Heritage, interviewed by Mary O'Hara, was passing on his awareness that change was not the same thing as inexorable decline, that resorts had diverse characteristics as well as common problems, and that there was plenty of scope for encouraging revival, even at that favourite symbol of seaside economic collapse, Margate.[4] All commentaries on tourism in Britain, however, whether at the seaside or elsewhere, highlight one universal problem when Britain is compared with rival destinations: the weather.[5] With all its unease and equivocation, this frame of mind was in striking contrast to the default media position on the British seaside that had evolved over the previous forty years and more (it was already evident a decade earlier in films like The Entertainer, The Punch and Judy Man and the Cliff Richard vehicle Summer Holiday). This was almost unremittingly negative, especially with regard to the old provincial popular resorts that suffered particularly from the 1970s onwards

from changing patterns of holidaymaking and the decline of old mining and manufacturing industries, together with their long-established town holidays associated with 'wakes', 'fairs' and 'tides'.[6]

Negative media assumptions and stereotypes about coastal resorts are particularly important in the light of current governmental sensitivities to media perceptions and coverage. They are palliated but not overcome by occasional positive coverage in colour supplements, by the early twenty-first century fashion for beach huts, and by the emergence of up-market outlets such as Coast magazine. The highly successful Coast TV series has, significantly, given relatively little attention to coastal resorts as such, although a recent programme has included assessments of the current state of Rhyl and Blackpool.[7]

Dominant representations of British seaside resorts in the later twentieth century pulled together a devastating combination of nostalgia and mockery. The 'traditional' seaside holiday was viewed as part of 'all our yesterdays', but therefore of nobody's tomorrows.[8] The British seaside was portrayed as if it were uniformly 'tired' (a label that became as big a cliché as its apparent opposite 'vibrant'), outdated and self-evidently unable to compete with the guaranteed sunshine, packaged exoticism or contemporary fantasy of the various incarnations of 'abroad' – whose inroads into core British holiday markets were assumed to have begun in earnest in the 1960s or even the 1950s as opposed to (as it happened) the later 1970s and early 1980s.[9] It was treated, in fact, as if it were as far beyond resuscitation as the coalfield and manufacturing industries that had also met their end at about the same time.

We know that this has never been the case, although we shall have to reserve judgement on the euphoric response to the early summer of 2009. The weather, and perceptions of it, remains crucial. But the work of Steve Fothergill, Christina Beatty and their colleagues at Sheffield Hallam University on trends in employment, migration flows and social problems at the larger British resorts since 1971 – to which we shall keep returning – has

shown that the picture was never as black as painted.[10] Nor, of course, was it uniform. British seaside towns are of all shapes and most sizes (up to around a third of a million residents, depending on how we define the boundaries of individual settlements, especially in coastal conurbations). They do have in common, of course, that their coastal location gives them a 180-degree (at best) catchment area, (although too much is probably made of this), most of them are peripheral in terms of distance from motorways and they are 'end-of-the-line' destinations.

The role of tourism in local economies varies markedly between coastal settlements, from insignificance to dominance, and attempts to quantify it are complicated by seasonal variations and by complex personal and household economies, which often combine different sources of income from different imagined sectors. This makes it difficult to define a 'resort' (or more broadly a 'seaside town') for practical purposes, which in turn makes the collection and presentation of statistics all the more problematic.

The Sheffield Hallam project recognised the element of subjectivity entailed in

defining a 'seaside town' with substantial tourism elements in its economy, and consulted the British Resorts and Destinations Association in marginal cases. It also noted the problems arising from resort areas being embedded in larger administrative districts, and made use of pre-1974 local government boundaries to focus on the distinguishing features of the coastal districts themselves. We shall return to the problems of defining 'seaside town' and 'seaside resort' in **Chapter 1**.

The 2003 report by Beatty and Fothergill forms the basis for the best studies we have, but it focused only on the 43 largest British or 37 largest English resorts. The threshold figure of 8,000 residents at the spring census of 1971 may seem small, but it excludes scores of smaller seaside settlements. To check on whether this might be distorting, an additional study of 37 seaside places with resident populations of between 1500 and 10,000 was undertaken in 2009; but although the smaller places contained a larger proportion of the elderly, they were otherwise little different from their larger counterparts. The most interesting development, in fact, was the uncovering of very high proportions of incapacity benefit recipients in the little Lincolnshire settlements of Mablethorpe, Chapel St Leonard's and Sutton-on-Sea; and it is tempting to associate this local effect with the area's close relationship with the former coal mining industry of the East Midlands.

In emphasizing coastal employment growth, moreover, Beatty and Fothergill may be glossing over the extent to which a lot of the work on offer has been low-paid and part-time. Their focus on quantifiable economic and demographic indicators provides a basic framework that was previously lacking, and they have performed the essential services of demonstrating that the British seaside remains important, that there is plenty of life in it, and therefore that it is a worthy recipient of policy initiatives. But they are unable to explain apparent anomalies like the curious case of Whitby, which was closely anchored to the bottom of their original performance indicator tables, even as it began to win awards for the quality of its amenities as a particularly attractive resort for weekenders and longer-stay visitors. We shall return to this example.[11]

Clearly there is more to all this than meets the eye: statistics tell only part of the story, qualitative as well as quantitative issues need to be weighed in the balance, and values can be conflicted as well as consensual. Moreover, it is one thing to describe the extent and distribution of the problems of seaside towns; it is another to attempt to prescribe solutions, especially for such a complex array of contrasting cases, each with its own history and identity, but each having significant characteristics in common with all the others.[12] As Beatty and Fothergill point out, the aggregate census population of the British resorts in their 2003 survey amounts to 3.1 million in 2001 (2.9 million in their later work on England). This is more than the whole of Wales, and as many as a small English region such as the North East, or even such a strongly defined 'nation without a state' on the European map as the Basque Country. On this basis alone, coastal towns would merit further examination.

We need then, to discuss ways of building on the 'Fothergill project' in its various incarnations (there have been local studies of particular resorts, and further pieces of research commissioned since 2003, as well as the original report) – noting in passing that, significantly, it started as a by-product of a study of unemployment in former coalfield communities. We need to pass from diagnosis of the current situation and recent trends to the pursuit of solutions, ameliorations and effective innovations. We must move beyond the existing firm, necessary and valuable grounding in economic and demographic indicators to incorporate culture and traditions. But first we need to investigate the context in which official interest in the problems of British seaside towns began to develop with gathering momentum from 2003 onwards, and to introduce the obstacles to that emergent interest being translated into intervention, especially of a joined-up and coordinated kind.

Dissemination of the first findings of the Sheffield Hallam team coincided with the English Heritage report, 'Shifting Sands', which drew attention to seaside heritage and the importance of the architectural and place-centred dimensions of regeneration, and the development from December 2004 of the Coastal Action Zone project, a Lincolnshire County Council initiative which drew support from European rural development funds and the East Midlands Development Agency, and originally focused particularly on the territory of East Lindsey District Council. Significantly, this grew out of issues that were identified as 'rural', and in April 2006 David Lloyd of East Lindsey argued that the existing rural/urban categories in policy formulation needed to be augmented by a third category – 'coastal' – which exhibited generic characteristics and problems that did not fit into existing structures.[13]

Meanwhile, the Select Committee on Coastal Towns for the Office of the Deputy Prime Minister: Housing, Local Government, Planning and the Regions, was set up after sustained prompting from Dr John Pugh, the Liberal Democrat MP for Southport, and reported in March 2007.[14] In the meantime the Coastal Action Zone held a weekend symposium in Skegness, in July 2006, at which a wide range of problems, responses and new approaches was ventilated across a broad front which embraced culture, architecture and the arts, as well as (for example) economic diversification, demographic issues and service delivery.[15] The Select Committee's membership was short on coastal MPs, with the members for Southport, Easington (an old mining constituency

which contained a coal port in process of regeneration) and Plymouth Devonport (a coastal constituency, but unusual in being dominated by a naval dockyard) constituting a small minority of the dozen in attendance. Nevertheless this did not temper the level of interest shown. Dr Phyllis Starkey, MP for the decidedly un-coastal constituency of Milton Keynes South West, proved to be an assertive and well-informed defender of its work.

The committee assembled an extensive array of evidence from coastal locations across England, with an additional input from Holyhead. It concluded that coastal towns, and especially seaside towns with a resort element in their economies, did indeed share a long list of often interconnected problems. These were associated with: peripheral location; poorly articulated transport provision; unemployment and significant seasonal fluctuations in employment (which the Department for Work and Pensions was at first unwilling to acknowledge); migration and population turnover giving rise to 'churn' in schools; high levels of incapacity benefit; high proportions of elderly people in the population; low

educational attainment and limited opportunities for young people; issues arising from the placement of vulnerable adults and children in coastal settings at a long distance from their places of origin; high levels of houses in multiple occupation; teenage pregnancies and other indicators of social instability; and problems of service provision and the recruitment of high-quality professionals and officials. Parts of some resorts scored highly on indices of multiple deprivation, and there were environmental issues around the maintenance and enhancement of coastal defences and the decay of the public realm and built environment. The extent of these problems was often masked by the vulnerable areas forming part of larger local government and other administrative units, which made the 'hot spots' less visible to analysts and policymakers.

The initial response of central government was to kick the report into the long grass, making much of the (valid) point that coastal experiences were diverse and that no 'one size fits all' approach would be appropriate. Using this as an excuse for denying the existence of a generic set of 'coastal' problems, it took refuge in the role of Regional

Development Agencies and in important initiatives like the British Urban Regeneration Association seaside unit, while passively resisting the recommendation that the RDAs might develop a 'coastal' as well as an urban and a rural category for policy analysis. Problems were referred on to local incarnations of national policies, with the remarkable statement that 'cities are where we will achieve social justice and social inclusion, and ... we do not have a coastal towns policy in isolation'. The assertion that 'no coastal town has seen a disproportionate shift in the proportion of people on incapacity benefit in the past 10 years' proved to be a particularly damaging hostage to fortune.[16]

This government response was met with widespread anger, and an unusual degree of parliamentary dissent. One outcome was the establishment of the Coastal Communities Alliance to argue for the recognition of distinctive coastal problems and the development of a coherent coastal strategy. Peter Hampson of the British Resorts and Destinations Association sent a particularly outspoken critique to Dr Starkey, who successfully urged Hazel Blears, the new Secretary of State, to impose a reconsideration of the response.

This led to a second response, issued in November 2007, which displayed a much greater willingness to engage with the issues the Select Committee had raised. It proposed: further research into the reasons for an embarrassing rise in payments for incapacity benefit, disability allowance and income support for disability in coastal towns since the complacent statement in the first response; a cross-departmental working group and coastal area network to provide overviews of coastal conditions and evidence of good practice; and further research from Steve Fothergill, whose reputation in the field was now established in government circles.

Performance was to be classified in three categories on economic, demographic and educational outcomes criteria – 'performing well', 'maintaining', or 'below average'. Particular emphasis was placed on regeneration, and note was taken of successful local projects, while national coordination of regional ventures was to be led by the South East England Development Agency (SEEDA) and to include contributions from the Commission for Architecture and the Built Environment (CABE), English Heritage, the British Resorts and Destinations Association (BRADA), and the seaside unit of the British Urban Regeneration Association (BURA).[17]

It was virtually impossible to cut through the maze of acronyms and initiatives that characterised regeneration policy, but here, it seemed, was some sort of coordinated national approach to urban coastal problems. But it was disturbing, and perhaps indicative, that it

had taken such an assertive reaction to reach even this point. Furthermore, the newly adverse economic climate that set in towards the end of 2008 made it all the more likely that, even as coastal issues began to attract increasing interest, it would be an uphill struggle to pull together the corresponding access to necessary resources, whichever party was in government. Professor Michael Parkinson's report *The Credit Crunch and Regeneration* emphasizes that, although regeneration projects are likely to continue where there is public sector involvement, potential new starts are at risk, and economically marginal projects are particularly unattractive despite the recognised need to sustain long-term initiatives in deprived areas. As elsewhere, direct reference to coastal concerns is conspicuous by its absence in this Department for Communities and Local Government (DCLG) report.[18]

Even so, the new governmental recognition that the problems of seaside towns are shared and generic, despite the wide variations in trajectory and interim outcomes, is an important development, grudging though it might appear, and slow though initial progress might be. It needs to

be seen alongside – indeed as an outcome of – a great deal of energetic and sometimes creative work at local and regional levels, and by non-governmental organisations. Regeneration has been under way, by a range of routes and in a variety of guises, especially at the local level, for much longer than the political debates that are chronicled here, as the evidence collected by the Select Committee (and elsewhere) demonstrates. But it does help to have some degree of national recognition of the existence of a defined set of distinctively coastal problems, which may provide better access to funding, expertise and transferable ideas and experiences.

We now need to build on these developments, and include the architectural research undertaken by English Heritage, which was well expressed in the book on *English Seaside Resorts* launched at the EH Hastings conference on 'Seaside heritage: colourful past, bright future' in October 2007, that followed on from two BURA events on seaside regeneration at Scarborough and Brighton in the spring of that year.[19] Fred Gray's distinguished study of the history of seaside architecture and design had appeared a year earlier.[20]

The first two Waves of the Commission for Architecture and the Built Environment's Sea Change initiative have channelled substantial funding into '[placing] culture at the heart of regenerating England's seaside resorts by investing in arts, public space, cultural assets and heritage projects', at locations as diverse as Blackpool, Bexhill and Jaywick, near Clacton. There are also large numbers of locally focused essays in coastal regeneration and 'positive gentrification', often involving public art and sometimes reaching out to the creation of innovative entertainment packages that respect but transform seaside traditions, as in the case of Vanessa Toulmin's 'Admission All Classes' at Blackpool, with its Arts and Humanities Research Council funding. Some of these initiatives will be discussed as case studies in the following pages.

Above all though, we need to pass from diagnosis of the current situation to the pursuit of solutions and ameliorations, and to move beyond the bridgehead that has been established in economics and demography when trying to broaden and deepen the engagement of a national government that is still far from convinced of the need for a suite of targeted and coordinated coastal regeneration policies. The approaches need to be interdisciplinary across a broad front, from meteorology (inevitably), geology, physical geography and engineering to architecture, entertainment and the arts. They need to pull together private and public spheres, engaging and coordinating local, regional and national government, private enterprise at all levels from the family firm to the multinational corporation, and include voluntary bodies and philanthropists; and they should be alert to appropriate and relevant developments beyond the British Isles.

This will be a complex task; and, at the risk of providing further ammunition to those who still wish to deny the importance and reality of a common coastal experience, we have to accept that there will be no 'one-size-fits-all' panacea – while remarking that this could never apply to 'the urban' or 'the rural' either. There is, however, great merit in mapping the resources and connections that are available, and presenting potentially transferable perceptions and approaches. This *Handbook* is intended to provide such a resource in accessible form, and to facilitate positive engagement

with coastal regeneration from the grassroots upwards. The word 'regeneration' has become familiar enough in English seaside settings, almost to the point of cliché. For example, a recent property column in the *Guardian*, focusing on Eastbourne, remarked that the town 'already has its own Cultural Quarter and attendant magazine, thanks very much, like any self-respecting regenerating seaside, and, indeed, a smattering of downshifted creative types'.[21] This is, of course, only one cluster of regeneration connotations, and, as we shall see, not the predominant one in the eyes of government. We must remain aware that 'regeneration' itself means different things to different people, both among those who seek to promote and facilitate it and among the intended beneficiaries, who are themselves far from uniform in age, outlook, culture and preference.

Regeneration also means different things in different kinds of place, so before we go any further we need to explore the problems of *definition*, and the related *diversity of experience and character*, which make the British coastline so rich and interesting, as well as so extensive and valuable, a resource.

At the outset, we must make the point that our working definition of regeneration goes beyond the current dominant assumptions of central government, as set out in the policy document *Transforming Places, Changing Lives: Taking Forward the Regeneration Framework* issued on 11 May 2009. This states the government's view (#3) that 'regeneration is a set of activities that reverse economic, social and physical decline in areas where market forces will not do this without support from government', and defines its focus (#4) on time-limited investment to create new economic opportunities and 'sustainable places where people want to live, work and raise a family'. The labour market is seen as key to achieving these outcomes (#5). The expectations in paragraph 6 are particularly interesting. It assumes a continuing increase in mobility, of people and businesses, and emphasises the need for places to compete to attract and retain skilled workers, and to support the health of the population *of working age*, while providing (unspecified) appropriate transport and communication links (might this concept include access to broadband?), and having the right public service infrastructure in place.

This does bring in health and social care on a broader front as health and well-being are not seen (#7) as *being part of* regeneration, but as contributing to it and being affected by its outcomes: it is not clear how marginal this makes them. There is clear recognition of the importance of local government and civic leadership (#8), and this resonates with recognition of the importance of distinctive *local* characteristics in a globalised world (#6). A response to feedback notes comments about the need to consider the problems of rural areas as well as concentrated pockets of deprivation in cities; but no voice is recorded from the coast, as such. (#10) This is all the more important in the context of recession, when it becomes clear that support for regeneration will be sharply targeted, based on local economic indicators of deprivation, socioeconomic characteristics and economic trajectory, and aimed at projects that can show clear economic outcomes, especially as regards employment. (#17, 18) The emphasis is on local initiative and local delivery, with an important role for RDAs; but how coastal areas, might access a share of the £6.5 billion on offer over the next two years, to promote growth and regeneration and prepare for the assumed upturn, is not clear. (#24, 40) In the absence of a clearly articulated coastal entity with power to make an impact at the sharp end, this is likely to be a struggle.

Two things are clear. Firstly the headline indicators for measuring progress in regeneration terms are *overall employment rates and the incidence of people of working age claiming out-of-work benefits* (p. 17, box). This does not engage promisingly with certain key characteristics of coastal settlements. Secondly, the commitments (#55) to recognition of the distinctiveness of each place, to valuing and making the most of the historic environment, and to ensuring that the right kinds (undefined) of cultural and leisure activities are made available, have the feel of an afterthought. So do the references (#40) to physical regeneration, including improved air quality, green infrastructure and healthy waterways (there is no mention of clean beaches or safe bathing water here).

What drives the government's vision of regeneration is, quite simply, *jobs*. This applies across a broad front. The Casino Advisory Panel, reporting in January 2007, noted that one of the considerations for granting casino licences was a 'need for regeneration' as 'measured by employment and social deprivation data'; but the report showed reservations about the narrowness of this, urging a more 'holistic' approach that would get beyond the physical and environmental approach through demolition and rebuilding that was associated with older definitions of 'redevelopment', and take into account a wider spectrum of social as well as economic considerations.[22]

Our definition of regeneration is broader than this, but it is important to recognise the nature of central government's agenda. At the key levels where policy is articulated, it still does not recognise the distinctive characteristics and problems of coastal towns; and its focus on employment is only part of the wider picture we embrace, which sees regeneration as involving and affecting all ages, and having cultural, leisure and environmental dimensions (built and natural) which are addressed only in a token way in this key document. We need to bear in mind that many of the attractive qualities of coastal environments are essentially non-commercial, based on the expectation of free access to beaches and coastlines, and the privatisation and commercialisation of space that is often associated with the preferred model of private/ public partnerships is likely to encounter resistance from both residents and consumers.

Nor is the pursuit of maximum rates of profit likely to resonate with community-orientated regeneration goals. It is no coincidence that the heyday of the British seaside coincided with that of municipal intervention and enterprise, and the established democracy of access to desirable

environments will need to be defended.

There is a long way to go to meet our aspirations, and a lot will clearly have to be driven from the local level, as has so often been the case in the past. Regeneration as a concept, after all, is about *renewal from within*. Dr David Green of Aberdeen University has usefully defined it as the 'redevelopment of an area to its former use by involving the community and stakeholders', in implicit contrast to the imposition of destructive innovation from outside by external agencies without a democratic mandate or informed consultation.[23] To pursue that goal, help and stimulation should be sought from wherever it may be available, but central government is unlikely to be a big player in coastal settings under current circumstances. The chapters that follow will have to take that harsh but potentially stimulating reality on board.

Finally, there is a further important context. We should be aware of the opportunities presented by European Union policies on coastal regeneration. In November 2008, a resolution on 'the regional development aspects of the impact of tourism

on coastal regions' was adopted by the Committee on Regional Development, with support from the Committee on Transport and Tourism. This characteristically complex measure included strong support for a range of integrated policies on coastal and maritime tourism development, emphasized environmental protection and cultural heritage issues, and lamented the lack of reliable statistics and comparative accounting that would enable needs and policies to be adequately evaluated. It called for the encouragement of public/private partnerships and for collaborative action between 'environmental groups, economic sectors linked to the sea, cultural organisations, the scientific community, civic entities and local residents'. It urged the Commission 'to ensure that the ongoing compilation by Eurostat of a socioeconomic database for the EU's coastal regions include data on tourism that is reliable, uniform and up-to-date'.[24]

This aspirational document offers a reminder that British governmental problems involving the recognition and capture of coastal issues are shared by other European countries, and by the EU as a whole. But it also suggests that European intervention in this field may at last be gathering momentum on a broad and inclusive front, thereby reinforcing the impression that this *Handbook* is appearing at a timely moment. The coverage of what follows certainly adds up to a close approximation, in the English setting, to the European agenda set out by these committees.[25]

Resorts created for Local Government Officers! - *Restructuring Coastal Tourism in Transitional Period in China*

The paper explores the rise and fall of Chinese coastal resorts in transitional period from the restructuring perspective. China is one of the largest oceanic nations in the world, with the coastal line stretching out as long as 18000 km. Since 1980s, coastal tourism in China has been developed at an unprecedented speed, creating numerous hospitality providers and beach resorts throughout the coastal areas. Most of them were created earlier in the century by government departments or state owned companies, and the customers catered for were mainly government officials staying at the beach resorts at public expense. That is to say, both supply and demand of Chinese coastal tourism development were supported and driven by government. Moreover, coastal resorts of this period were poorly planned and managed, developing in the spontaneous and unplanned manner. Silver Beach Resort in Beihai, Guangxi Province is typical in this government dominated development, which has been deeply studied by the author. Until mid-1990s, as transition reform from planned economy to market economy was getting deeper all over the country, financial support and clients of coastal resorts were sharply cut down. More and more restrictions on government investment and spending relative to coastal resorts development were launched, causing most coastal resorts to get into trouble and some severely declined. Chinese coastal resorts were facing great challenges and need to be restructured to adapt to the new market-oriented supply and demand situations. Since the new century, some coastal resorts are successfully redeveloped in Hainan Island, which lies in southern China and is famous for amazing tropical beach resources. Further comparative research should be made on these resorts to learn more about restructuring of Chinese coastal resorts. In short, the rise and fall of Chinese coastal resorts happened under the background of transitional reform. Therefore, the causes, consequences, and mechanisms of coastal resorts decline and restructuring are completely different from UK and need to be addressed more specifically. Market reform should be hold on to rejuvenate the Chinese coastal resorts, and the role of local governments should also be adjusted.

Liu Jun and Ma Fenghua, South China Normal University, China

This extract and the others which are distributed around the book are from papers presented at "Resorting to the Coast: Tourism, Heritage and Cultures at the Seaside", Blackpool 25-29 June 2009. The CCA are grateful to Professor Mike Robinson and the Centre for Tourism and Cultural Change at Leeds Metropolitan University for permission to use. If you wish to obtain more information on any of the extracts, please visit: www.tourism-culture.com.

Chapter 1

English seaside towns: past,
present and future

by John K. Walton

Before we pull together our ideas about regenerating seaside towns, we need to be clear about where and what kind of places we are talking about, as well as what exactly we mean by 'regeneration'.

Our focus is on English seaside towns with some element of tourism and resort activities in their economies, following a pattern of development that can be traced back to the eighteenth century and forming part of the world's first Industrial Revolution. Some understanding of the complexities of a variegated past is necessary if we are to place their current situations in perspective and develop a convincing position on what their future might be.

English seaside resorts cannot compete internationally on climate, and depend almost entirely on domestic markets (as has always been the case). Nevertheless, they can lay claim to attractive topographical and historic identities, including architectural and cultural heritage, together with traditions associated with popular culture and entertainment (their 'intangible heritage'). They need to be able to retain (where appropriate) and carve out market sectors and niches that are founded on authenticity and distinctiveness – features that respond to native cultural traditions in contrast with the 'Fordist' mass-produced resorts such as the Mediterranean, from the 1960s onwards, although those destinations have their own histories and are not as uniform as stereotypes about 'mass tourism' suggest.[1] That is another story.

But the English seaside also needs to overcome the adverse aspects of the legacy of the past, especially the lack of innovation and loss of media credibility over the last two generations, and the associated social pathologies of local stagnation and decline.[2] This affects the working definition of 'regeneration' that this *Handbook* adopts – which will need to go beyond the government's preoccupation with labour markets (without denying their importance), to be sensitive and responsive to local and regional identities and traditions even as it revives, refreshes, reconstructs and innovates, and to take account of existing residential interests and visitor markets, even as it seeks to replace or supplement whatever may be lost or failing. So this chapter sets out: what kinds of coastal or seaside town are at issue; how the 'resort' element in their economies fits into past trajectories, present circumstances and future options; to what extent the problems we identify in the early twenty-first century are new; what options are available; and what kinds of intervention might be helpful across a broad spectrum.

We begin by emphasising that we cannot understand the present or plan for the future without an understanding of the past.

- Where have the tremendous number and diversity of English seaside towns come from, how did they develop, and what were the key influences on them?[3]
- As the first network of towns of this kind to develop in the modern world, how do they compare with subsequent models and patterns of development in other countries and parts of the

world, as the beach holiday has become a global phenomenon?

- What can we learn, positively and in terms of what to avoid, from past practices and processes, from how we got to where we are now, and from alternative trajectories and models of development beyond our shores?
- What can we learn about demand flows, branding, marketing, the provision of amenities and entertainments, the creation, protection and enhancement of desirable environments, the management of space and conflict, and the relationships between private enterprise and local government, the citizen and the developer, or local democracy, political legitimacy and economic development?
- What are, have been and might be the roles of diversity, of competition and complementarity between and within resorts and resort clusters, of transport systems, and above all, of perceptions of distinctive character and identity, as expressed through that topophilia that invests emotion and nostalgia in buildings and locations?[4]
- How might an understanding of the

trajectory of the seaside, not least in terms of past or recurrent problems, be harnessed to the satisfying and economically successful generation of new futures?

There are a lot of questions here. Some will be tackled directly in this chapter; others will inform subsequent discussion in what follows.

First of all, where are we talking about? When we look at most lists and definitions of 'coastal' towns and communities in England, or indeed in Britain, we find a tendency to include every local government district or parliamentary constituency that has a stretch of tidal waters within its boundaries. Charitably, this must explain (for example) the inclusion of Sherwood, a former mining district close to the very centre of England, in a list of 130 'coastal' parliamentary constituencies: the River Trent is tidal for a very long way inland. But this raises a general question – should we regard tidal estuaries as 'coastal' for present purposes? If so, London is a coastal city, although none of its constituencies is listed among the 130. So too are Bristol, Liverpool, Birkenhead, Newcastle-upon-Tyne, Hull, Middlesbrough, Ipswich and Goole, and many other towns and cities that are, or have been, important ports on estuaries and tidal river systems.

Where should we draw a notional line?

Sited more explicitly on coastlines rather than estuaries there are also, of course, maritime industrial and commercial cities, some of which contain, or have contained, naval dockyards and commercial shipyards, such as Barrow-in-Furness, Sunderland, Portsmouth and Plymouth; or have been industrial deep-sea fishing centres as well as commercial ports and import processors, such as Lowestoft and Fleetwood; or whose past prosperity came mainly from coal exports and heavy industry, like Workington in Cumbria. We might regard such places as towns that are 'on the coast', rather than coastal towns. We could reserve the category 'coastal town' for a different kind of place: one whose economy and identity depends, and has depended, to a significant extent on seaside tourism, and the extended influence of a seaside tourism tradition on related activities or identities (commuting, retirement, fishing and maritime heritage), and on enterprises that are mobile because they deal in ideas, intangibles or easily portable items, which draw people to coastal locations because that is where, given a choice, they prefer to live and work.[5]

This is the kind of distinctively 'coastal' setting that justifies the adoption of an additional category for evidence-based policy analysis, over and above those 'urban' and 'rural' areas that happen to be on the coast or include some coastline. But it has been difficult to isolate the targeted evidence on which to base the policies. A surprising number of 'coastal' parliamentary constituencies are shaped to contain a small stretch of coastline whose salient characteristics are swamped by an overall dominance of agriculture, industry or suburbia. This also applies to local government districts, especially since their reorganisation into larger units in 1974, which often provided a recipe for enduring local jealousies and strife over priorities and resource allocation. As Beatty and Fothergill have understood, and Fred Gray reinforces; to identify key characteristics and problem hot-spots we have to go to the smallest available statistical outputs and build upwards from them.[6]

It is even harder to develop a united coastal voice when coastlines and individual communities are perceived as being in conflict with each other, although in many cases they actually provide complementary offers for differing constituencies and niche markets, even on the same coastlines. This kind of regional resort system has a long history, growing out of older histories of diverse provision for almost all the population of adjacent industrial regions, negotiated between developers, holidaymakers and transport services according to local characteristics and demand flows. But it remains difficult to generate a united voice behind a shared set of identifiably 'coastal' interests, as the British Resorts and Destinations Association (BRADA) has found. It is difficult, but necessary.

'Coastal towns', as defined above, are the places whose economies and demographic systems Beatty and Fothergill have analysed. There are a lot of them, and they go back a long way. Most of them have dual or mixed economies, and (as Fred Gray has noted) most have developed as 'stand-alone' urban centres – which means that they necessarily pull together a variety of functions and social strata, and have complex small-scale internal geographies.[7] Some date, as resorts, from the earliest days of seaside tourism around the middle of the eighteenth century, often developing around existing port and harbour settlements. Some participated in the first great surge of seaside town growth during the first half of the nineteenth century. Many are products of the Victorian railway age – what might be called the first 'democratic seaside' – arranged around railway stations, piers and promenade tramways. A few were twentieth-century late-comers, especially the informal so-called 'plotland' settlements and caravan resorts.[8] Some, like the late Victorian speculation on the cliffs at Ravenscar in North Yorkshire, never got far beyond the initial property auction in the first place, and are now of archaeological interest.

Most contain elements of some or all of the above, as they have grown by accretion and adjusted piecemeal to new fashions and new markets, from bathing machine to (in a few cases) naturist beach, and from the Assembly Rooms ball to the club scene.[9]

My own efforts to count and tabulate such places between the mid-nineteenth and mid-twentieth centuries, concentrating on those for which runs of census population figures were available, put together 122 along the English coastline, 13 of which had census populations of fewer than 1,000 in 1911.[10] But as early as 1885 a national guide to 'seaside watering-places' listed 170 in England alone (including the Isle of Wight but not the Isle of Man or Channel Islands).[11] These included major maritime cities like Southampton and Plymouth at one extreme, and at the other tiny fishing hamlets like Staithes and Prussia Cove, and even coastal villages in coal-mining districts, such as Ryhope in County Durham. Here the local tourist 'industry' was run by a Mrs Salkeld, who rented out boats and the solitary bathing tent, and presided over a 'sort of marine grotto' where she sold refreshments. Already, too, there were places that had seen better days and needed to be revitalised. This is not a new problem!

Many 'coastal' resorts, of various sizes, are themselves on estuaries: Arnside, Cleethorpes, Lytham, New Brighton (whose decline as a resort is an important case study in itself),[12] even Southend or Weston-super-Mare. Moreover, how should we deal with places that develop on separate sites within the boundaries of a larger local government district, or that are subsumed into larger entities through local government reform (especially that of 1974), or that form distinctive enclaves within existing larger towns (like, on an unusually large scale, Cleethorpes within Grimsby, or Southsea within Portsmouth)?

These problems of identity and classification are important if we want to build a precise and convincing (or at least consensual) database of 'coastal towns', sensitive to change over

time. But in the absence of agreed definitions or precisely calibrated statistics, an element of subjectivity must always creep into the calculations. This applies equally, of course, to the imagined and shifting boundary between the 'rural' and the 'urban', which is being increasingly recognised as problematic as academics and policymakers investigate the spread of suburbia, exurbia and the 'rurban'.[13] The concept of the 'rural' in Britain had become so complex by 2001 that the Office of National Statistics commissioned a special report to clarify the terminology. The report noted a tendency to categorise the 'rural' as a residual – whatever is 'not urban' – and to use the category as a 'matter of convenience'. This is a reminder of the frailties of the existing urban/rural divide for policy purposes. Further, we should note that one of the ONS's own area classifications was 'coast and service', which combined 'coast and country resorts'.[14] If the government accepts the category 'rural' as a basis for policy formulation, it is hard to understand why it should deny the validity of 'coastal'.

Beatty and Fothergill are well aware of these issues, and recognise the element of subjectivity in their own classifications and calculations, as of course do I as regards my own contribution to these

discussions. Under all the circumstances it is clear that theirs is the best list to work with, not least 'because it is there' and to discard it would be to abandon an essential baseline and comparator. It deals with current circumstances, and is certainly not demonstrably inferior to any conceivable alternative. The limitation that in its original form it dealt only with the larger resorts, which may not have been representative of coastal experiences and problems, is now dispelled by the supplementary report of July 2009. Its coverage still adds up to 'only' 74 places in England, leaving up to 50 of the smallest out of account – but they really are probably best left in the existing 'rural' category for present purposes, reinforcing from the other side the point that not everywhere on the coast is a 'coastal' or 'seaside' town. Put together, their populations would add up merely to a single medium-sized town, distinctive though their collective experiences might be.

The places on the Beatty and Fothergill list have many core characteristics in common, but they display a spectrum of current fortunes and historical trajectories. We need to understand the reasons for their current circumstances before we can intervene to try to change them.

Even without the smaller settlements, there is a very wide distribution of sizes among these towns, from Greater Bournemouth with over a third of a million, and Greater Brighton and Greater Blackpool with well over a quarter of a million, to a cluster of places that just cross the qualifying barriers of 8,000 (in 2003, based on the 1971 census) or 10,000 (the additional 'benchmarking' exercise of 2008).[15] They contain nearly six per cent of England's population, but the proportion who have visited them or lived in them will be very much higher, especially given the tendency for seaside residence to be seasonal or a life-cycle stage, especially late in the life course (but also early in it, before moving away in search of higher education or a career).

The largest towns are actually seaside conurbations, containing within their boundaries several smaller places that would feature well up the league table in their own right, such as Christchurch and Poole within Greater Bournemouth or Lytham St Anne's within Greater Blackpool. All (perhaps especially the largest) have complex economies, combining in varying degrees tourism, fishing, seaport, retirement, residential and industrial functions, and often sustaining intricate family economies

as opportunities fluctuate seasonally in ways that may not be captured by benefit claimant statistics. For example, I suspect that seasonality of employment is still more widespread than statistics based on the implicit assumption of 'one person, one job' – and failing to pick up on seasonal migration – may lead us to believe.

Collectively, seaside towns grew more rapidly than the national figure throughout the twentieth century, although the motors for growth changed over time. However, since 2001, although still growing, they have lagged behind the rest of England. The long history of growth, to varying degrees, is significant in itself, and may help to explain the relatively high proportion of seaside inhabitants of pensionable age (24 per cent against a national figure of 19 per cent), although this discrepancy has been a long time in the making.

How are the larger seaside towns currently faring? The 'benchmarking' exercise found that, according to its primarily economic criteria, several were performing strongly, with a concentration along the south coast (of all sizes, from Greater Bournemouth to Sidmouth), but also outliers at Southport, Whitley Bay on Tyneside, and Whitstable on the Thames Estuary. Others

were deemed economically weak, with a string of poor performers along the east coast from Clacton to Bridlington and then Whitby, together with Thanet, contrasting examples in Devon (Torbay and Ilfracombe),[16] Penzance in Cornwall, and the Lancashire resort of Morecambe. Of the largest urban areas in the category, Thanet fared worst, followed by Torbay, Hastings, Greater Blackpool, the Isle of Wight (which contains several small seaside towns of varying character) and Southend; while at the top were the three south coast conurbations based on Brighton, Bournemouth and Worthing.

Several aspects of these findings call for comment. First, there is no exact fit between the fortunes of regions and seaside towns. The south coast, from West Sussex to east Devon, has concentrations of current economic success, which seem to be affected not only by widespread economic growth in south-eastern England but also by ease of communication with London. Significantly, Hastings (with more difficult metropolitan access), and resorts like Folkestone which formerly doubled as cross-Channel ferry ports, do not reap discernable benefits from regional prosperity. Round the corner on the Thames estuary is Thanet, where the loss of early comparative advantage in transport access has contributed to serious and sustained decline since the later twentieth century. Just a little closer to London but on the same coastline, Whitstable is deemed to be doing well. In the North West, residential Southport appears to be prospering, while Greater Blackpool is probably only kept out of the 'economically weak' category by its comfortable residential components along the Ribble Estuary, especially Lytham, which mask the well-known pockets of poverty in some of its central wards, and Morecambe continues to struggle.

It seems that the patterns are based less on the fortunes of resorts' surrounding regions than on the character, social composition and markets of individual places. The most 'difficult' category, indeed, might be defined as *old provincial popular resorts that historically had regional industrial visitor catchments*. This would include most of the struggling east coast resorts north of Southend, as well as Morecambe and the historic resort core of central Blackpool – which was, however, a holiday place for the whole of the North of England before the First World War and for most of Britain by the 1930s, though always deriving its dominant character from the old textile and mining centres of Lancashire and West Yorkshire.[17] The resorts of the Bristol Channel, extending as far south-west as Ilfracombe, might fall into this category, and so might post-war Torquay and Paignton, which also came to draw strongly on the industrial north and midlands, and even Southsea, Weymouth and the Isle of Wight. Redcar, on Teesside, would fit the pattern were it not so tied into manufacturing industry that it is omitted from the Fothergill statistics. Thanet might even be assimilated into it, as through trains and indeed coach services from manufacturing districts in the North and Midlands brought substantial numbers of visitors during the 1950s and 60s. Going beyond our present geographical remit, the North Wales coast, Aberystwyth, Pwllheli and the Isle of Man would also fall into the same category.

Another useful label might be *'resorts that have developed strong residential functions as prosperous retirement and commuter centres'*, as opposed to the less prosperous retirement that takes former industrial workers, often with long-term illness and disability, to the old popular resorts and (for example) the caravans of the Lincolnshire coast. This might help to account for the strong showing of Whitley Bay, near Newcastle-on-Tyne, and Southport on the Fothergill criteria, as well as extra-metropolitan Brighton, Worthing and a Greater Bournemouth that includes the highly prosperous areas of Christchurch and property hot-spot Sandbanks.

We might also consider a third category of *'smaller resorts with attractive harbours, fishing, boating and distinctive landscape and heritage assets'*. A list of the top ten resorts in the Holiday Which? competition for the best British seaside resort for 2006 suggests that this may be a valid, and in some senses highly successful, category. Whitby, to which we shall return, came first; but its success was part of a wider renaissance of small British seaside resorts that were perceived to have distinctive

character and atmosphere, and to be the bearers of attractive, evocative traditions from the history of the English seaside, into the beginning of the new millennium. The other resorts in the top ten were all small and presented some claim to distinctive character: Wells-next-the-Sea in Norfolk, Frinton in Essex (with its reputation, dating from its inter-war heyday, for exclusivity, bowls and lawn tennis), expensive and equally exclusive Swanage and Sidmouth in Dorset and Devon, artistic St Ives (home of the Tate Modern gallery, on the site of the old gasworks) in Cornwall, the little Welsh resorts of Tenby and Abersoch, Rothesay on the Isle of Bute in western Scotland, and Portrush in Northern Ireland.

Only Sidmouth, St Ives and Swanage joined Whitby among Britain's '43 principal seaside towns' as defined by Beatty and Fothergill, and they all featured among the six smallest, with census populations between 10,200 and 13,800.[18] They were all relatively difficult to access from major population centres. Even Frinton, easily the nearest to London, tried to discourage visitors with 'alien values' by suppressing attractions and activities deemed 'inappropriate' and using its rail crossing as a kind of unofficial frontier post.[19] The others were far from the nearest motorway, and any rail journey, if available, necessitated connecting with a rustic branch line. Wells-next-the-Sea, Swanage and Portrush were not only 'remote', especially from a London media perspective, but also had close connections with steam railways, a particularly popular and evocative form of 'heritage' attraction in Britain. A visit to Rothesay involved a short sea crossing – it had a long history as a popular destination for Glasgow area holidaymakers travelling down the Clyde estuary, initially by paddle steamer.[20] In these cases the journey was a positive aspect of the overall experience, even part of the attraction, not least because it acted as a filter on the 'wrong sort' of fellow holidaymakers or residents.

Small resorts with 'character', and offering – in the 'top five' cases at least – large numbers of beach huts, that fashionable accessory to holiday living at the seaside in the early twenty-first century, were clearly of the essence.[21] A measure of eccentricity and the capacity for catering for niche markets also seemed to help. Above all, what mattered was to be able to connect with a sense of nostalgia for a secure, rich and interesting past that could be transmitted to a new generation through the revival of an idealised family holiday in a 'traditional' and evocative seaside destination – essentially relieved of all the associations of dullness, dampness, incompetence and poor service that had plagued the British seaside in the late twentieth century, but were no longer seen as inevitable, as the predominant tone of media coverage began gradually to shift from mockery towards celebration, from denigration towards affection.[22]

Nor was this kind of resort confined to the top ten in this competition, interesting though its outcomes were. Whitstable's current high profile, for example, is associated with similar characteristics; and other seaside places with less promising economic profiles, such as Hastings, are now making a virtue, and a selling point, of their more attractive eccentricities and idiosyncrasies. But Whitby is a particularly good example of a coastal town whose current reputation as a tourist destination is in tension with its position in the economic and demographic league tables. It was consistently at or near the bottom of all the economic and demographic performance tables in the original Seaside Economy report of 2003 (although it is interesting that the subsequent 'benchmarking' study in the aftermath of the Report of the Select Committee on Coastal Towns, which updates the picture using statistics from 1998/9 to 2005/6, shows the town in a much more positive comparative light). Its employment level increased by 16 per cent during those years, putting it seventh among the chosen towns, while it was fifth in the relative importance of the classic tourist trade occupational categories in distribution, hotels and restaurants. It was also strong on gross value-added per capita, coming tenth, and it was making excellent progress in reducing its working age claimant rates. It was pulled down by issues connected with age structure, educational attainment and housing amenities, but it finished in the top half of the survey when overall comparative deprivation levels were calculated. Even so, it still featured in the Department of Trade and Industry's list of 'declining' coastal towns in 2008, on the basis that its employment rate was more than 3 per cent below the figure for England as a whole, a measure that Steve Fothergill rightly described as 'one-dimensional'.[23]

This apart, the recent evidence confirms impressions that were already current in the mid 1990s that Whitby was turning a corner. But it should also remind us that this kind of evidence is only part of the story, presenting a warning not to put too much trust in the quantitative and seemingly quantifiable. Whitby has enhanced its reputation as a popular weekend destination for seekers after distinctiveness and 'authenticity'. Its day-tripper markets from old industrial areas of North East England and West Yorkshire have been augmented by touring coach parties and more distant affluent visitors, keeping tourism buoyant through times that were harder in other resorts. Like all British seaside resorts, its visitors are overwhelmingly domestic tourists, despite attempts to build an international public around associations with Captain Cook.[24] It won the Holiday Which? 'Best Seaside Resort' title in 2006, when newspaper publicity was supportive, referring to the town's 550,000 visitors per year, tourism employment running at one in five of the population, sandy beaches, quaint harbour, abbey ruins, picturesque cliffs, fossils, jet ornament manufacture, kippers, folk festival, Goths (responding to the Whitby setting of Bram Stoker's Dracula), regatta, literary and historic associations. The Yorkshire Post emphasised the town's recovery from high unemployment rates in the mid 1990s, with extensive new investment, especially around the harbour. It went on to come top of the Observer '50 best holidays' list in 2007, and a year later it won an Enjoy England Award as the best town in England for a day out. At the beginning of 2009 an article on a new hotel venture, again in the Observer, was full of praise not only for Whitby's 'retro' charm, but even for the mysterious mists associated with its classic Yorkshire coast sea frets.[25]

Why focus on this case study of a small northern coastal town? In the first place, it reminds us that economic and demographic indicators, valuable as they are (and central to government thinking), do not tell the whole story. Regeneration is about jobs, enterprise and services, but it is also about reputation, distinctiveness, attractiveness and aura. Fothergill has noted the existence of 'competing perspectives' on what matters in assessing performance and proposing interventions:

- the socioeconomic indicators in which his primary expertise lies;
- the significance and promotion of tourism (despite the difficulty in assessing its role in an economy, in the absence of reputable statistics);
- architecture and the built environment;
- the natural environment.[26]

Others, such as the 'intangible heritage' of tradition and association, might be added. It would be better, of course, if these considerations were to be regarded not as competing,

but as complementary, to be brought together in a holistic set of policies that transcend departmental and administrative boundaries. This is what we advocate, and why this *Handbook* covers so many dimensions of its subject.

We should also recognise that Whitby is attractive for its history and associations, informal as well as formal. These are expressed partly through a distinctive urban maritime environment on each side of the harbour, involving the survival of narrow cobbled streets, eighteenth-century cottages and 'yards' set back from the main streets and climbing the lower levels of the cliffs. The ambience associated with this untidy quaintness, which gives a sense of communing with an imagined past that is accessible without detailed historical knowledge, is marketable to a range of visiting publics, and generates a great deal of affection among repeat visitors. This has been shown at various points since the early 1930s, whenever 'Old Whitby' has been threatened by

redevelopment or commercial innovation, and the present state of the harbour area is itself the result of several decades of conflict and compromise.

The current popularity of Whitby reflects the importance of a sense of uniqueness and authenticity, of the atmospheric and memorable, and such intangible assets are of the utmost value to a resort. In this context it is also important that Whitby's recovery has gone forward without recourse to heavy-duty master-planning or heavy-footed demolition and redevelopment. It has benefited rather from external investment in greatly improved water quality on the beaches and in the harbour, and it has seen investment in new accommodation and expanded marina facilities in the upper harbour. Above all, it has built on its existing assets and reputation, and modernised its offer within an established attractive framework, without damaging its fragile core environment.[27]
These points, and options, do not apply only to old harbour

towns and fishing communities. Other kinds of coastal town have their own histories, ambience and versions of authenticity. Blackpool, the world's first 'working-class seaside resort', has its own unique heritage, both tangible and intangible, architectural and cultural, based on the surviving piers, theatres and pleasure palaces from its explosive late Victorian growth phase, its streets of Victorian and Edwardian holiday hotels and boarding houses, its inter-war modernist architectures of play and relaxation (including the extensive developments of the 1920s and especially the 1930s at the Pleasure Beach and Winter Gardens), and of course its evolving tradition of hedonistic popular enjoyment. There is a credible basis here for a UNESCO World Heritage Site bid, provided that nothing further of major significance is lost. The streets of Victorian boarding houses are a particular problem, as the economics of adaptation to new tastes and expectations with limited access to capital present daunting challenges.[28]

But there are similar splendid survivals all along the coastline, a growing number being adapted to contemporary needs and sustained as local landmarks, magnets and active sites of regenerated memory, as in the cases of Morecambe's Midland Hotel, Bexhill's De

La Warr Pavilion and (now) Scarborough's Spa complex. How this is done, in what kind of relationship between the public and the private, the third sector and different tiers of government, is less important than that it is done, provided that the places concerned remain accessible. How do we bring new, contemporary life back to Hastings Pier, or Morecambe's long-neglected Winter Gardens, or Margate's threatened (and fiercely defended) Dreamland? And how do we reconcile the needs and desires of an older generation of seaside visitors, and retired residents who may have come to the coast to escape change, with the need to build new markets and cater for the rising generation of young residents who are now in evidence in (for example) Morecambe?

These were the iconic buildings of earlier phases of coastal tourism. What might their equivalents be for the early twenty-first century? The building types and styles did not have to be unique to a particular place to generate attachment in their habitual users, at a time when it was realistic to expect to build a regular, returning clientele from the same streets and factories. Every substantial resort had its pier, and every pier had its own idiosyncrasies within the genre. Many resorts had Winter

Gardens, but each developed a different architectural style and a unique entertainment tradition, again within a shared grammar of expectations. Even Blackpool Tower was not a unique project, and its rival at New Brighton was actually built, to a greater height, while the venture at Morecambe was nearly half finished.[29] The proliferation of seaside swimming pools and lidos during the Edwardian and inter-war periods, most of which have now been lost, similarly encapsulated a sunny vision of open-air pleasure and freedom in a variety of detailed ways.[30] The equivalent coastal investments of the early twenty-first century seem likely to be art galleries, as pioneered by the St Ives Tate, or maritime museums like the Falmouth branch of the National Maritime Museum, or the various displays of public art associated with public realm regeneration initiatives, as with the Glitterball and subsequent installations on Blackpool promenade, or the Eric Morecambe statue, Tern project and Stone Jetty installations at Morecambe.

What can private enterprise provide to offer novelty and excitement, responding to seaside traditions and environments and making coastal towns worth visiting for an arresting, distinctive but recognisably 'seaside' experience, at a point of

intense competition between destinations, a fragmented set of markets and the loss of old certainties? This will be a key question for regeneration promoters. What will not suffice is a proliferation of off-the-peg shopping malls or residential developments that could be anywhere. Getting to the coast requires effort and organization, and it needs to be made worthwhile. There is no point in providing buildings and facilities that could be anywhere, except as parasites on interesting and distinctive neighbours. Anna Minton's recent book reminds us of the perils of cloned developments, 'blandscapes', non-places, the privatisation of space (especially at the British seaside with its tradition of free access to the shore), and what Jonathan Glancey calls 'hard and shiny playthings designed for maximum profit'.[31] The key is to regenerate the democratic excitement that made the seaside an exciting destination for earlier generations.

Many coastal towns can also capitalise on other kinds of maritime building and spatial organization, constructed for purposes other than the tourist but attractive to the discerning (or even the less discerning) gaze of those who value evidence of age and identification with particular settings or functions, and who seek to conjure up romantic pasts that may or may not be historically specific in the mind of the beholder. Harbours, dockyards and their surrounding 'fishing communities' or other maritime quarters, with commercial piers, lighthouses, capstans, warehouses and perhaps distinctive kinds of old vessel – restored, rebuilt or replica – are all grist to this mill.[32] So are fortifications, gun emplacements and other relics of the sea and the seaport as defended frontier; and so, more peacefully, are the houses built for opulent inhabitants, summer visitors or those who speculated in renting to them.

There is hardly a branch of architecture that does not have a distinctive seaside incarnation, although in some cases it would be hard to define precisely what is 'seaside' about it apart from the location: piers, promenades and aquaria are easier to attach to a distinctive 'seaside' branch of 'heritage' from this perspective than, for example, residential buildings (even hotels or purpose-built villas or boarding houses) or entertainment centres. This is not just a matter of iconic buildings that define key aspects of the identity of resorts, like the Brighton Pavilion or Blackpool Tower or the De La Warr Pavilion at Bexhill. Such signifiers of place identity and myth are highly important in constituting, in MacCannell's terms, 'sacralized' sites or

spaces, or in those of Bale as promoting 'topophilia', that emotional attachment to locations associated with personal histories of pleasure and pain that can be identified with tourist sites as well as the sports stadia to which Bale's arguments are applied.[33]

At least as important, however, are the less immediately impressive but characteristic and cumulatively defining buildings and artefacts that not only make up the backcloth to the iconic sights, but also generate the atmosphere and the sense of uniqueness that set a place apart and generate emotional attachment to it. This theme is most obvious in the older areas of 'traditional' fishing harbours, with their small scale, intricate detail, inviting rather than alienating and vulnerabe to wholesale redevelopment or piecemeal attrition.[34] But it applies not only to the workaday elements of such townscapes, as increasingly intertwined with their tourist elements, but also to the purpose-built holiday areas that might at first sight be dominated by massive sea defences, concrete promenades, long terraces of hotels and boarding houses, and the substantial pleasure architecture of piers, Winter Gardens and the like. Kenneth Lindley, in a delightful book, made this point very well in the early 1970s, with particular reference to the

promenade, using attractive plain language that anticipated the subsequent coinages of 'liminality' (the shore as gateway and intermediate zone in which the usual rules of property and propriety are suspended or at least relaxed) and 'topophilia', while treating nostalgia with unworried indulgence:[35]

"The indefinable character we think of at the mention of the word seaside is nowhere more apparent than along the strip of no man's land between beach and buildings, the promenade. The name conjures up memories of walks along breezy cliff tops; of evening concerts by brass bands, the fairy lights reflected in polished buttons and instruments; of bank holiday picnics on the greensward ... of obstacle golf and paddling pools... . It was the promenade which gave a town its particular character. Along it you would find that strange collection of objects ranging from cast-iron shelters to flagmasts which together made up the seaside image. Here, the massive functionalism of seawalls combined with the frivolities of rustic fencing or fancy ironwork. Much of the detail is ephemeral in character, even if it has lasted a century, and it has an appropriate jollity. It is mainly composed of that strange mixture of nautical functionalism and

the joyfully unrestrained which is the key to the charm of urban seaside landscape".

The nostalgic attributes here associated with place identity at the seaside have moved on by a generation, but the point stands. This commentary also reinforces the importance of the seafront as central to urban coastal identity, the need to rescue it from decline and dilapidation and, where there are problems, to focus sufficient regeneration effort in this signature area.[36]

As Lindley also pointed out, again, the exact nature of the details varied noticeably from place to place, as did the atmosphere conveyed by the mix of stalls, capstans, wartime mines used to collect pennies for the lifeboat, net stores, fortune-telling booths, ice-cream kiosks, promenade shelters and crab pots, some ubiquitous, some reserved for particular kinds of place or particular places: a mix that shifted over time as items were lost or added or changed their shape, form and position, but all within a shared grammar of memory and expectation.

This is a reminder that, in order to survive, revive and prosper, established resorts need to retain the loyalty of their remaining established customers while recruiting the next generation and reaching out to new or lost constituencies. So they cannot afford to change too completely, even under conditions where the old expectations of loyal, enduring regional markets were shattered in the later twentieth century by the rise of new competitors (within Britain as well as beyond it) and the fragmentation of a widely shared popular pleasure culture into niches organised around age, gender and specific entertainment preference as well as class and (to some extent) ethnicity. These smaller, more unpretentious elements of these coastal landscapes, especially those that represent the 'heritage of the recent past', are particularly vulnerable to sweeping, 'one-size-fits-all' developments, as recently demonstrated at Scarborough's North Bay.[37]

Regeneration of the built environment and of spaces of pleasure and relaxation, residential as well as recreational, thus has to tread carefully lest it treads damagingly on people's dreams. We need to resist the notion – which is propagated by the enduring influence of the 'tourism area life-cycle' – that British coastal towns have come to the end of the inexorable working out of the 'product cycle', are now overdeveloped and tired, and need either to be abandoned to their fate, to be converted into something else, or to regenerate themselves completely according to the currently favoured recipes. That would of course leave everywhere looking like everywhere else and destroy the essential element of contrast and distinctiveness.[38] Many of the most successful English coastal resorts have not run through all the imagined phases of the cycle, but have settled comfortably and successfully as small and middling places with renewable niche markets, loyal regular visitors and retired residents, and attractive natural and built environments. This is not to be disparaged: it is the fate of many of the smaller resorts which have performed well both on the demographics and in terms of recognition as desirable destinations. Here as elsewhere, regeneration needs to be piecemeal, carefully considered, sensitive and interdisciplinary.

A corollary of this is that many coastal problems are not new. Low wages, precarious small businesses, extended working hours, unemployment, part-time work and seasonal economies (the last of which should be recognised as more of an issue than the present statistics make it look) have been staple problems of English coastal towns since the beginning of their tourism industries. They have also affected the older maritime industries, compounded by the difficulty of organising labour to protect its interests and defend its working conditions. Women's work has been particularly exploited, not least by small employers.

Schooling has always been problematic for those who fell outside the orbit of the private schools which made their own contribution to the particularity of the more up-market resorts, and attendance levels were disrupted throughout the twentieth century by the demands and opportunities of summer work. The distortions of the age pyramid, as retirement to the coast became attractive, were already becoming apparent in places like Budleigh Salterton, Grange over Sands, Hove and Hastings before the First World War, to be amplified and extended considerably in the inter-war years and especially in the 1960s and 70s.[39] Sewage pollution of beaches and bathing water was already a problem in many coastal towns by the late nineteenth century, and is perhaps closer to resolution than it has ever been, although other problems of the coastal environment remain more intractable.[40] But the identification of bird and dolphin-watching, and walking coastal paths, as significant income generators for coastal businesses and communities, is a recent and promising

development. This, together with a growing appreciation of seaside architectural heritage, should remind those who protected sites as barriers to development that, viewed positively, they are assets with tremendous potential.

It is tempting to argue that novelty resides not so much in the issues as in their visibility: it sometimes seems as if the most effective role of the Welfare State has been to generate statistics, although this does not prevent some problems from remaining invisible to those who do not want to take responsibility for them. But there is no doubt that new and persistent challenges did emerge alongside the old during the last third of the twentieth century. Houses in multiple occupation are the heirs to the Victorian common lodging house or tenement of one and two roomed dwellings; but their multiplication at the seaside, in areas that previously provided holiday accommodation, has been disruptive and sometimes catastrophic, as in Morecambe's West End or parts of Margate or St Leonard's. The transferability of benefits has worsened this trend, which has filled the gap in property revenues that arose from the decline of the old working-class holiday market. The advent of so-called 'care in the community', with the decline of the asylum and

other 'total institutions' since the 1970s, has fuelled this development: some seaside streets have become dumping-grounds for those who were previously in segregated, controlled accommodation, as well as for children and adolescents 'in care'. Alcohol has always presented problems, but the growth of new kinds of drug abuse has heightened the impression of 'inner city' problems exported to the coast, helping to generate significant pockets of crime and fear which, like other localised problems, tend to be lost in broader averages.

Here we see a downside of the idea of the coast as 'liminal' space as mentioned above, a gateway between elements, experiences and life-cycles, a place where the usual inhibitions and constraints can be cast aside.

A key theme here, which is not peculiar to the coast but finds its own expression there, is a loss of the security and predictability which matter a lot more to people than the ideologies of choice, consumerism and individualistic competition would have us believe. Until, perhaps, the 1970s there was a regular rhythm to play as well as work. The holiday seasons were quite precisely defined, based on Easter, Whitsuntide, and a summer that largely coincided with school holidays, but was inflected by the (established) traditional industrial holidays that brought particular towns to particular places in designated weeks. These patterns fragmented with the collapse of the old industries and their holiday schedules, which coincided with the opening out of private transport and new holiday destinations, and shattered the security of recurrent visitors coming for predictable blocks of time. Generational differences in leisure preferences also came to the fore, in step with the invention of the teenager and the rapid expansion of seaside retirement. It became much more difficult to plan ahead, whether as a boarding house keeper, an entertainment company or a local authority, and it has proved very difficult to adjust to the new unpredictability. Effective regeneration policies will need to take account of these frailties. They are not crippling, but they need to form part of the equation.

For the time being, too much of this analysis remains speculative. We still do not have an adequate framework for analysing the complexities of coastal towns, and we conspicuously lack a set of convincingly reliable tourism statistics for any English coastal resort. We have a range of local studies, conducted for differing purposes and using contrasting methodologies. These and related points will be developed in **Chapter 8**. A genuinely holistic approach to regeneration, working in a steady and measured way along a broad front, is capable of making a tremendous positive difference. That said, we do need to be aware of the richness and variety of what coastal towns have to offer, and of the perspective provided by a longer view of the communities and practices in question.

Marketing cultural events to support cultural tourism and helping to diversify the economy through sector support:

One of Hastings' strengths, evidenced by visitor feedback, is its cultural event programme, and the Borough Council invests over £100,000 specifically to fund large events, which are generally focused on the quieter, off-season, months. This includes support for the International Chess Congress (December/January), Hastings Half Marathon (March), Jack in The Green Festival of Morris Dancing (May), Old Town Carnival Week (August), Coastal Currents Arts Festival (September), Hastings Seafood & Wine Festival (September) and Hastings Week, including torchlight procession, bonfire and fireworks (October).

These events can attract upwards of 20,000 visitors, and most fill the town visitor accommodation to capacity. The Hastings Seafood & Wine Festival received a Tourism South East award for tourism excellence in 2008.

The events are heavily promoted on the towns websites including www.visit1066country.com, in the area's holiday guide, which emphasises the events programme with stunning photography, and also in journalists' 'fam trips,' which are specifically arranged to coincide with these events where possible.

Marketing is aimed at promoting the image of Hastings as a cultural destination. The target market is those taking short breaks. The town is now being seen as a unique 'must visit' destination. Hastings has had much positive national press coverage of late and was recently among British Airways High Life Travel Magazine's 50 most authentic places on earth

Hastings Borough Council and partners are investing in targeted sector support, particularly towards the creative and cultural industries, such as art, design, film, retail, tourism and hospitality. These will help 'brand' our town for potential investors, residents, students and visitors. The Foodlocal project initiated by Hastings Council has boosted the town's reputation for a destination for high quality food, with restaurants, cafes, bakeries, butchers, greengrocers, deli's, fish shops, and organic and ethnic food shops, all contributing to the diversity of the offer for visitors and residents. The Thursday Late & Live late night shopping initiative which was set up by Borough Council and partners to boost the evening economy, was awarded a national Association of Town Centre Management prize in 2007. Small grants are offered to assist the development of small and medium 'cultural' enterprises in the town. The local enterprise agency offers a programme of support aimed at the independent retail, tourism and hospitality sectors. Hastings also has a 'Creative Media Centre' which opened in 2004-05, consisting of purpose-built serviced town centre office accommodation and support services for creative industries. The new Sussex Coast College in Hastings will have state-of-the-art catering facilities, and an art gallery and design studio.

Contact: kboorman@ hastings.gov.uk

Chapter 2

Coastal issues and the select
committee inquiry into
coastal towns

by Patrick Browne

There are three barriers to overcome when seeking to raise the profile of coastal town problems. The first is *quantitative* – that is to say, national statistics have diluted coastal resort problems within large area analysis. The second is *time and scale* – the economic decline of our seaside resorts has not been as dramatic, nor as political or unionised, as the closures of coalfields, shipyards and other historic manufacturing sectors.

The third barrier, as has been vividly described, is *emotive!* Our love of the coast and our attachment to the seaside often make it difficult for negative messages to penetrate the layers of national nautical affection. It is rather like a reluctant family being told that a loud and favourite uncle,

who filled our childhood with lollies and laughter, really has some rather dodgy habits and relationships. As with seaside resorts, many would not want to know.

A spring tide of satisfaction, therefore, greeted the news in late 2005 that there was going to be a Select Committee Inquiry (SCI) into coastal towns. This was particularly satisfying for those coastal MPs, local authorities and coastal networks who for many years had been articulating the need for national action to address the growing socioeconomic problems of seaside resorts. Not least among these were: the MPs for Sefton and Blackpool South, Dr John Pugh and Gordon Marsden; the LGA Coastal Special Interest Group, whose *On the Edge: The Coastal Strategy* started the decade with

a call for 'integrated solutions for coastal problems';[1] and the Centre for Regional Economic and Social Research (CRESR) team at Sheffield Hallam whose coastal economy research of 2003 provided a framework for analysis.

When Dr Phyllis Starkey MP, the chair of the then ODPM Select Committee Inquiry into Coastal Towns , reported their findings in February 2007 to a spray-lashed room of coastal practitioners at the Spa Complex in Scarborough, Max Jaffa – the once long-serving bandleader at the venue – would have had little difficulty in recruiting a *Hallelujah!* chorus.

However, the jubilation was cut short when the government dismissed the report and its recommendations.

Coastal people, places and maps

There are around 3.5 million people living in or near the 113 seaside resorts (population > 1,000) spread around the

6,250 miles of English coastline. The resorts are administered by 49 district councils, 14 county councils and 23 unitary

authorities. Figures 2-1 and 2-2 show England's resorts and the coastal local authorities.

Figure 2-1 113 Coastal Resorts

Spittal
Alnmouth
Whitley Bay
Silloth
Redcar
St Bees
Whitby
Seascale
Scarborough
Arnside
Filey
Grange-over-Sands
Silverdale
Bridlington
Morecambe
Hornsea
Fleetwood
Thornton-Cleveleys
Withernsea
Blackpool
St Annes
Southport
Cleethorpes
Birkdale
Mablethorpe
Hoylake
Sutton-on-Sea
Skegness
Wells-next-the-Sea
Sheringham
Cromer
Hunstanton
Mundesley
Great Yarmouth
Lowestoft
Southwold
Aldeburgh
Felixstowe
Harwich
Frinton on Sea
Walton-on-the-Naze
Clacton-onSea
Southend-on-Sea
Portishead
Canvey Island
Birchington
Margate
Ilfracombe
Clevedon
Gravesend
Combe Martin
Broadstairs
Mortehoe
Lynton
Minehead
Weston-super-Mare
Whitstable
Ramsgate
Herne Bay
Deal
Northam and Westward Ho!
Porlock
Burnham-on-Sea
Shoreham
Walmer
Watchet
Lancing
Hastings
Dover
Instow
Bexhill
Sandgate
Clovelly
Bideford
Worthing
Hythe
Folkestone
Lyme Regis
Charmouth
Christchurch
Bognor Regis
Eastbourne
Bude
Sidmouth
Bournemouth
Exmouth
Bridport
Littlehampton
Seaford
Padstow
Dawlish
Seaton
Southsea
Brighton and Hove
Teignmouth
Budleigh Salterton
Hayling Island
Newquay
Paignton
Weymouth
Isle of Wight
St Ives
Torquay
Looe
Brixham
Fowey
Dartmouth
Swanage
Mevagissey
Salcombe
Penzance
Falmouth
Marazion

Figure 2-2 Coastal Authorities

☐ County and District Authorities
▨ Unitary Authority

Why have a Select Committee Inquiry into coastal towns?

Following prolonged and concerted pressure from MPs and others, the then Office of the Deputy Prime Minister (ODPM) decided to hold an SCI, with the brief 'to examine current government policy affecting English coastal towns'.

Select Committees are appointed by the House of Commons to examine the expenditure, administration and policy of government departments and their associated bodies. In the case of the Department for Communities and Local Government, their Select Committee inquiries range from local government finance, the central/local government power balance, through planning, housing and waste management; down to the provision of public toilets!

During 2006, the coastal towns inquiry called for evidence and received 66 written submissions on coastal issues from local authorities and coastal organisations, visited several resorts, and invited experts to a number of oral evidence sessions at Westminster. This work has established a formidable body of evidence on the circumstances of English coastal towns in the first decade of the twenty-first century.

The committee published its findings in March 2007, highlighting specific issues and making the following recommendations for government action.[2]

The SCI recommendations

- **National policy.** The lack of cross-departmental working on coastal towns is disappointing. The government should establish a permanent cross-departmental working group on coastal towns.
- **Vulnerable adults and children.** Placing authorities should communicate in advance with host authorities, consider the impact of placements on the receiving communities, and take responsibility for the financial impacts of placements.

- **Tourism.** It was recommend that the government should conduct an immediate study on coastal tourism, including evaluating the levels and spend of domestic and inbound visitors.
- **Benefit claimants.** The government should investigate the trend whereby coastal towns have experienced a disproportionately high rise in the number of people claiming sickness and disability benefits. It was 'unacceptable and extraordinary' that the

government should have no knowledge of this situation.
- **Diversification.** Coastal towns need to diversify and the government should encourage the sharing of best practice on economic diversification.
- **Seasonality.** It was surprising that the significance of seasonal work in coastal towns was not recognised by the Department for Works and Pensions. This is suggestive of a wider lack of understanding in government of the specific employment patterns

in many coastal towns.

- **Housing.** Resort housing is often characterised by a dual economy of high house prices and low-quality private rental sectors. Coastal houses in multiple occupation (HMOs) provide cheap, short-term accommodation that contributes to the transience in many coastal towns. Local authorities should use the powers available to manage HMOs where they contribute to social problems and costs.
- **Affordable housing.** The shortage of affordable housing can be exacerbated by inward migration and the purchase of second homes.
- **Climate change.** The government should put in place a fair and transparent national approach to coastal adaptation to enable local communities to plan their futures, be it behind enhanced defences or planning for managed retreat.
- **Sea defences and regeneration.** The Department for Communities and Local Government (DCLG) and the Environment Agency (EA) should work together to maximise the regeneration potential of sea defences.
- **Physical isolation.** Physical isolation is a considerable barrier to

economic growth, development and regeneration in many coastal towns.

- **Demographics.** The in-migration of older people to coastal resorts can place significant additional demands on public services, particularly health and social care.
- **Transient populations.** Coastal resorts experience a higher than national average level of transience populations: inflows and outflows of individuals and families attracted by seasonal employment, cheap rental accommodation and/or the quality of resort life. This can have negative consequences for education, public services, regeneration initiatives and social cohesion.
- **Regeneration.** The government should support a permanent network to facilitate the spread of best practice in coastal town regeneration.
- **Funding.** The government should evaluate the impact of the termination of any funding streams on coastal town regeneration with a view to addressing any funding gaps.

This long list of coastal-specific issues will be expanded on below, and elaborated on, from various perspectives, in the following chapters.

The Select Committee also noted that there was no standard definition of coastal towns for policymakers or practitioners, and that government departments and coastal organisations use a variety of topographies to define coastal settlements for their purposes. This means that it is extremely difficult to compare national and local coastal resort research over time, and between areas, if standardised definitions and datasets are not employed. This situation requires resolution if the reality of coastal resorts is to be articulated and available to inform national policy and programmes.

While the Select Committee used the broadest definition of coastal towns – settlements by the sea, excluding ports – in order not to restrict its scope, this book is concerned with coastal resorts, that is to say, seaside settlements that evolved as, and are still predominantly, tourist destinations.

Figure 2-3 colour codes the 2007 Indices of Multiple Deprivation for England, which illustrates how deprivation rings the country. The map also shows that many northern resorts service large urban areas that also experience above-average deprivation. If we were to roll up the English coast into its own region, the level of compressed deprivation would qualify the area for substantial European Union and national regeneration funding. As it is, many of the dispersed pockets of coastal deprivation fail to qualify for such support because of their size and their location.

Figure 2-3 Multiple Deprivation 2007

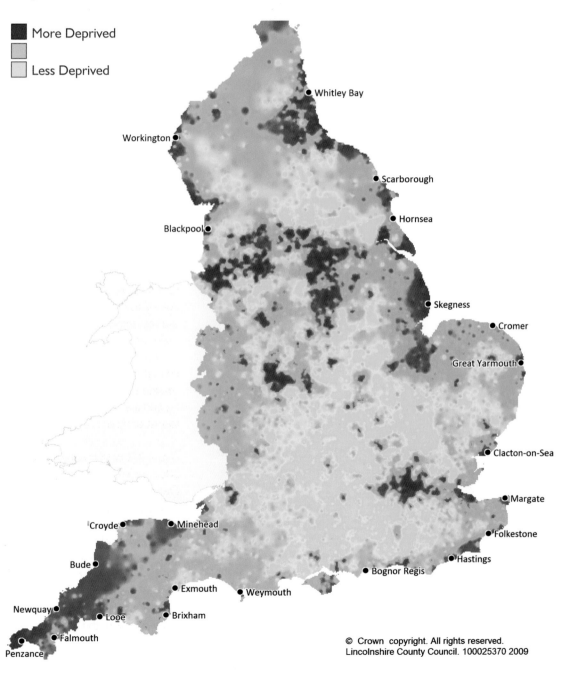

The Select Committee's recommendations came as no surprise to coastal practitioners, but some inlanders could argue that, with the exception of, say, erosion, seasonality and elderly migrants, most of the issues highlighted are experienced, to some degree, throughout the country. This may be true, but it is the concentrated mixture of rural and urban problems, within peripheral, undynamic economies and reduced hinterlands, that combine to create the unique deprivation of our seaside resorts, and which require unique solutions.

For example, resorts suffer from the rural problems of poor communications, isolation, poor access to services and jobs, lack of opportunity, recruitment issues, and access to affordable housing. Added to these are the urban deprivation issues of transient populations, poor housing, worklessness, poor health, low educational attainment, crime and lack of community engagement. It is the consequences of this cocktail of social and economic problems, often in attractive settings, that require new thinking and new approaches.

All coastal resorts are affected because, while they may be diverse by size, prosperity, access, popularity, culture and prospects, they all share the consequences of the 'seasonality – low wage – cheap housing – transience' nexus that distinguishes resort deprivation and places unrewarded costs and burdens on coastal local authorities and other public service providers.

The scale of resort deprivation can range in intensity from being the dominant and debilitating characteristics of many smaller resorts, such as marginalised Mablethorpe, to being almost submerged beneath the cosmopolitan vibrancy of Bournemouth and Brighton, or the niche market prosperity of towns such as Salcombe. It could be argued that the socioeconomic problems of coastal resorts produce the conditions for sustainable deprivation!

For example, the availability of cheap rental housing maintains a transient population that can be very disruptive in schools, where the turnover of pupils can reach 40 per cent during a year. Similarly, the ageing coastal population and the influx of summer visitors can make considerable demands on medical and social services, as indeed do higher teenage pregnancy levels, high numbers of benefit claimants, and established coastal worklessness. The additional demands placed on coastal public services can be further compounded by the difficulty of recruiting public and private sector professionals in many coastal areas. *Chapter 11* debates coastal health issues while *Chapter 12* describes the ageing coastal population and the opportunities they may create, while *Chapter 11* debates coastal health.

Location and transport links often defy efforts to diversify resort economies, as do the lack of critical masses in customers, skills and business culture. In addition many coastal towns lack connections with the economies and dynamics of major conurbations, except for visitors and retirees. Often businesses that are attracted to resorts move away because of costs, distance, recruitment issues and an undynamic business environment.

The funding available for regeneration may not be conducive to resort development, in so far as coastal outputs are often dearer to achieve than in larger urban areas, and this can influence funders where set targets are their priority. Also, current thematic EU funding assumptions, with the focus on innovation, R&D, technology and the environment, reduce opportunities for support in resort areas where tourism-related employment fails to qualify.

The quality of coastal education provision can be undermined by transient populations and low attainments can be another barrier that maintains deprivation. The lack of further education in many resorts is also a disincentive to retaining the young and talented, while efforts to retain young people can be expensive and time-consuming for limited success.

Poor education provision can deter families from moving to coastal towns.

Compounding the effects of resort deprivation is the local authority funding formula that does not cover the costs generated by transient populations, looked-after children, mental health issues, homelessness, housing benefit dependence and worklessness; while services such as waste collection, street cleaning and car parking need to be elastic in dealing with the volume of resort visitors.

There is also the national issue of regeneration and deprivation timescales. As the coalfields, and many other former industrial areas have shown, with sufficient resources land can be developed and jobs relocated, but the impact on deprivation can be marginal and it may require years of effort to improve community

aspirations, education and skills. As in the case of many national deprivation issues, these problems are magnified at the coast, where they may be less responsive to conventional regeneration stimulation. For this reason, coastal regeneration and deprivation require a national debate, particularly relating to economic growth, deprivation and wellbeing. *Chapter 6* outlines the challenges of 'enterprising the coast'.

Deprivation is, therefore, a major challenge and burden for coastal local authorities, particularly district councils. Overstretched service budgets can undermine efforts and the resources available for community engagement, developing attractions, stimulating business growth and engaging in the costly uncertainty of inward investment promotion.

The government's responses to the coastal towns report

The government's first response created outrage among coastal local authorities, stakeholders and, not least, members of the Select Committee itself. This led to protesting MPs meeting in Westminster, a powerful and effective missive from the British Resorts and

Destinations Association (BRADA), the formation of the Coastal Communities Alliance (CCA) and, indirectly, to this publication.

The anger and the lobbying, coupled with a change of Prime Minister and new departmental ministers, provided the

opportunity for the government to take a second look at the Select Committee report. This produced a more positive response and an acceptance of the distinctiveness of coastal town issues that embraced some of the recommendations, and led to:

- a governmental cross-department working group on coastal towns;
- the Regional Development Agency (RDA) Coastal Best Practice Network;
- the commissioning of socioeconomic research into the larger coastal resorts;
- the creation of the first coastal-specific regeneration fund.

Chapter 5 reviews the actions of coastal LAs, organisations and networks and their barriers and priorities in coastal regeneration.

Why did it all go wrong?

If the 1930s and 50s were the heyday of the coastal resort, then the 1970s and 80s witnessed the social and economic changes that impacted on established resort structures and mores, as staying visitors declined, holiday accommodation became cheap housing, and urban-bred social problems came to the seaside.

The 1960s may have been the last days of coastal community stability, and the last decade of rail domination that fed the growth of resorts, when, paradoxically, seasonality was more defined as the regimented summer season ending in September and was followed by shutdown as traders, landladies and residents hunkered down for the deserted winter. While poverty and the poor must have existed, their details were not refined into Indices of Multiple Deprivation – misery was mostly your own and went largely unrecorded.

The 1960s were also the cusp of the modern era as more money, more cars, more planes and more media meant more choice, a more liberal society, more mobility, more welfare support and more individual freedoms. It also meant less collective community activity, fewer class barriers, fewer trains, fewer works outings and fewer pre-booked mass holidays. There is something poignant in the fact that the mainly northern resorts that serviced belching industrial heartlands have experienced the greatest decline in their economic fortunes, and have developed some of the worst social problems.

There is also something poignant about local authorities, among others, who are seeking to grapple with the modern tide of coastal issues with often diminishong resources and increasing expectations. The last 30 years have seen the range of coastal problems broaden, presenting more complex and costly challenges to local authorities and public service providers. Table 2-1 lists the coastal issues that underline the SCI recommendations and which coastal regeneration practitioners seek to address.

Table 2-1

Coastal issues highlighted by the Select Committee Inquiry into Coastal Towns:

Coastal erosion and flooding
Sea defences and regeneration

Lower employment levels
Higher sickness and disability benefits

Affordable Housing, HMOs, caravans
Placing vulnerable people in resorts

Seasonality of the poor coastal economy
Need for economic diversification

In-migration of older people
Out-migration of younger people

Peripherality issues
Transport connections

Low educational attainment levels
Poor health issues

Enhancing the public realm
Attracting investment

Low skills and wage economy
Public and private sector recruitment issues

Business development
Tourism support sector

The responsibility for addressing these disparate but interconnected issues resides with numerous national, regional and local organisations, who are often focused exclusively on their core services and prescribed targets. Meanwhile, the collective impact of resort problems are experienced by local authorities who are expected to provide leadership and solutions for issues and forces that may be beyond their budgets and influence. This is often the burden of local democracy and one that is being reinforced with the new 'place shaping' agenda, which tasks local authorities with leading on generating a collective vision for the development of their areas. This is a formidable challenge that will require strong leadership, realistic assessment of potentials, and significant cultural shifts in partnership working.

To recreate the 1950s 'golden age' of the seaside resort would require the removal or amelioration of a number of those social and economic changes that have emerged over the past 50 years. If this retrospection were possible, would it be desirable? For what purpose are we seeking to regenerate our coastal resorts? What forces are at work here and what countervailing forces are available to support visions for coastal futures? What futures are available? Can coastal regeneration move from reactive to proactive at a time when 'diminishing resources' could be added to the menu of woes? *Chapter 4* reviews coastal regeneration – past, present and future.

The challenges facing coastal regenerators can be divided into three broad areas:

- dealing with the social, cultural and economic costs of deprivation;
- maximising the quality and income of existing resort assets;
- diversifying the economic base of resorts.

Conventional wisdom regards economic growth as one of the main weapons in addressing deprivation, and a great deal of European and national regeneration resources are directed at business innovation, skills development and productivity. Coastal resorts however are generally not attractive to inward investment and new sector developments. Conventional regeneration wisdom is not working at the seaside.

Building on existing resort assets and demographies appears a more realistic business development approach to improving the local economy and the quality of the visitor offer, as later chapters demonstrate. Notwithstanding the necessity to maximise existing assets and the drive to diversify, there is perhaps a greater need for a more coordinated approach to addressing resort deprivation as a route towards improving the wellbeing of coastal communities and reducing public sector costs. This in turn could raise local aspirations and pride and inform new visions.

The next section reviews how coastal local authorities are currently seeking to deal with the coastal forces that mould the social and economic circumstances of resorts.

Coastal Forces

Seaside resorts are exposed to many interacting forces that vary in intensity by location. These include:

- physical forces – eroding cliffs, sand dunes, infrastructure and investment;
- human forces – bringing the elderly and transient in

and luring the young out while keeping staying visitors away;
- economic forces – maintaining seasonality, polarising housing markets;
- social forces – contributing to transience, low pay and worklessness;
- cultural forces – defining the 'personality' and meaning of

resorts;
- forces of inertia – that can maintain the status quo of decline.

What are the countervailing forces for change to help regenerate our coastal resorts? Unfortunately the one outstandingly popular countervailing uberforce of regeneration – money – is no longer as readily available as hitherto, and will become even scarcer in the coming years as what remains of public resources are diverted to reducing the national debt.

It is therefore ironic, just at a time when coastal issues are commanding national attention, when local government is being given the task of articulating local visions, and the national framework for regeneration will enable flexibility in national programmes for local circumstances, that the economy is static and public spending and regeneration resources are being reduced. Asking coastal practitioners to deliver more with less, despite the fact that many coastal resorts did not benefit economically during the 'good times', raises the question as to whether the menu of coastal issues has become too large and complex for the resources and structures available. **Chapter 15** lists potential friends for austere times.

Much is also made of the power of partnerships to deliver greater outputs and outcomes in regeneration. This concept will be tested as resources shrink and the fragmented 'industry' that serves, or could serve, coastal regeneration is culturally challenged to view the world differently and work to deliver a clear, realistic and agreed local vision. Achieving the latter will be the first regeneration challenge of the decade. Local leadership, harnessing the energy of the many regeneration organisations and cultures that exist to enhance aspects of our coastal towns, can re-focus and energise resort regeneration.

While the economy may not be buoyant, stronger local leadership can facilitate the maximising of resources and drive coastal renaissance through liberating cooperation and realistic visioning.

Impacts of four major coastal issues

- *Tourism and business*

Tourism is the *raison d'être* of resorts – it is their history, but is it their future? The dominant position of the low-wage tourism industry in most resorts maintains a lower standard of living for many coastal residents and undynamic economies that are unattractive to other business sectors.

There are many tourism quality initiatives under way and these will need to be maintained to increase the value of the tourism offer and raise the income of the sector. However, there are formidable barriers to tourism quality development, particularly the fragmented nature of the industry, with large national companies at one extreme, some SMEs, and a vast volume of individual and family businesses, making quality improvement initiatives costly.

A further barrier is the lack of high-quality, policy-oriented tourism research. National information is required on

the size, economic value, employment levels and importance of the tourism industry in national coastal resorts. Such intelligence could inform policy and local actions.

Matching efforts to developing the existing resort sectors is the need to attract new business sectors that offer skilled and well-paid employment. Diversifying the local economy in order to create quality year-round employment and increase the vitality of the local economy remains a priority for most resorts.

- *Affordable housing, HMOs and caravans*

The demand for retirement and second homes in many resorts raises the price of property and reduces the availability of houses to buy for low-paid local people. This situation can force people into cheap rental accommodation which also provides flexible and affordable accommodation for seasonal employees and for the increasing number of people who are attracted to resorts out-of-season.

As with many coastal issues, housing problems vary by type and intensity by location. Affordable housing is a major concern in many resorts in the South East and South West of England. HMOs are a major issue in Blackpool, while the Lincolnshire coast contains the largest number of holiday and residential caravans in Europe

Purchasing a caravan home can provide an attractive capital gain for people wishing to retire to the coast who sell an inland property, and high-quality caravan parks are proving popular with new residential markets and for their employment creation. However, the sheer volume of caravans in some east coast areas, and the confusions about residential status, raise concerns about the number of 'residents' in an area, their health and service needs, and the additional demands they can make on public services providers.

While there are a range of national initiatives on affordable housing that could assist resorts, the financial and housing market situation is currently diluting activity. HMOs are a major concern in coastal deprivation, and the reduction or the upgrading of current cheap rental accommodation could dramatically change the levels of transience, the resulting costs on public services, and the quality of resort environments. In the case of caravans, there is a national need to understand their role in the housing market and also the needs and characteristics of coastal caravan residents. *Chapter 11* reviews coastal health issues, including caravans.

Blackpool HMOs: *Improve or sell up*

To address housing market failure in Blackpool, the council has embarked on a selective licensing strategy, which demands that HMOs meet higher standards. 'What we hope is that if we say to a landlord that your property needs £50,000 worth of work to make it fit for occupancy, then they will decide to sell it and move on so that we can then intervene,' says Ian Hassall, director of land and property at urban regeneration company ReBlackpool. Hassall says that more regulation can ease the problem and only radical intervention will bring the change needed. 'We estimate that there are around 13,000 surplus beds in Blackpool's hotel industry, which are all potential HMOs, so just tinkering around the edges is not going to work,' he says. 'We need to be bold and that will involve demolition, clearance and the creation of the family housing, gardens and community facilities necessary for a sustainable community.'

Former national regeneration agency English Partnerships has allocated the council £35 million to begin the process of tackling the problem, and ReBlackpool is developing plans to create housing pilots in the north and south of the town. 'We will be creating neighbourhoods of the highest possible quality, with a balanced mix of tenure, and hope in that way to catalyse further development,' Hassall says.

Hassall adds that these pilots will build on an ongoing flagship project developed by Lancaster City Council and English Partnerships to fundamentally improve the quality of the housing stock in Morecambe's West End, which suffers similar problems to Blackpool in the form of high concentrations of HMOs, benefit dependency, high levels of transience and rising crime. One pilot, at Chatsworth Gardens, involves removing around 70 poor-quality and inappropriate properties and replacing them by constructing 172 residential units and 101 family homes. 'We will aim for a similar impact,' Hassall says. 'We will do this by taking out inappropriate housing supply that is driving decline and replacing it with modern high-quality homes which will help to provide stability for the local community and encourage further investment.'

But Hassall acknowledges that, while radical housing market interventions are crucial, more will be required to solve Blackpool's problems. 'What we need is a year-round sustainable economy. That has to be the goal.'

- *Higher numbers of sickness and disability benefit claimants*

One irony about coastal resorts is that they began life as therapeutic venues for the upper and middle classes, but now contain above-average numbers of unhealthy people. In the poorer resort areas of the East, North East and parts of the North West of England, the availability of cheap retirement homes and caravans attracts retirees who often have health issues. Also, the availability of cheap rental accommodation is attractive to many benefit claimants, and these families and individuals can place an additional burden on health, social and educational services.

The inflow of summer visitors (lost medication, sunburn!) and hedonistic young binge drinkers (lost youth, lost night!) also can make extra demands on seasonally stretched coastal health and other public services.

Barriers and priorities by practitioners

A survey of coastal local authority practitioners for this *Handbook* asked them to list (a) their barriers to coastal regeneration, (b) their priorities for action, and (c) to state, self-effacingly, their particular and sharable coastal regeneration specialisations.

The main barriers to coastal regeneration were considered to be, in order of seriousness:

- the nature of the local economy;
- lack of investment in infrastructure and transport links;
- the levels of deprivation;
- the lack of regeneration funding;
- the nature of the housing market;
- peripherality;
- climate change.

In the 'other barriers' section were: an ageing population, local resistance to change, the image of the area, and a lack of community strength found in industrial, mining and shipping areas.

While the barriers to regeneration were spread across a range of issues – the economy, deprivation, location, transport, housing – practitioners' priorities for delivering coastal regeneration were almost exclusively concerned with economic issues. These included diversification, inward investment, sector development, employment and skills, premises, business development and start-ups, with isolated references to housing need, reducing benefit claimants, enhancing the public realm, raising aspirations and improving partnership working. This is both understandable and a concern. It is understandable because national policy, regeneration funding and the strong desire for tangible outputs focuses effort almost exclusively on stimulating economic activity. It is easier to audit breeze-blocks and NVQs than measure wellbeing, security and local pride. On the other hand, the emphasis on the 'economic' as the solution to coastal deprivation is a concern. Until the current recession, the United Kingdom had experienced almost 15 years of unprecedented economic growth that had enriched many of our towns and cities. However, the rising economic tide did not reach the majority of our coastal towns, and while there have been a number of notable regeneration projects in the larger resorts, deprivation has actually increased in many coastal areas.

Given this relative failure to induce market forces into our seaside economies, and a predicted future of low or no economic growth, coupled with reduced public and individual spending, what should be the priority for coastal regeneration?

If the solution is not exclusively economic, should the emphasis for coastal regenerators be 'quality of life' and 'local distinctiveness' issues, rather than 'standard of living'? Could it even be that a focus on the quality of people's lives and the environment in coastal communities (for example, reducing transience, improving housing, reducing crime, enhancing the public realm, improving health and lifestyles) could actually lead to 'social regeneration' by attracting new residential groups and new priorities to the area? Should the economic totem of Gross Domestic Product be replaced by Gross Domestic Happiness for coastal resorts whose product is "pleasure"?

Enterprising the coast

This is not a cry to abandon the economic challenge, for there are products and services that coastal areas could develop to maximise on the location and the existing demographics. One of the key tests for resort regeneration, especially in the smaller resorts, will be the ability to generate niche markets based on demography, leisure, risk, authenticity, history, culture, design and the environment. In order to develop these niche market opportunities, strong local leadership, an enhanced environment and clear vision are required.

The one market force that appears to favour seaside towns is the influx of the elderly and retirees. Professor Heinz Wolff, the former 'TV scientist', is a passionate advocate of the use of technology to improve the health and independent living of an increasing elderly population.

He states:
"There are gaps in the market for seaside resorts that embrace elderly people by actively seeking to build communities that can deal with a high level of elderly by providing services, security and leisure that reinforce health, mobility and independent living. ... Local leaders who understand the strengths and weaknesses of the local economy are vital if a vision of change is to be communicated, and followed through".

At the other end of the age range, there are business opportunities in a risk-averse society for leisure, adventure and sports facilities that have controlled risk elements. Seaside resorts and the coast could be natural bases for such new markets. Energy generation and bio-fuels present green opportunities for coastal areas, while seaside entertainment is another potential area for enhancing the offer of resorts, with their existing infrastructure for entertaining summer visitors. The potential role of seaside heritage and historical experiences in promoting distinctiveness and authenticity is also worthy of exploration.

Climate change and flood risk provide regeneration opportunities, but first there must be a clear national statement on which parts of the coast will be defended and where there will be managed retreat. Sea defences that integrate with public realm and regeneration projects could have a powerful positive impact on coastal regeneration. In fact, many areas claim that the lack of clarity on sea defences is inhibiting investment in coastal areas.

Coastal realism and Gross Domestic Happiness.

The leadership of an area that promotes a realistic vision of what can be achieved can inspire and harness the resources and goodwill of other coastal organisations by providing clarity and direction.

Often, 'brainstorming' events on the future of resorts, and other areas, for that matter, undermine the exercise, and the confidence of partners and the community, by debating *unattainable goals*. Places, like people, need to be realistic about their aspirations and potentials. Much of this *book* is about maximising the existing potential of resorts, raising local pride and enhancing local distinctiveness to improve the quality of life for residents, businesses and visitors. In a world in which economic forces do not favour the coast, and where most resorts would be near the bottom of the Gross Domestic Product League, should the realistic regeneration goal for our popular resorts be GDH? Happiness is what they were made for!

Gross Domestic Happiness - *New ways to measure coastal wellbeing?*

The notion of Gross Domestic Happiness (GDH) was created by Bhutan's King Jigme Singye Wangchuck when he ascended the throne in 1972. It signalled his commitment to building an economy that would serve his small mountainous Himalayan kingdom of 700,000 people and retain Bhutan's unique culture permeated by Buddhist spiritual values.

GDH seeks to define prosperity in more holistic terms and to measure actual wellbeing rather than consumption. By contrast the conventional concept of Gross Domestic Product (GDP) measures only the sum total of material production and exchange in any country. At present most developed countries plan their affairs based upon a model of continous economic growth, despite the evidence of environmental and social damage. However, there is growing pressure for an infusion of moral and cultural values into the existing economic growth model.

In 1961 Bhutan opened its doors to the world. The Bhutanese quickly learnt that in the pursuit of economic prosperity, many countries had lost their cultural identities, their spirituality, and compromised their environment. From a Buddhist perspective the burst of consumer-driven economic growth and consequently the explosion of affluence in industrialised nations had resulted in wide-spread spiritual poverty. The Bhutanese recognised that economic growth alone did not bring contentment.

However, the government, also knew that change was inevitable. So Bhutan had to come up with a different approach to development - something that would monitor and regulate the nature and pace of change without compromising the essence of its citizens' well-being. GDH is not against change. It proposes development that balances economic growth with the preservation of the environment and religious and cultural heritage. The message is that the country should not sacrifice elements important for people's happiness to gain material development. In short, GDH takes into account not just the flow of money but also access to healthcare, free time with family, conservation of natural resources and other non-economic factors.

Hastings - *Attracting external capital and revenue funding:*

Hastings is active in local, regional and EU partnerships to attract funds for coastal regeneration, and has been very successful in this. Significant national and European funds have been secured for urban and social and cultural regeneration; and for sustainable development initiatives. Partnerships are key not only to unlocking funding, but also to transferring expertise, and the Interreg IVA programme now offers the opportunity to do this with partners from both sides of the entire Channel Coast. Increasingly the impacts of climate change will offer both challenges and opportunities for coastal communities, and there are significant EU funds available for those who can develop innovative and enterprising solutions to these. The 'Arc Manche' cross channel political network offers a means of sharing expertise on coastal regeneration on a cross-channel basis: www.arcmanche.com

It is felt that the following ways of working have assisted the Borough Council's success in securing external funding:

- Effective partnership working.
- Realistic assessment, understanding and communication of needs.
- Using good background information to evidence needs, such as: consultation, research, evaluation and data.
- Making a good business case.
- Effectively showing the strategic fit.
- Providing good evidence of previous experience.
- Successful interpretation of the aims and requirements of the funding body.
- Effective management of consultants or contractors involved.
- Researching what has successfully been funded elsewhere.

Contact: dmorrison@hastings.gov.uk

Chapter 3

Regeneration players and coastal networks

by Patrick Browne

Nobody is solely responsible for coastal regeneration – a nebulous and all-embracing term that means different things to different organisations at different times. The responsibility for coastal regeneration is chiefly borne by local government as the democratically elected upholder of the common good for their area. However, there are scores of other organisations that contribute directly and indirectly to some aspect of coastal regeneration and for a variety of reasons.

This chapter reviews the coastal regeneration 'industry' by outlining the roles of local government, regional bodies and departments of state, before listing some of the many interest groups concerned with coastal issues and whose enthusiasms and resources could be further harnessed to enhance coastal wellbeing and 'regeneration'. But first a concern about "regeneration"

Before outlining the players there are issues about the regeneration concept that are particularly relevant to coastal resorts. Firstly, the objectives and outcomes of regeneration activity can be difficult to assess. For many practitioners and funding organisations, regeneration is exclusively about economic growth, with the expectation that success will address deprivation issues.

However, a recent review of the 25 years of coalfield regeneration activity claimed success for developing industrial land and creating some employment opportunities, but the communities have not being regenerated and deprivation was still depressingly high. (Regenerating the English Coalfields. 2010.Author: National Audit Office.) The coast, too, reflects this situation where – despite years of national growth – deprivation remains stubbornly unchanged.

The term needs unpacking from being an all-embracing palliative for complex social and economic issues and there is national confusion as to whether regeneration resources should be focused upon economic opportunity or community need. Prior to the current recession much of national policy was beginning to focus upon worklessness and its causes, an important coastal resort issue, but circumstances have diverted attention and reducing resources to supporting existing financial institutions, businesses and maintaining employment. While breeze-block regeneration can be quickly achieved , the building blocks that change community values, aspirations and spirits may not be achievable with the same regeneration 'package'. Decoupling 'economic growth' regeneration from deprivation

regenerationmay be a new start, particularly on the coast, where the deprivation needs may be greater than the economic opportunity.

Notwithstanding the ambiguity about the term 'regeneration' and given the problems of coastal resorts and the emotive energy that the coastline generates, it should be no surprise to learn that there are many national, regional and local departments, authorities, organisations, networks, partnerships and acronyms involved in some aspect of our coastal resort inheritance.

The latest members of the acronym club are the XDWGCT and the RDA Coastal Network, who join the LGA Coastal SIG, the CCA, BRADA, BURA, CoastNet, IDeA and CABE, among many others, whose status, influence and objectives can confuse even seasoned coastal practitioners. Some of the activities of these bodies are listed below and in *Chapter 15*.

Harnessing the skills, interests and resources of these organisations remains a challenge for "place shaping" local authorities.

We start our review of coastal players down on the promenade, where buffeted local authorities seeks to contain the tide of coastal issues. We then move inland to the regional foothills of strategy and funding streams, before heading for the capital hill of policymaking and perceived coastal detachment.

The local government hotchpotch

There are 45 district councils, 14 county and 23 unitary councils who are responsible for the local government administration of the 113 coastal resorts around the English coast (see Figure 2-1 and 2-2 on page 30 and 31). The district councils share service delivery responsibilities with their overlaying tier of county councils, while the unitary authorities are responsible for all local government services in their areas. Unitary Authorities can range in size from large, historic and predominantly rural counties to high-density, urban coastal settlements. What do such structures and geographies mean for coastal regeneration? What can a front-line district council expect to influence and achieve for its coastal resorts when faced with limited financial and staff resources, the competing demands from traditional inland rural communities, the priorities of members, and the political cycle that can promote expediency over a long-term vision?

Do servicing the unitary needs of large areas, such as Cornwall and Northumberland, present different regeneration challenges from servicing compact coastal urban areas, such as Bournemouth, Blackpool, Hartlepool or Torbay? Suffice to say that, as with many coastal issues, there is a lack of information by which to evaluate the most cost-effective, relevant and community-engaging structure for coastal regeneration. However, the new powers of local authorities for 'place shaping', for producing local economic assessments, and the ability to form Local Area Agreements (LAAs) and, probably more relevant for resorts, coastal-hugging Multi Area Agreements (MAAs), provide the opportunity for informing the debate, testing new structures and stimulating new coastal leaderships and visions.

Structures apart, the effectiveness of coastal regeneration by LAs will be influenced by the financial and staff resources available, by the quality of local leadership and management that attracts national and regional support and galvanises established, and hitherto marginal, partners into delivery agreed objectives. Understanding the processes that lead to effective local delivery is one of the main objectives of this book and is the subject of a CCA website debate. Your views are welcomed on www.coastalcommunities.co.uk. Below is an excellent return from North Somerset Council in response to the CCA questionnaire. Please feel free to provide answers to the questions posed and contribute to the debate.

The CCA Coastal Regeneration Questionnaire – Sample Response

Name: North Somerset Council, Unitary Council: Population 204,700 (Census 2001). Coastal resorts in your area, and their populations: Weston-super-Mare – 71,759, Clevedon –21,957, Portishead – 17,130.

Do you think that coastal issues merit special attention in regeneration plans?

There are characteristics within coastal towns that require a different approach. These include:

- Sea and coastal defence & enhancement programmes
- Climate change & rising sea levels
- Perceived remoteness – 'end of the line' perception of potential investors and economic development
- Public realm projects
- Seasonality
- Transient populations
- Age profiles of populations
- Specific health and housing issues
- Cultural
- Identity, profile and public perception

Do you have an explicit coastal regeneration plan/strategy?

No specific coastal plan or strategy but there are a number of ongoing areas of work relating to the coastal regions of the district

- Business website with distinct identity
- Sea front flood defences and enhancement work
- Weston Area Action Plans
- Civic Pride
- 'Sea Change' project to promote the seafront and parks
- Port Marine, Portishead

If the Severn Barrage goes ahead then this will have huge implications for North Somerset district and coastal areas in particular across a range of issues. Two of the short listed options are –

- Middle Barrage from Brean Down to Lavernock Point – known as the Cardiff – Weston barrage
- Bridgwater Bay lagoon – on the English shore between Weston-super-Mare and east of Hinkley Point

What are the barriers to coastal regeneration in your area?

- Lack of resources and funding
- North Somerset district is mostly prosperous which masks pockets of high deprivation including the two most deprived wards in the district, located in Weston-super-Mare. There have been no Neighbourhood Renewal or Working Neighbourhood Fund allocations in the area, apart from a small SSCF neighbourhood management programme in one of Weston's most deprived wards (ends March 2010).
- Low wages compared to high house prices
- Traditional employers in the area that employed high percentage of local people (aviation and shoe making) now gone
- Intergenerational worklessness

- High unemployment and levels of incapacity and other benefit claimants
- Area is seen as dormitory area to Bristol with high % of residents commuting to work there
- Transport infrastructure including lack of capacity at Junction 21, M5 motorway
- Rail connections in Weston-super-Mare are on a loop line and off main London – Bristol – Exeter – Penzance route. No stations at Clevedon or Portishead. Campaign running to re-open Portishead – Bristol line as infrastructure still in place
- High levels of HMOs (houses in multiple occupation)
- High levels of mental health and drug/alcohol dependency
- The number of people sent to area from other areas to undertake drug rehabilitation treatment (Weston-super-Mare has 11% of drug rehab places in UK)
- High transient population
- Seasonal nature of tourism related employment

Weston super Mare

As with many Victorian coastal towns, Weston Super Mare has issues around people on benefits and drug/ alcohol rehabilitation. This has built up over many years due to a number of factors including location by the sea, access from around the country and a large supply of Victorian buildings suitable for conversion to smaller units. Other towns and cities have preferred to send their rehabilitees on rather than dealing with them locally. Also large job losses in manufacturing during the 1990s has led to high levels of low-skilled unemployed people and benefits claimants in the town.

A number of actions have been and are being taken to reduce impact of the issues, these have included: use of Townscape Heritage Initiative (THI) to improve older buildings which have resulted in some being converted from bed-sits to more modern apartments; Single Regeneration Budget (SRB) used to address health and safety issues in HMOs as well as conversion of bed-sits into affordable housing units; targeted action at drug dealers and closing down of rehabilitation centres not meeting assessment requirements. A Ready4work programme provides re-training and re-skilling for long term unemployed in the Weston and surrounding areas.

Neighbourhood Management in South Ward has made a major step change in terms of community engagement and empowerment to ensure local residents have more say and influence over decisions taken in the area and service delivery.

General

There are signs that key sites in the coastal towns will be redeveloped soon - early discussion with developers is encouraging. Ensuring the retail and service industries are fit for purpose alongside increased town centre residential development is essential. Each of our three coastal towns is different and one challenge is to maintain that local and cultural distinctiveness.

What are your priorities in coastal regeneration?

- Economic development and attracting investment – attracting high quality new businesses to the area (private and public)

- Employment led planning policies relating to new housing developments
- Employment - tackling worklessness and getting people off benefit (programmes include Ready4Work and bid submitted for Future Jobs Fund)
- Health – reducing inequalities in areas of deprivation in coastal communities
- Education – supporting local primary and secondary schools to be able to raise the aspirations of children and young people
- Perception and identity – raising and changing profile of coastal areas being a good place to live and work
- Visitor economy & visitor experience e.g. short break themed holidays attracting wider range of visitors, 'a Taste of North Somerset' local food promotion
- Visitor attractions that are open all year round – thus providing permanent employment rather than seasonal

Have you developed expertise in addressing specific coastal resort problems?

- Sea front flood defence and enhancement works
- Work of drug action teams
- Partnership working to tackle issues including housing, anti-social behaviour, tourism

Can you provide details of regeneration successes and good practice in your area?

- Attracting funding from CABE Sea Change fund – successful bid for Weston-super-Mare
- Regional Development Agency funding for Civic Pride, public realm improvements in Weston super Mare
- Knightstone Island, Weston-super-Mare
- Port Marine, Portishead
- Portishead public art programme (www.publicartportishead.co.uk)
- Clevedon Pier (Grade I listed)
- Sea front enhancement programme, Weston-super-Mare including rebuilding of pavilion (in private ownership) on Grand Pier (Grade II listed), following fire in 2008
- T4 On The Beach event now in 4th year at Weston-super-Mare – this Channel 4 event has increased the profile of the area and attracted in young people from across UK. Council has worked very hard to hold onto event, against stiff competition from other resorts
- South Ward Neighbourhood Management Programme

Can you provide details of enterprising coastal businesses in your area?

- Cove Restaurant in Weston has secured a place in the Which Good Food Guide and has been awarded an AA Rosette only 18 months after opening, and achieved good coverage in national newspapers. www.the-cove.co.uk
- Clevedon Pier Trust http://www.clevedonpier.com/history2.htm
- Portishead Pool Community Trust http://www.portisheadopenairpool.org.uk/

Contact: Marian Barber, Head of Economy and Regeneration.
Email: marian.barber@n-somerset.gov.uk
Tel: 01934 42 6670

Government Offices and RDAs

Moving inland, Government Offices (GOs) and the Regional Development Agencies (RDAs), with their influence over large amounts of European Union and national regeneration funding and their connections with government departments, are clearly important partners for LAs in securing project funding, promoting coastal issues, supporting project delivery and addressing deprivation.

A sample of coastal activities by GOs include:

- coastal studies of flood risk;
- supporting LSPs and LAAs;
- processing projects for the SeaChange initiative;
- addressing coastal housing issues;
- facilitating a Seaside Violent Crime conference;
- supporting delivery vehicles, such as the Blackpool Task Force, and promoting the Flyde coast MAA.

Regional development Agencies (RDAs). England's nine RDAs were established in 1999 to bring a regional focus to economic development. As with GOs, RDAs work in partnership with public, private and voluntary organisations to deliver their strategic objectives. Among coastal projects that RDAs have been involved in are:

- developing coastal strategies;
- promoting renewable energy research;
- supporting tourism research;
- developing resort action plans;
- supporting heritage initiatives.

A fuller review of GOs and RDAs' coastal regeneration activities appear in *Chapter 15*.

However, given the economic-growth emphasis of regional players, the intense competition from urban areas, and the relatively undynamic nature of many resort economies – coupled with higher-output, inland urban claims – can make coastal areas less attractive for funding streams that support opportunity over need. Strong coastal leadership, direction and creativity is required to compete and to relate local visions to regional objectives.

At the national level, all government departments impact on coastal resorts to varying degrees, as indeed they do in all areas, in delivering substantial programmes of public service and maintaining employment. However, as previousely stated, it is the interlocking issues of low educational attainment, poor health, lack of business development, growing worklessness and increasing incapacity benefit claimants that contribute to coastal deprivation, and that merit government policy reviews on service delivery.

The XDWGCTs and the RDA Coastal Network

The Select Committee Inquiry (oft cited!), in recognising the lack of coastal awareness among some government departments, recommended the establishment of a Cross-Departmental Working Group on Coastal Towns (XDWGCT). Because of the undynamic nature of resort economies, they also proposed the setting-up of an RDA Coastal Network to disseminate best practice on business diversification, skills and employment creation. These groups are reviewed below.

Established in 2007, the XDWGCT is intended to provide a mechanism for the exchanging of information about coastal settlements between all departments of state. A small team at the Department for Communities and Local Government (DCLG) administers the working group, who have already delivered a valuable service in commissioning two pieces of research into the socioeconomic circumstances of the largest coastal resorts in England. The working group have also invited a range of coastal and regional stakeholders to present at their meetings, including the CCA, Brada and the Coastal SIG. They have also provided financial support for the production of this *handbook*.

Despite the determination of the people involved in the XDWGCT and the Regional Development Agency Coastal Network, both have met some resistance from government departments in supporting their work, often on the basis that the government departments' role is about *policy*, while the delivery and impact of their national programmes are the responsibilities of regional and local delivery agencies. The fact that many coastal resorts over-consume some public programmes (e.g. incapacity benefits and health services), while other programmes have limited impact in some resorts (e.g. business services, education and skills development), requires further analysis and a national policy response.

Unfortunetly, the global recession has influenced the development of these national coastal bodies, in two negative ways.

- First, before the global financial disaster, and following a long period of rising national employment and economic growth, there was evolving a concerted national programme focused on addressing worklessness, which is a substantial and growing problem in coastal resorts. However, the scale of the financial crisis resulted in government departments having to divert attention and resources to dealing with the failings of the banking system, supporting industry and responding to rising unemployment.

- Meanwhile, the RDAs were having their funds diverted into housing and their powers and morale undermined by structural reviews. Even the highly valued and well-received new funding stream, SeaChange, has felt the machete of public cuts!

Despite the existence of the XDWGCT and the RDA Coastal Network, the CCA considers there is a need for a nationally resourced and independent Coastal Intelligence Unit to support coastal regeneration practitioners by articulating the social and economic circumstances and needs of coastal resorts, supporting topic groups, highlighting good practice and informing and lobbying for policy reforms.

Coastal interest groups

This section provides brief pen-pictures of a range of membership and subscription organisations concerned with some aspect of our coastal resorts and coastline. Fuller details of some of these organisations appear in **Chapter 15**, 'In their own words'. We start with the Local Government Association Coastal Special Interest Group whose support has contributed to the production of this publication.

The LGA Coastal Special Interest Group (SIG)

Its Mission

The Local Government Association's (LGA) Special Interest Group (SIG) on Coastal Issues champions coastal issues and represents the collective interests of all maritime local authorities. It seeks to increase awareness and debate at a national and European level of environmental, economic and social issues and concerns that directly affect or which may so affect coastal, estuarine and maritime interests by:

(a) bringing pressure on the Government to achieve a step change in the level of funding to overcome present and future problems;

(b) use every opportunity to secure full involvement of local Government at all levels of policy formulation concerning the coast;

(c) strongly oppose any changes which take responsibility and decision making powers out of the hands of democratic leaders.

Its membership

Currently chaired by Councillor Roger Thomas (East Sussex County Council), the SIG comprises elected members and officers from maritime local authorities throughout England. This blends the experience, skills and expertise of practitioners with the influence, leadership and direction of decision-makers. By way of its broad geographical representation, the group has extensive experience of a wide range of coastal and estuarine related fields and disciplines. The group can call on ecologists, flood defence engineers, coastal planners and economic development practitioners.

Its work

Coastal Policy – the SIG's 'On the Edge' strategy (2001) drew attention to the challenges and threats to the coast, particularly in light of climate change as well as the potential impacts of both on and off-shore development.

The SIG's accompanying action plan seeks to influence emerging policy and legislation notably the raft of new Government policies aimed at modernising and streamlining the management of the coast and our inshore waters. Two key pieces of legislation are currently being developed; the Marine and Coastal Access Bill and the Flood and Water Management Bill. The SIG provides comprehensive responses to these and other key consultations with the aim of:

• raising the profile of Local

Authorities within key policy areas;

- commissioning surveys and studies to raise awareness of policy implications for Local Government;
- ensuring full democratic accountability and the allocation of adequate resources for their implementation.

Coastal Risk – the SIG commissions studies and publishes reports to help inform coastal management, e.g. "Managing Coastal Risks" Study, LGA Coastal Risks Pack and publication of a comprehensive report into Shipping Incidents and implications for Local Government.

Lobbying – the SIG has developed close working relationships with Government Ministers and MPs (its champion in the House of Commons is Norman Lamb MP for North Norfolk) together with statutory organisations such as the Environment Agency and agencies such as the Local Government Information Unit.

Regulation – local authorities play a leading role in managing the coast (e.g. planning and licensing, coast protection and beach management). As the SIG comprises councils specialising in managing beaches and foreshores, it collates and shares best practice through e.g. a Bathing Water Directive Conference and information pack.

Research – it continues to support and commission a comprehensive research programme highlighting challenges to the coast and sustainable coastal management, a list of which is highlighted on its website.

Partnerships – it has representation on Defra committees and the Environment Agency led Coastal Forum and works closely with Coastal Partnerships and Regional Flood Defence Committees. The SIG continues to work with all agencies to represent the position of Local Government.

Finance – in response to the challenging current financial climate it published a report on the financial benefits to working in partnership at the coast, with Defra and the Coastal Partnerships Working Group.

Regeneration – as well as contributing to the Government's Coastal Inquiry the SIG has contributed to the development of the Coastal Communities Alliance's Regeneration Handbook together with support for the All Party Parliamentary Group Coastal and Marine Inquiry into deprivation and disadvantage in coastal rural areas. Its particular areas of interest include fisheries, offshore renewables (e.g. windfarms) and dredging alongside wider economic regeneration. In continuing this theme, the SIG's 2009 Conference in June was focused on the coastal towns of east Kent.

Looking forward the SIG will work closely with partners such as the CCA that share its vision for a vibrant, dynamic, sustainable, democratic, thriving and natural coast.

Key SIG contacts:

Secretary: Kate Cole (kate.cole@eastsussex.gov.uk)
Phone: 01273 481621
Address: East Sussex County Council, Transport & Environment, County Hall, St Anne's Crescent, Lewes, East Sussex BN7 1UE

Economic Development and Regeneration issues:
Nick Churchill (nicholas.

churchill@canterbury.gov.uk)
Phone: 01227 862052
Address: Canterbury City
Council, Military Road,
Canterbury, Kent CT1 3YW

See www.coastalsig.lga.
gov.uk for its strategy, work
programme, current activities
and membership

- *Coastal Communities
  Alliance (CCA)*

The CCA is a UK-wide
umbrella network that focuses
on the socioeconomic and
regeneration issues of all coastal
communities, not just seaside
resorts.

Membership of the CCA
is open to all coastal local
authorities and to all public and
private sector organisations
engaged with coastal
communities (including BRADA,
BURA and the Coastal SIG).

The CCA operates as a
brokerage organisation that
serves to connect up the
activities of partners (specifically
Coastal SIG, BRADA and
BURA) and to articulate the
issues, lobby for change and
promote solutions for coastal
problems.

Membership is free.
The website is www.
coastalcommunities.co.uk.

- *British Resorts and
  Destination Association
  (BRADA)*

This is a national body that

operates as a trade association
representing the wider interest
of local authority sponsored
tourism. Membership includes
local government authorities,
regional and local tourist
boards, and commercial
organisations that are suppliers
of services either to the public
or to the industry itself. The
association does not promote
the interests of major built
coastal resorts exclusively; many
are major rural destinations.
The common link between
all members is an ingrained
tradition of hosting visitors
– and therefore a tendency
towards a much higher
local social and economic
dependency on a vibrant
tourism industry.

Originally set up and run as a
lobbying and advisory body,
since its reorganisation in 1993
the association has expanded
its offer to include a wide range
of services. These vary from
national advertising campaigns,
through PR and press initiatives,
to employee benefits, such as
low-cost travel insurance.

Membership is by subscription.
The website is www.
britishresorts.co.uk.

- *British Urban Regeneration
  Association (BURA)*

This is a membership
organisation championing
physical regeneration. Its
membership is formed from the
private, public and community
sectors. BURA's core areas of
businesses are:

- leading the policy debate,
  influencing and shaping
  future policy;
- training regeneration
  practitioners;
- identifying and promoting
  excellence in regeneration;
- providing a knowledge,
  evidence and research base;
- building national and
  international networks of
  practitioners.

Membership is by subscription.
The website is www.bura.org.
uk.

- *CoastNET*

CoastNET was established
in 1995 and has evolved to
provide a multidisciplinary
network for the exchange
of information, ideas and
expertise in the sustainable
management of the coastal

and marine environment. In 1997, CoastNET became the UK branch of EUROCOAST, a pan-European network that stretches from the Atlantic to the Baltic. Current members include coastal industries, policymakers, marine consultants, local authority staff, researchers from universities and colleges, and non-governmental organisations (NGOs). CoastNet is also the secretariat of the All Party Parliamentary Group of coastal MPs.

Membership is by subscription. The website is www.coastnet.org.uk.

- *Improvement and Development Agency (IDeA)*

IDeA is owned by the Local Government Association and works for local government improvement so councils can serve people and places better.

Working with national, regional and local partners, the agency helps councils work through local partnerships to tackle local priorities such as health, children's services and promoting economic prosperity. The agency advises councils on improving customer service and value-for-money. IDeA also promotes the development of local government's workforce. IDeA has financially supported the production of this *Handbook*.

The website is www.idea.gov.uk.

- *Wildlife Trusts*

There are 47 local Wildlife Trusts across the whole of the UK, the Isle of Man and Alderney, with 765,000 members. Collectively, they are the largest UK voluntary organisation dedicated to conserving the full range of the UK's habitats and species, whether they be in the countryside, in cities or at sea. Objectives are:

- to stand up for wildlife and the environment;
- to create and enhance wildlife havens;
- to inspire people about the natural world;
- to foster sustainable living.

The website is www wildlifetrust.org.uk.

- *Royal Society for the Protection of Birds (RSPB)*

The RSPB is an environmental charity specialising in birds and biodiversity, working for a better world for birds, other wildlife and people. It gives nature a louder voice. The RSPB have more than 200 nature reserves, covering more than 130,000 hectares (500 square miles).

The website is www.rspb.org.uk.

- *Marine Conservation Society (MCS)*

This is a UK charity dedicated to caring for our seas, shores and wildlife. MCS campaigns for clean seas and beaches, sustainable fisheries, and protection for all marine life. Through education, community involvement and collaboration, MCS raises awareness of the many threats that face our seas, and promotes individual, industry and government action to protect the marine environment.

The website is www.mcsuk.org.

- *Standing Conference on Problems Affecting the Coastline (SCOPAC)*

SCOPAC works to promote sustainable shoreline management, and to facilitate the duties and responsibilities of local authorities and other organisations managing the coastal zone of central southern England. SCOPAC's aims are:

- to give sound advice on coastal issues;
- to be a strong influencer in optimising strategic and sustainable policies, plans and programmes to best manage the risks from coastal risk management;
- to be a natural and chosen forum for coastal practitioners to discuss

coastal defence problems and share best practice;

- to be efficient in operation and provide best value for the public purse.

The website is www.scopac. org.uk.

- **UK Beach Management Forum (UKBMF)**

UKBMF was formed in 2004 to bring together under one umbrella a forum that enables all beach operators to share best practices, to ensure that our beaches (resorts/rural) are presented at the highest standards. There are two key objectives:

- to raise the standard of UK beaches by sharing best practice and ensuring dialogue between beach managers;
- to represent the interests of UK beaches by providing a united and cohesive voice to promote the management, quality and sustainability of beaches and the coastline.

The website is www.ukbeach. org.

- **National Piers Society**

The National Piers Society was founded in 1979 under Sir John Betjeman, at a time when some of the finest piers were threatened with demolition. Over the years the society has grown steadily and has become well established as the leading authority on piers. Through its efforts, several piers that would otherwise have vanished remain for the enjoyment of everyone.

The society's aims are to promote and sustain interest in the preservation and continued enjoyment of seaside piers. It publishes Guide to British Piers and a quarterly magazine, and advises heritage bodies, lottery boards, local authorities and the media on pier matters. It maintains links with the British Association of Leisure Parks, Piers and Attractions (representing pier owners) and the Paddle Steamer Preservation Society, whose ships operate excursions from pier landing stages. The society has instituted an award scheme for engineering achievement in pier restoration. It organises visits and talks and holds its annual general meeting in a different resort each year. In the longer term, the society wishes to establish a network of regional branches and a National Piers Museum.

Membership is by subscription. The website is www.piers.org. uk.

- **Royal Town Planners Institute (RTPI)**

The Royal Town Planning Institute is an organisation that attempts to lead the way in the creation of places that work now and in the future. The RTPI's work involves:

- promoting good planning;
- developing and shaping policy affecting the built environment;
- raising the standards of the planning profession;
- supporting members through continued professional development;
- education and training for future planners.

Membership is by subscription. The website is www.rtpi.org. uk.

- **UK Climate Impacts Programme (UKCIP)**

UKCIP helps organisations to adapt to inevitable climate change. While it is essential to reduce future greenhouse gas emissions, the effects of past emissions will continue to be felt for decades. Since 1997 UKCIP has been working with the public, private and voluntary sectors to assess how a changing climate will affect construction, working practices, demand for goods and services, biodiversity, service delivery, health, and more.

The website is www.ukcip.org.

- **Coastal & Marine Union (EUCC)**

The Coastal & Marine Union (European Union for Coastal Conservation) is an association with 2,700 members and member organisations in 40 countries. Founded in 1989 with the aim of promoting coastal conservation by bridging the gap between scientists, environmentalists, site managers, planners and policymakers, it has grown since then into the largest network of coastal practitioners and experts in Europe, with 14 national branches and offices in seven countries. The working area is Europe, the Mediterranean and Black Seas and other neighbouring regions.

The Coastal & Marine Union is dedicated to conserving and maintaining healthy seas and attractive coasts for both people and nature. It advocates best practice by developing coastal and marine policies, mobilising experts and stakeholders, providing advice and information, and implementing demonstration projects.

The website is www.eucc.nl.

• *Cozone*

Cozone is a national network for UK marine and coastal scientists and engineers. The aim of the network is to provide a forum through which the coastal community can identify and tackle issues raised by both the research

community and practitioners. The main objectives are to encourage new multidisciplinary research collaborations and to bring together an extended community of researchers and end-users of research. These objectives are achieved through a programme of meetings and a website.

The website is www.cozone.org.uk.

• *CoaST*

CoaST is a social enterprise whose aim is to work towards one-planet tourism – a type of tourism that provides benefits to the people, economy and environment of Cornwall, and that operates within our social, financial and environmental means.

The website is www.cstn.org.uk.

• *Institution of Civil Engineers (ICE)*

The Institution of Civil Engineers is a registered charity

that strives to promote and progress civil engineering. The institution believes that civil engineers are 'at the heart of society, delivering sustainable development through knowledge, skills and professional expertise'.

Those with an interest in the diverse aspects of coastal zone management are facing increasing challenges as a result of development pressures, environmental impacts as well as increasing risks arising from the impacts of climate change. The institution has papers available that cover the full range of coastal management topics, including:
• coastal policies and management arrangements;
• managing the dynamic coast;
• mapping, monitoring and new technologies;
• coastal and estuary engineering;
• coastal environmental management and enhancement;
• achieving better integrated coastal zone management.

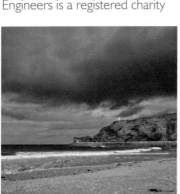

Membership is by subscription. The website is www.ice.org.uk.

Further information on organisations involved with the coast appears in **Chapter 15**, "In their own words". If you wish your organisation to feature on the CCA coastal database, please send the details to:

Patrick.Browne@lincolnshire. gov.uk. Thank you.

As one acronym among many, the CCA is aware of the confusion that exists even among seasoned practitioners on the status, objectives, resources, responsibilities and activities of the very many coastal organisations. In order to clarify the situation, the CCA will collate details on all such organisations, evaluate their services, and promote participation on the website with the objective of maximising the skills and resources available for coastal regeneration. Please contact the website to contribute to this service.

From Blue Rinse to Hedonism? Drinking in 21st Century Bournemouth Will Haydock Bournemouth University UK

This paper looks at how young people behave and think about drinking. My research was based on conversations with 113 drinkers and professionals, such as the 'club chaplain', youth work professionals, two drug and alcohol professionals, one bar manager, five bar workers, one door supervisor, the two MPs for Bournemouth and the night-time economy coordinator.

Bournemouth developed in the nineteenth century as a seaside resort for the middle classes and invalids, and can thus be contrasted with other resorts more oriented towards pleasure and indeed the working class. However, in recent years Bournemouth has gained a reputation for being a destination for stag and hen nights and heavy drinking,

with the mayor describing it as a place where 'blue rinse' and 'hedonism' live side by side.

Alcohol is certainly important to the local economy, being worth £125 million per year, and support 4,000 jobs. The council has stated that the borough has 'the greatest concentration of night-time activity outside London' The Lonely Planet's is less favourable: '...it.....is now a hedonistic paradise of stag-and-hen party hell.....it parties so hard it's a nation's drinking problem personified'

In this paper I argue that this characterisation of the night-time economy as hedonistic does not tell the whole story - some young drinkers employ ideas of responsibility and decorum that might be familiar to the refined residents

of nineteenth century Bournemouth.

The Carnivalesque and the Everyday

I found that employing two ideas of 'drinking styles' made sense of the variety of ways in which people talked about drinking to me – referring both to their own and other people's practices. The two styles can be understood as the 'carnivalesque' and the 'everyday'. The carnivalesque implies a world of altered norms of behaviour and social interaction. The everyday, in contrast stresses the continuity with standard societal norms. To give an example, funny stories of being drunk such as Hannah's tale of emerging from a pub toilet with her trousers and underwear still around her ankles are celebrated in the carnivalesque approach to drinking, whereas they would be considered embarrassing or degrading – or at least undesirable – according to the everyday approach.

One important point is that as well as the idea of dissolution of everyday hierarchies and norms, the sense of public display and community associated with the carnivalesque moves it beyond simply 'hedonism' which has associations with individualism and immediate, sensory pleasures. Moreover, where participants almost universally distanced themselves from the figure of the 'binge' drinker, the idea of the carnivalesque is a more ambivalent concept which can be embraced or rejected on the basis of cultural, aesthetic approaches. The carnivalesque can be understood most simply as the application of an alternative set of norms from everyday life.

This apparent shift in norms is frequently understood as being amusing and was frequently directly to the consumption of alcohol. Ollie, for example, explained how 'unusual' events were the main attraction of going out, as these made a night 'legendary' – it generated stories that could be told again and again. He told me that alcohol was essential to such nights out because without alcohol people would not behave in the 'unusual' way necessary for these stories.

or further information on this paper, please visit: www.tourism-culture.com

Chapter 4

Regeneration policies and
their impact on coastal areas

by John K. Walton

It is clear that national regeneration policy, as it focuses on or otherwise affects coastal settlement, needs to be examined in all its dimensions and at all levels. What are, and should be, the relationships between European funding bodies, government departments, Regional Development Authorities (RDAs), local authorities and entities such as HLF and English Heritage, the National Trust and the Royal Society for the Protection of Birds? How do, and how should, relationships between the public, the private, the hybrid and the voluntary sector play out in regeneration programmes? How far should they be prescriptive, how far enabling, and what should the balance be under given sets of circumstances? How do we make national regeneration policies agile, flexible and interactive at the local level? And what, for these purposes, is special about regeneration policy at the coast? How can national policies be encouraged to take account of the difference and distinctiveness of coastal settlements and of each coastal settlement within a common framework, and how can we overcome the obstacles to recognising this distinctiveness, which still meets with resistance and even rejection at national and RDA level, as evidenced by the first response to the Coastal Towns report? What can we learn

from the successes and failures of the past, perhaps especially the recent past, and how can we feed these understandings into current and future policy? And what can we learn, in positive and negative terms, from national regeneration policies (or the lack of them) in other countries?[1]

This chapter cannot engage with all these issues in equal depth, and must be selective. We are fortunate to have a new overview of urban regeneration in the United Kingdom, which sets the theme in historical context and examines a wide range of issues and problems.[2] This is particularly useful because it charts a course through the bewildering array of initiatives that are revealed by a trawl through the literature, as layer upon layer of past proposals, approaches and agenda swim past the investigator's gaze. This was already being described as 'the regeneration maze' nearly a decade ago.[3] We also have a new collection of international essays, with genuinely global scope and adopting a variety of approaches, which is particularly concerned with the avoidance of inequity and the inclusion of ethnic minorities and the poor, and which will help to rescue us from insularity by encouraging comparative perspectives. It even includes an important essay on a historic coastal city, Salvador da Bahia in Brazil.[4]

This offers a reminder that we must resist the temptation to regard the regeneration of seaside towns as a uniquely British set of issues; nor, indeed, is it peculiar to so-called 'cold water' resorts with nineteenth-century origins. There are plenty of comparable cases on the French Channel Coast and on the 'Jersey shore' of the north-eastern United States, for example; but we can also find them on the Spanish Mediterranean coast, where early 'mass tourism' resorts have needed extensive intervention, and on Italy's Adriatic coast, where the 'colonie di vacanza' of the inter-war years have left a fascinating architectural legacy that resists easy adaptation to new holiday tastes, preferences and needs. They are also evident in Florida and on the Gulf Coast. There is no room to develop this theme here, but it is worth reminding ourselves that good practice in coastal regeneration may be found outside England if we care to look for it.[5]

The focus of most work on regeneration, however, is still overwhelmingly on cities and their problems; and it is interesting to see how cities, 'inner cities', 'urban neighbourhoods' and estates have dominated the regeneration literature on Britain, whether critical, descriptive or prescriptive. A word-search of book titles in the British Library on-line catalogue, which is an indicative if imperfect approach to analysis, communicates this message very strongly, while revealing lesser preoccupations with rural regeneration, market towns and docklands. These last are the only 'coastal' examples, and are mainly associated with maritime cities like Liverpool, Bristol and, of course, London. 'Coastal regeneration', as a word-search category for books, produced not a single hit. This is a little misleading, in that local coastal regeneration initiatives have been in train for the last quarter of a century in particular places. But it is very interesting to see how recently a generic interest in coastal regeneration, as a focus for involvement and investment, has emerged.

The most visible initiatives, apart from the work of the Coastal Communities Alliance and its component organisations, have been sparked by, or coincided with, the report of the Communities and Local Government Select Committee on Coastal Towns in 2007, and the angry response to the government's attempt to evade the consequences of its conclusions. Thus, in November 2007, we saw the establishment of the coastal regeneration fund, led by CABE, which offered £45 million up to bidders during 2008–10, and the

cross-departmental working group which constituted the response of the Department for Communities and Local Government to the Coastal Towns report. Meanwhile English Heritage, whose interest in the seaside has a longer pedigree (like that of the Coastal Communities Alliance and its antecedents), produced its report on regeneration in historic coastal towns, and the Historical Environment Local Management (HELM) scheme signposted a local dimension to the initiative. Local initiatives are, indeed, proliferating, such as the interventions by Roger de Haan at Folkestone. Now is clearly a propitious moment for taking matters further.

But this is jumping the gun slightly. In the first place, we need to return to the question of what we might understand by 'regeneration'. This chapter presents a particular point of view. At the core of the concept should be the idea of giving a new, fresh lease of life to something that is already there, enabling it to rejuvenate itself and grow in ways that are new, dynamic and sustainable, but recognisably drawing on existing identities, resources and vitality.

Regeneration, as a concept, is not about destroying what is already there in order to replace it with something completely different, on the

model of the 'slum clearance' programmes of the middle decades of the twentieth century. That kind of operation may sometimes be necessary and even desirable, but the appropriate label for it would be 'redevelopment' or 'replacement', in association with rebranding and place-making on a scoured and levelled site. 'Renewal' is also a relevant descriptor, which in practice also tends to be associated more with demolition and rebuilding than with the idea of regeneration envisaged here. In most parts of most coastal settlements we should not be thinking in such drastic terms: these are not brown-field sites whose former identities can be swept away and buried, but, as Beatty and Fothergill have demonstrated, communities whose historic identities are still recognised and whose capacity for generating employment, attracting migrants and conjuring remembered pleasures is still powerful. So 'regeneration', in this sense of reviving and revitalising rather than destroying and replacing, should generally be the order of the day at the British seaside. This is not always understood by those who intervene in coastal urban settings, especially when they are not embedded in the communities in question. Neil Lee's report for the Work Foundation on the importance of 'distinctiveness' reinforces the concerns of, for example,

English Heritage in support of these contentions.[6]

Regeneration is also more than just an economic concept, a key point that is also often overlooked. Economic questions are at the core of it, but they are not the whole package. Local jobs and spending power need to be created and sustained, and ways of dealing with unemployment and benefit dependency, together with shortages of decent affordable housing, lack of consistent, reliable incomes, and lack of demand to sustain local businesses, are necessarily central to regeneration policy. Interventions in these fields appear to offer measurable yardsticks and outcomes, which are particularly important when central government is evaluating apparent fitness for purpose; and, in this respect and others, they are in tune with dominant values, with the result that preoccupation with the necessary economic basis for action may become exclusive and overriding, without accounting for the whole picture.

It is perhaps unfortunate that government policy on regeneration is so firmly focused on economic development and performance as an end in itself, and on benchmarking against neighbours and averages. These are useful indicators of state of play and trajectory of change, but they cannot be satisfactory as apparent 'ends' in themselves, especially when they are necessarily abstracted from the ways in which localities are experienced 'on the ground'.

We also need to remember that, while it is right to regard the distinctiveness of coastal employment and demographic profiles and (for example) the related health problems as requiring attention, they are also identified with the peculiarities of the coast as a hidden 'region', and we should not expect to be able to iron them out: they are part and parcel of the necessary diversity of the English whole, and interventions need to aim at managing variations rather than aspiring to remove them. Related issues involving, for example, the need to tackle crime and antisocial behaviour,[7] under-achievement and lack of opportunity, seasonality,[8] population instability and 'churn', are likewise high on the agenda. National policies are available to engage with many of these interrelated sets of problems, but they need to be adjustable to take account of regional and generic distinctiveness, and especially local circumstances. Coastal towns, and specifically coastal resorts, have generic issues that are specific to them as a 'family' of towns, while varying in extent and nature on different coastlines and according to the experiences of individual resorts, with their various markets, social profiles, environments and histories. Regeneration initiatives need to recognise this variety, which is expressed through a range of attributes that may need to be safeguarded, respected and nurtured when decisions that affect localities are made, at whatever level and along whatever axis of power they are taken. Such attributes are likely to include architecture (especially the architecture of enjoyment), amenity, layout, industrial history, the informal paraphernalia of established activities, traditions of festivity, entertainment and the occupation and use of space, and free access to places of shared pleasure. A good deal of 'regeneration' literature does indeed focus on such issues, especially architecture, art and performance; but it needs to be connected more systematically with the other components of this polymorphous concept, and especially with the dominant emphasis on economic performance and service delivery.[9] Regeneration, as such, needs to be conceived in a holistic way. Moreover, it will be successful only if it works with the grain of existing local cultures and preferences, and sustains the positive distinctiveness of place-myth and local identity for residents, visitors and those who may be

in transition between the two conditions.

The key players 'on the ground' in coastal regeneration are often (and perhaps increasingly) going to be local, even when the nature of the exercise is to find the best ways of negotiating appropriate ways forward with a government whose instincts are (still) centralising, cascading policy from the top down and the centre outwards through what is in many ways the preferred (and often catastrophic) model, the line management system with prescribed targets (leading to game-playing and misdirection of effort) and (pseudo-) quantitative checks on outcomes. Even so, this is where decisions have to be made about which of the bewildering array of options will be worth pursuing, with which partners, and to what ends, not least because of the enduring lack of joined-up thinking higher up the chain of command. It is encouraging that government policy on SNR (Sub-National Economic Development and Regeneration), as reviewed

in July 2007, recognises the importance of the sub-regional level of economic decision-making. The need to focus on the local level applies to coastal communities with particular force, and government's historic reluctance to recognise the importance of this kind of settlement, the distinctive problems that the coast poses (beyond the obvious technical ones of sea defences), and the need for 'coastal' to become as established a category as 'rural' for policy purposes, were made only too clear in the initial response to the report of the Coastal Towns Commission. The most dynamic and successful period for England's coastal towns in general was probably the later nineteenth and early decades of the twentieth century, perhaps between about 1870 and 1939, when municipal government was at its strongest and most self-confident, accessing advice and expertise from an increasingly effective central government civil service on matters of technology and best practice, developing a proud tradition of local public service

and expertise among elected representatives and officers alike, and installing a remarkable array of infrastructure to sustain the health of what was still, predominantly, a locally owned and run private sector. This period, and these processes, were not conflict-free, and nor were local authorities uniformly successful, effective or free from conflicts of interest. We should add that the key decades at the turn of the century were economically and politically propitious, especially at the seaside.[10]

Decline probably began to set in during the 1930s, becoming sustained and serious after the Second World War and cumulatively disastrous after 1979, as the financial autonomy of local government was eroded and central controls were steadily intensified. This has not been solely a British set of problems: it has also been apparent, for example, in the United States.[11]

The heyday of local and municipal government cannot return, at least in its previous form. But a retrospective view offers a reminder that restoring a measure of civic pride and autonomy to municipal government requires the reconstruction of a measure of trust and prestige (which has, in its turn, to be earned), and of a cadre of experienced, competent and trustworthy civic leaders, as well as initiative and financial independence, that has been progressively and cumulatively lost over the last half century.[12]

It is therefore exciting, at precisely the point where the currently orthodox approach to recession threatens the spending power of local government, to highlight the appearance of a report (by Tom Symons and Chris Leslie) that emphasises the need for local action and empowerment through access to new sources of capital.[13]

One indicator, among many, of the likely impact of the funding crisis in urban regeneration is the projected collapse in land sales receipts for the Home and Communities Agency, the regeneration quango that replaces the Housing Corporation and English Partnerships, with a decline of around 90 per cent in prospect and a likelihood that very little money will be available to bidders in the 2010/11 round.[14] Symons and Leslie emphasise the necessity for continued infrastructure investment as part of wider regeneration initiatives. They suggest that local authorities should be able to bypass the Treasury and go direct to capital markets through bond issues, while finding creative ways to access capital and manage financial reserves. Potential strategies

include the generation of revenue streams through user charging, and – more positively – the taking up of new trading opportunities as 'permissive powers of wellbeing and general competence become available'. A shift away from the notorious Private Finance Initiative is advocated, through alterations in the conventions to provide a level playing field offering greater local choice; and the establishment of a new collective fund for council reserves is advocated.
What this adds up to is the dismantling of restrictions on local authority activity and the emancipation of councils from dependence on central government. Such suggestions are all the more stimulating because they open out the possibility of a return to the heyday of local government, when it was able to innovate, trade, manage natural monopolies for the benefit of either consumers (through price controls) or ratepayers (by ploughing back profits), and invest for the future.

In other words, this is nothing new, whether the preferred label is 'municipal socialism' or 'municipal capitalism'. An interesting pointer to changing times is Blackpool Council's proposal, announced in December 2009, to seek national and European regeneration funding in support of a municipal takeover of the

Tower, the Winter Gardens and other central amusement and entertainment facilities in the resort: this is not 'nationalisation', as reported in the Daily Mail, but a proposed reversion to (and extension of) older models of municipal involvement in essential aspects of resort economies.[15] Whatever the label, this worked very well in the late nineteenth and early twentieth centuries, especially at the seaside, and it could work well again now.[16] In the earlier incarnation, though, we should reinforce the point that it benefited from generally expansive coastal economies, the availability of able and experienced councillors often drawn from local backgrounds in large-scale businesses, and the development of a rooted and experienced cadre of local officials with a public service ethic, while well-informed though invariably cautious advice and counsel were available from the Local Government Board.

The Symons and Leslie report also resonates with aspects of the report of the Business Panel on Future European Union Innovation Policy, which emphasises the need to extend the concept of and vehicles for innovation from business to social models, involving charities and social enterprises and looking to promote social innovation. These proposals are still under discussion, but they point the way towards alternative approaches to regeneration that go beyond the narrowly economic and technological, and bring neglected actors into play.[17]

Giving space, scope and encouragement to local responses to local situations, informed by 'best practice' and drawing on external partnerships, creativity and expertise where appropriate, should be a key theme in coastal regeneration, especially in the hard times that are arriving. But a further essential element is the nature of the political processes involved in regeneration.

In many coastal settings the coastal settlement itself is part of a larger administrative entity, especially since local government reorganisation in 1974, which created amalgamations such as that of the old county and industrial city of Lancaster and the coastal resort of Morecambe, generating enduring conflict over tourism policy, or brought together resorts of contrasting character under a single umbrella, as with Thanet (Margate, Ramsgate, Broadstairs) or Scarborough, which also includes the smaller coastal resorts of Whitby and Filey. Under such circumstances all proposed developments (or withdrawals of support for established assets) are likely to become controversial, as local interest-groups complain of discrimination, neglect or lack of understanding.

A good example is the outrage that erupted in Whitstable in the summer of 2007 when proposals for 'regenerating' a profitable working harbour by destroying the existing ambience of the South Quay to make way for a hotel, supermarket and theme pub were published under the auspices of Canterbury City Council. The plans, submitted in competition by external developers, were rejected after a fierce and popular local campaign, and Whitstable Harbour Watch was established to keep an eye on future developments, recognising the need to preserve the distinctive and unusual character of the working harbour while sustaining its economic viability. This was one of many examples of a local authority failing to recognise the individuality of its component communities and seeking to impose a standard scheme on an enjoyably untidy area of attractive character. The politics of regeneration, especially in terms of facilitating debate and acting on its outcomes, are an essential part of the process.[18]

This also applies in nearby Thanet, where the efforts of the local authority to meet economic targets and promote development according to government criteria have not always been appreciated by elements of local opinion.[19] This can be illustrated by the comments of Christine Tongue as part of the publicity for her 'Thanet on Film' exhibition, a compilation of films of holiday Thanet in past times which 'shows what we once had and how it's all been left to decay.'[20] This theme of lost assets and enjoyments – and how they might be recovered or renewed – is common to many seaside campaigners, as are problems associated with neglect of the public realm, together with the sense that well-targeted investment and effective management could restore their attractiveness and promote regeneration without expensive wholesale redevelopment, at a time when all the signs suggest that domestic tourism is itself regenerating.

Recently, however, Thanet Council has also been supportive of the genuine regeneration of Margate's Dreamland cinema and amusement park complex: the former closed in November 2007, in the face of competition from the new multiplex at Westwood Cross, and the latter in 2003. The Dreamland Trust's proposals for an open-air amusement park museum on the site, which are attracting development funding and have strong support from the

English Heritage Urban Panel and the Prince's Trust, offer an authentic, locally rooted opportunity to regenerate Margate's popular tourism industry.[21] The plans are grounded in a historic local attraction which had been in place since 1920 and developed from earlier popular entertainment uses of the site.[22] That contrasts with the proposals for redevelopment put forward by external consultants in 2004, focusing on routine housing, retail and car parking in a key coastal location. Existing amusement park operators are clear that the demand is there.

Nearby Arlington House, an early and distinctive seaside tower block of 1963 with spectacular sea views, provides another interesting Thanet example of conflicting attitudes to heritage and regeneration. Despite its bad local reputation, which arises from sustained neglect, it is a really impressive piece of post-war architecture, and in another setting it would be highly valued.[23] A similar seaside tower block in Cesenatico, on the Adriatic coast in Italy, completed in 1957, has become an emblematic element of the local tourist townscape and of the resort's publicity.[24] Refurbishment rather than demolition seems to be on the agenda for this building of character, a classic example

of the 'heritage of the recent past' which generates strong opinions for and against, but can certainly not be accused of blandness.[25]

Buildings like these, and – more conventionally – those of Margate's Old Town and early resort area, help to give a coastal town a sense of identity and identification. Margate has lost so much that it needs to cherish what remains, while regenerating imaginatively and 'in character' around and within it. The Turner Contemporary cannot stand alone, any more than Morecambe's regenerated Midland Hotel can do so. And, as the Midland Hotel, the De La Warr Pavilion or Blackpool's Winter Gardens complex demonstrate, there is no point in losing genuinely iconic buildings and amenities, especially if you have nothing of value to put in their place. Despite the escalating costs of restoration and refurbishment, it generally comes cheaper than demolition and new build. It also attracts a more up-market public with scope for generating local multipliers, as is beginning to happen around the Midland Hotel in Morecambe. Those local multipliers, whose importance emphasises the need to minimise 'leakage' from the local economy into the coffers of national and multinational business, are crucial to spreading the benefits of regeneration into local

pockets.[26]

This focus on an important case study draws attention to what Thanet in general, and Margate in particular, has to offer as an example of the tensions surrounding the articulation of regeneration policies. These emerge through the local (party and other) political dimension, the complex interactions between the locality and external organisations (county, regional and national government agencies, private developers, NGOs, hybrids, lobby groups and the media), and the relationships between economic, cultural and 'heritage' criteria as drivers of regeneration. Local authorities need to resist the temptation to take whatever developers are prepared to offer, and to regard all promises of increased employment as plausible and cost-free; and they need to pay genuine heed to the wishes of local residents and visitors, even when the signals are mixed and confused, as is the case with many of Thanet's critics.

The 'reputation for power' of big international developers, with their ability to hire expensive legal support, to exhaust the appeals procedure and to threaten determined opponents with crippling costs, constitutes another widespread set of problems, in coastal locations as elsewhere. Pressure from higher tiers of government, especially to meet targets defined in narrow economic terms, may help to exacerbate these problems, and the tensions that can result are well illustrated in the case of Exmouth, where supermarket-led regeneration proposals in 2004 generated conflict between Devon County Council, East Devon District Council and Exmouth Town Council, and eventually gave way to a much less ambitious and intrusive set of proposals.[27]

We seem to be moving, in the last few years, towards a broader understanding of what the coast has to offer, and how to enhance or at least ameliorate what is there rather than sweeping it away root and branch. English Heritage has been helpful and supportive here. Hastings' efforts to market itself as a 'cultural destination', and its encouragement of – and financial support for – annual events that draw in visitors and become identified with the town's image, is an example of a widespread and long-lived tendency to develop niche marketing, for events that may or may not have a clear coastal resonance (seafood but also wine, an Old Town Carnival – and an illuminated heritage trail – but also a chess congress and a morris-dancing festival).[28] In some respects recession may be a blessing in disguise, as it discourages disruptive large-scale projects – especially those that are founded on unrealistic

expectations of the competitive attractiveness, in locations that are relatively difficult of access, of standardised development packages. In turn it may encourage local ventures that reinforce existing loyalties and identities while making them expansively available to others, but in sustainable ways.

Rachel Cooke, writing about these issues for the *Observer* in August 2009, showed a refreshing awareness of such resources and opportunities on the south coast, and this kind of media coverage seems to be gaining ground, hand over fist, against the older default mode of dismissive contempt (although a week earlier Cooke herself, in drawing attention to the need for seaside SMEs to cater more cheerfully and imaginatively for their customers, resorted to that very tone of authorial voice in writing about a visit to Broadstairs).

Media perceptions are of vital importance. Changing the grammar of expectation and reporting about the coast in general, and about specific destinations, constitutes an essential element in making regeneration effective at the level of image promotion and, indeed, brand management. The role of *Coast* magazine, and its competitive awards for best seaside attractions and businesses, is potentially

significant here. But the tendency of journalism to focus on individual examples, and to enjoy amplifying unpleasant experiences, reinforces a general point. Regeneration initiatives need to engage with enhancing the attitudes and expectations of local business and service providers, as well as providing infrastructure and reinforcing systems.[29]

Finally, several other themes should be emphasised across the range of disparate but connected issues that make up the 'regeneration question', here as in other settings. They are: simplification; sustainability; inclusiveness; collaboration; topophilia; and above all the importance of taking a holistic approach, or looking at the problems and solutions 'in the round', going beyond isolated box-ticking exercises and assessing how things fit together and what the overall impact of initiatives has been. Simplification, or streamlining, is highly necessary, not least to prevent duplication of effort and unnecessary competition for shrinking resources, but also to ease information flows and workloads by reducing the sheer volume of opportunities to evaluate and information to accumulate.
It is to be hoped that the DCMS 'single conversation' approach may prove helpful here. Sustainability needs to engage the active and informed

participation of residents and local businesses, and, in a financial environment that will be less conducive to large-scale redevelopment initiatives, it will be best pursued in ways that generate local employment in support of local economies. Labour-intensive projects for the improvement of the public realm, in the form of parks and promenades, or loans for amenities and enhancement for local SMEs (such as seaside boarding houses) to make them more attractive and competitive, should be on the agenda, as should financial support for museums and other cultural attractions that sustain distinctive facets of local identity.

All this kills two birds with one stone. It offers employment opportunities while making places more attractive. Water quality, litter removal and efficient waste disposal management are all ongoing housekeeping concerns that local people respond to positively, and that improve the local environment in ways that encourage repeat visits. Sprucing up and spicing up existing assets should be part of this process. Subsidising and supporting the public realm through affordable and flexible transport options should also be in tune with the spirit of the times, and of course it is particularly relevant to access to and travel within coastal locations, which are hard to reach and often both scattered and elongated in their development patterns.

This is regeneration through modest expenditure on good housekeeping, something that has often been neglected as big 'iconic' projects catch the official and political eye. An expanded local taxation base, which would be best and most equitably funded by a return to the fully graduated property taxes or 'rates' which were foolishly abandoned a generation ago, would make such proposals easier to fund and more accountable locally.

Such activity should also promote inclusiveness, which entails providing a welcoming and accessible environment for all who are attracted by what the coast, and particular incarnations of it, has to offer. This will not be everyone, and it need not be everyone: openness is a necessary and life-enhancing virtue, but trying to alter the character of seaside places to appeal to everyone is an illusory goal. Looking after existing residents and visitors, including the unfashionable but often lucrative older demographics, and expanding their numbers, should take priority over speculating in imagined new markets – unless there is strong evidence (especially in the larger, more diverse and cosmopolitan resorts) of demand.

Moreover, the dangers of sealing off gated communities, and setting the barriers of access and acceptance in desirable places too high, are now becoming apparent. Gentrification needs to be inflected by democracy, perhaps particularly at the seaside, where the traditions of open access to public tidal beaches and their adjacent commons is so strong and culturally pervasive. Privatise such spaces at your peril.

A related theme should be that of collaboration. As many contributors to the discussions in this *Handbook* have emphasised, working together with the full range

of government organisations and NGOs, at all tiers of representation, is of central importance, from sharing skills and knowledge to presenting coastal regions as shared systems of assets that are more attractive than their individual components taken in isolation. That also applies to businesses within destinations. Done well, and with democratic awareness of local wishes (which are, of course, sometimes divided and contradictory), this should promote that essential concept of *topophilia* – emotional attachment to a place through the shared enjoyment of memory, nostalgia and the power of association – that is fundamental to successful regeneration. It defies quantification, but it is the essence of a holistic approach to local improvement, engagement and practical sustainability. Lose that and you have lost the battle. Sustain it, enhance it, transfer it to new publics who can then pass it on, and England's coastal settlements have a future.

SNR and the Framework for Regeneration
by the Department for Communities and Local Government

The government published its review of the Sub-National Economic Development and Regeneration (SNR) in July 2007. This set out a framework that would enable central and local governments and partners to work together more effectively to tackle future economic challenges. The review stressed the need for local authorities to play a stronger role in economic development and regeneration. It argued that as different places face different economic challenges and opportunities, *much economic development activity needs to be tailored locally or sub-regionally.*

The ability of local authorities and partners to deliver sustainable economic growth and to respond to economic challenges in their areas depends heavily on their ability to assemble a robust and well-informed economic evidence base. The SNR proposed that a new duty be placed on county councils and unitary district councils to assess the economic conditions of their areas. The proposed new duty is included within the Local Democracy, *Economic Development and Construction Bill,* currently before Parliament.

The government published draft statutory guidance on the new duty in August 2009, available at www. communities.gov.uk/ publications/localgovernment/ localeconomicassessments. This sets out the government's thinking on how local economic assessments should be carried out and the issues they need to address. This is complemented by more detailed guidance, launched in October and prepared by the Improvement and Development Agency (IDeA)

As the draft government guidance explains, local economic assessments should equip local authorities and partners with a common understanding of local economic conditions. It should enable them to better understand the strengths and weaknesses of their local economy and the local constraints to economic growth and employment. Local authorities and partners already assemble a range of data and evidence to support their economic interventions. Local economic assessments should provide a mechanism for bringing this evidence together within a common evidence base that tells the story of a place.

Through their local economic assessments, coastal areas should specifically draw out the wider social, environmental and geographical factors, such as seasonality of attractions, connectivity and peripherality

to other centres, that impact on their economic growth. They should also use their assessments to identify the economic linkages between their area and the wider economy – thereby establishing their functional economic area. Assessments also provide an opportunity for coastal areas to benchmark their economic performance against neighbouring coastal areas and regional averages, and try to establish the reasons why their area has performed better or worse than other areas.

The SNR also stressed that sub-regions are in many respects the key spatial level around which economic growth is concentrated. It stated that increasing the extent to which economic development decision-making is concentrated at sub-regional level is an important means of improving economic outcomes.

We have already seen the establishment of Multi Area Agreements (MAAs). These are voluntary agreements between groups of local authorities and partners to deliver economic development improvement targets. The Local Democracy, Economic Development

and Construction Bill further strengthens the ability of local authorities to work at a sub-regional level in the pursuit of economic development. The Bill enables the establishment of MAAs with duties, which brings MAAs on to the same statutory footing as LAAs. The Bill also enables the establishment of economic prosperity boards and combined authorities. These would provide a formal structure for sub-regional collaboration between relevant authorities on economic development and regeneration (and transport in the case of combined authorities). They would provide a stable mechanism for long-term, strategic decision-making on economic issues across the whole functional economic sub-region.

The Framework for Regeneration

Regeneration has been primarily concerned with improving outcomes for places that underperform across a range of measures. The priorities attached to tackling different aspects of underperformance have varied over time, but the DCLG's activities to support this agenda broadly fit into the following categories:

- housing-led regeneration (broadly led by the HCA);
- provision of key infrastructure (broadly led by RDAs);
- economic renewal (broadly led by councils through funds in ABG such as Working neighbourhoods Fund and LEGI).
- improving prospects for areas of multiple deprivation through neighbourhood renewal (broadly led by councils through funds in ABG such as Working Neighbourhoods Fund and LEGI).

These activities have delivered striking improvements in recent years, particularly in the post-industrial cities. However, the wider economic situation has impacted significantly on our ability to deliver this form of activity, largely due to:

- falling land and property values;
- loss of secured occupancy;
- reliance on a single private developer;
- cash flow problems;
- high operational costs for developers.

The government has remained committed to regeneration, and is still planning to spend over £6.5 billion to support local ambitions over the next two years. In response, the Pre-Budget Report 2008 announced that we would be bringing forward £180 million to support key regeneration projects – £100 million from RDA budgets and £80 million from HCA budgets. BIS is working closely with the RDAs to monitor regeneration activity brought forward.

To promote better alignment of resources and a clearer focus for regeneration activity during the downturn, the government published Transforming Place, Changing Lives, a framework for regeneration for consultation in July 2008. This set out a vision for regeneration, by:

- setting out a clear definition of regeneration – reversing economic, social, and physical decline in areas where market forces will not do this without support from government;
- setting out the steps government is taking now to keep regeneration moving in the current economic conditions;

- retaining a clear focus on tackling deprivation – which is central to the government's approach;
- focusing on tackling the underlying economic challenges that hold back too many places through joint HCA and RDA action;
- setting out clear expectations from the regional strategy in prioritising areas for investment, and aligning capital funding in support of these areas.

DCLG responses to questions raised by the Framework for Regeneration

Will the focus of regeneration funding be on economic areas of opportunity as opposed to deprived areas of need?

We don't believe the two are mutually exclusive. The framework is clear that investment needs to be targeted where it will have most impact by supporting those communities where the most severe poverty and worklessness persists and where there is the opportunity to deliver long-term change.

What will the national regeneration budget be in the future and who will control the budget? With major public sector cuts forecast by all, what will be the scale of impact on the totality of the regeneration budget?

As Professor Michael Parkinson's report indicated, the tough economic conditions are now making life challenging for the regeneration sector, and are affecting projects across the country. While the work of our programmes is necessarily long-term, they will of course be affected by trends in the wider market. But much good work is still going ahead. It is neither possible nor desirable to support every regeneration project in the current economic environment. However, we are taking the necessary steps to ensure that critical projects continue, by making available additional resources for housebuilding and bringing forward funding for mixed-use projects. The RDAs and the HCAs will be working to support those projects that offer the best value for money and are capable of providing real help now for communities.

Our definition of regeneration covers a wide range of area-based interventions. It therefore encompasses both city and sub-regional level interventions as well as the more localised neighbourhood renewal interventions. In 2007/8, CLG alone had responsibility for delivery of the following streams:

- New Deal for Communities;
- Local Enterprise Growth Initiative;
- Neighbourhood Renewal Fund;
- Stronger Safer Communities Fund;
- Thames Gateway;
- Housing Marker Renewal Pathfinders;
- RDAs and LDA;
- English Partnerships;
- European Regional Development Fund;
- Coalfields.

We cannot anticipate the spend in the future.

DCLG responses to issues raised in this chapter

National regeneration policy needs to be examined in all its dimensions and at all levels. Who should we identify as the players? What are, and should be, the relationships between government departments, RDAs, local authorities and entities such as HLF and English Heritage?

The 'players' are those organisations that can contribute to three success measures – against which all regeneration should be judged in future. They are:

- improving economic performance and tackling worklessness, particularly in the most deprived areas;
- creating the right conditions for business growth which could include investment in infrastructure, land use, and a better public realm;
- creating places where people want to live and

can work and businesses want to invest.

The relationships between the various organisations at different spatial levels should be predicated on desire to devolve responsibility to the right spatial level and as close to the communities as possible.

How do, and how should, relationships between the public, the private, the hybrid and the voluntary sector play out in regeneration programmes? How far should they be prescriptive, how far enabling, and what should the balance be under given sets of circumstances?

What's important is not the issue of the relationships between various sectors (which inevitably will vary from area to area) but whether the success measures are achieved.

That said, there is a vital role for better coordination of public sector work at the regional and local levels, working in partnership with the private sector. And the chances of success are greatly enhanced where the public sector and its partners agree on and work together with the private sector and third sector towards a shared strategy, rather than in narrow remits or silos.

How do we make national regeneration policies agile, flexible and interactive at the local level? And what, for these purposes, is special about regeneration policy at the coast?

By following the Regeneration Framework! At local level, LAAs led by local authorities offer the key mechanism to deliver a targeted and strategic approach. MAAs, and the new regional strategy provide similar opportunities at sub-regional and regional levels. These will complement the establishment of employer-led Employment and Skills Boards, usually at city-region level, bringing much greater powers for local partners to direct public funds to achieve local employment and skills priorities.

How can national policies be encouraged to take account of the difference and distinctiveness of coastal settlements and of each coastal settlement within a common framework, and how can we overcome the obstacles to recognising this distinctiveness, which still

meets with resistance and even rejection at national and RDA level, as evidenced by the first response to the Coastal Towns report?

The Regeneration Framework allows for flexibility to adapt to local needs and opportunities. A key plank of the framework is that regeneration activity needs to be driven at the right spatial level – and as close to communities as is practicable, making the most of opportunities that already exist.

The proposed Local Economic Assessment duty would help ensure that all local authorities have a clear understanding of the conditions required for business to flourish in their area and for people to take advantage of economic opportunities.

What can we learn from the successes and failures of the past, perhaps especially the recent past, and how can we feed these understandings into current and future policy? And what can we learn, in positive and negative terms, from national regeneration policies (or the lack of them) in other countries?

Despite successes, targeted regeneration programmes in the past have been less successful in bringing about a significant reduction in the number of people without work in some places and deprivation remained intense in some areas.

The SNR identified failings in past regeneration activity and has proposals at the local, sub-regional, regional and national levels to:

- strengthen the local authority role in economic development – including the proposed statutory economic assessment duty;
- support effective collaboration by local authorities across functioning economic areas – for example by establishing MAAs;
- sharpen the focus of central government – with regional ministers; and clearer central government objectives and responsibilities.

Chapter 5

The view from the beach

Mike Goodman MBE, Weymouth

Richard Samuel, Thanet

Alison Penn, East Lindsay

David Archer, Scarborough

Hugo Swine MP, East Devon

Weymouth and Portland by Councillor Mike Goodman MBE, Leader of Weymouth & Portland Borough Council

Over recent years it has become clear that the longstanding economic activities of virtually all of our coastal communities have faced rapid and unprecedented change. Centuries of fishing, ship and boat building and repair, coastal shipping activity, traditional family seasonal holidays and even military operations have largely gone. The result is frequently an imbalance of financial wellbeing between the resident population and those who move in for leisure or retirement.

With the possible exception of the established conurbations, coastal communities tend to share a number of distinct differences from their inland counterparts. In general they experience significant shifts in both population and economic activity according to the season. Not only does this mean that work opportunities fluctuate between summer feast and winter famine, but it can also mean that local facilities provided for the seasonal visitor are closed in the off season for refurbishment or their operators take their break in the sun. Service providers find it hard to plan a steady or even predictable income stream, not least local authorities. In turn, these fluctuations also make it hard for employers to provide longer term training for their workforce, leading to seasonal recruiting, sometimes from abroad, for trained personnel.

Many coastal towns are literally at the end of the line. Not for us the motorway leading virtually to the centre of town, the main line railway connections giving a choice of direction to travel or even a reliable and high-capacity broadband link. Instead we are more likely to be hours removed from potential customers or even cut off completely from certain economic activities. Property prices are frequently distorted by a near constant stream of cash-rich second-home or retiring buyers, while clusters of old-style boarding houses being converted for multiple occupation can generate problems of their own. Some have been fortunate to switch from minor polytechnic to modern university with the boom in tertiary education or even become a Mecca for followers of certain fish restaurateurs, but most have to deal with the situation as best they can.

In Weymouth and Portland we have been able to take advantage of a fine harbour recently vacated by the Royal Navy with immediate access to challenging open-water sailing conditions. With help from our friends in the Royal Yachting Association, the South-West RDA, many local businesses and London winning the right to stage the Olympic and Paralympic Games of 2012, we gained a major advantage for inward investment at a crucial time. We will host the sailing events for both games and are proud to be able to report that the venue is ready with over three years to spare. With our partners we are seeking to maximise this opportunity to expand our share of the leisure marine sector, its technology and enhanced skills base. Even so, there is much to be done to switch a whole economy from one significant strand to a more diverse but hopefully more resilient option. Not only that, it would be foolish in the extreme to switch from one dependency to another.

I have no doubt that the leadership of all councils face similar problems in shifting priorities from one discretionary spending area to another without alienating the electorate and the established business community. In two-tier areas this is where we must ensure that adjacent districts and the county council join the campaign for our mutual benefit and to expand their own markets. We know it must be done; there is no pot of gold to enable spending to increase and for most, if not all, we will also be under pressure to cut costs at the same time.

We have taken every opportunity to network with those who have been successful in managing change from a historic economic pattern to something entirely different. Our team, led by a councillor well versed in the world of big business, has travelled all around the country taking soundings and stealing ideas. The experience I shared with him on a visit to the inward investment team at Sheffield clearly demonstrated the key elements that are essential in changing the future. First and foremost is a detailed analysis of all the strengths in the old system that can be built upon plus an unshakeable faith in the place itself. We all produce our Local Plans and more recently our Core Strategies to allocate space for the business and people of the future; but unless we have a development, investment, infrastructure and marketing plan to show to potential new businesses we will not be in the best situation to compete for their investment.

Where there is a clear deficiency locally we have got to minimise its effect or use it to our advantage. If, for example, our local age profile is heavily biased towards the high end, we can try to rebalance by developing training and education establishments, or we could consider using it to our advantage by increasing direct provision for the needs of the elderly. Either way, the essential element is to recognise the situation and deal with it. It is no good ignoring a problem and hoping that change will occur naturally; the only natural occurrence is decline.

Another key tool to explore is that of partnership. The most successful companies and service providers are those that can identify common objectives, not only with potential clients but also with other providers to get the competitive edge. It is no coincidence that most new computers come pre-loaded with popular software; it is because both hardware and software manufacturers see commercial value in the arrangement. Local authorities need to be able to do the same. Thus a new sports facility might be impossible to fund by a school or a district council, or even a leisure company alone, but together they may be able to generate the necessary capital and even find that together they can share revenue costs and maybe even profits! In looking for

investment partners it may be advantageous to look beyond our immediate area. I am sure that we have all experienced at some time a sense of frustration when dealing with local small businesses and chambers of commerce, wedded to the past and unable to see the inevitable change coming towards them. How often has a poor season been put down to the weather when it is just as likely to be the progressive change in customer expectations of a holiday that is the real reason?

There will always be a place for the providers of seasonal services around our coasts, but without some positive effort now to generate alternative year-round economic activity it is hard to see how such services can be improved to the extent that they become the reason for the visitor to come at other times. Not only that, central government needs to be aware that coastal towns need to be treated differently from their inland counterparts; a coastal resort is not a market town with a beach! First, the grant formula must reflect the population, public service demand and economic activity shifts that occur seasonally. Second, the effects of being at the end of the line must be countered as much as possible; it is not just a question of average traffic flows by road, rail or the internet, it is more a question of what is holding up future development. And finally, it is an acknowledgement that enhanced economic development along the coastal fringe will generate more cash for the exchequer from balanced and contented communities who live, work and take their leisure all in the same place.

Thanet by Richard Samuel, Chief Executive, Thanet District Council

In many ways the decline and rise of the Thanet towns is typical of the problems and opportunities experienced by many coastal communities. Nevertheless it is worth describing the story because it provides the clues that tell us how the problems can be tackled better in the future. In parallel to this story is a brief commentary on the effectiveness of the public service environment and how in the past this may have hindered delivery and hastened the economic decline of our area.

I joined the council as Chief Executive in 2002 and found an authority striving to deliver significant economic and regenerative change against a background of tight resources, inadequate partnerships, weak strategic positioning for investment, and poor corporate management. Undoubtedly the political will was present to effect change but the managerial capacity and quality of performance was poor. In due course this was to lead to a weak Corporate Performance Assessment rating in 2004. In summary, the council was not delivering for its community on its services, nor was it gaining the key support from key partners such as Kent County Council and the then recently formed regional development agency, SEEDA. There was also no area-based strategy to tackle the worst area within the district: the wards of Margate and Cliftonville. Here, as then, the wards stand at the top of the rankings of the indices of multiple deprivation in the South East region.

However, to return to the longer term economic history of the area. The Thanet area was originally an island cut off from the mainland of Kent by a marshy corridor through which the Wantsum and Stour Rivers passed. The channel was navigable and in Roman times was guarded by substantial forts at Richborough and Reculver. Access to Thanet was via a causeway and ferry. The land round the river route gradually became drained and eventually the Isle of Thanet became part of the mainland. It is helpful to repeat this history if for no other reason than to explain the island culture that still strongly exists in the local community.

Thanet thrived in the eighteenth century, particularly Ramsgate (a Napoleonic Wars port), Broadstairs (a delightful fishing village) and Margate (one of the first and finest seaside resorts). In Margate the fashion of 'taking sea waters' to benefit health flourished in the eighteenth and nineteenth centuries, and Ramsgate became a Royal Harbour in 1821.

The holiday industry continued to grow to its peak in the 1930s but was still strong in the 1950s after the Second World War. The greater part of the local economy revolved around tourism with little need to diversify. Even in the 1960s the tourism industry for 'bucket and spade' holidays remained buoyant, but the storm clouds were gathering.

It all ended so quickly. Suddenly Freddie Laker's Skytrain arrived and UK holidaymakers could experience the dubious delights of holidays in the sun. The tourism began to shrink and by 1980 the area was in terminal decline. Once fashionable hotels closed their doors to reopen as cheap rented accommodation, and by the

At this point I arrived to work for the council, coming from a background of urban renewal in London and Bristol with housing as my career pathway. My early analysis was that a number of key changes needed to happen before the council could take its regenerative work to the next level.

early 1980s the area had been dubbed Costa del Dole.

At the same time the closure in the 1980s of the Kent coalfields, which employed many Ramsgate miners, and changes to agriculture and fishing meant suddenly a crisis had developed. By the early 1990s nearly one person in five was out of work across Thanet and in some wards unemployment was around 60 per cent. The lack of a diverse economy was a key factor in the inability of the area to absorb the changes.

Throughout the period of rapid economic decline there was little national focus on the problems experienced by this type of coastal area. Policy focus in the 1980s was very much on the big cities and the smaller coastal districts were largely left to fend for themselves.

The winds of economic change came in the end from Europe with the award of European regional assistance funding to the whole Thanet area in 1993, coinciding with the introduction of the Single Regeneration

Budget (SRB) programme.

The Regional Assistance programme in particular forced a more strategic approach to regeneration, although the generally low intervention rates requiring the raising of considerable matched funding could prove difficult to implement. The council embarked on a wide range of EU-funded initiatives, some aimed at stimulating the tourism industry, some at creating employment opportunities, some at celebrating the area's heritage. The European programme finally ended in 2008 after 15 years of benefit.

One stunning early success at this time was the building of the first university centre in Thanet by Canterbury Christ Church University, funded through the EU/SRB programme and the HEFC. The Broadstairs campus seven years on is home to over 1,000 students, mostly local, who could never have aspired to a higher education previously. Alongside the council built Kent's first innovation centre.

- First, the emphasis needed to shift to achieving practical actual delivery of jobs on employment land. This could build on the innovative idea of the East Kent Spatial Development company that was a key part of Thanet's 2000–2008 European programme.
- Second, an area-based approach was needed for the worst wards, in particular Margate Central and Cliftonville West.
- Third, partnerships and funding from Kent County Council and SEEDA needed to be developed more strongly and the strategic context within which those organisations operated needed to highlight Thanet. The support of the Government Office was also a key success factor.
- Fourth, the council needed to improve as an organisation, particularly in areas of basic services such as waste and street cleaning, and front-line customer services. This was as crucial to economic recovery

as any regeneration project because it supported residents' key concerns about the area. Good public services sit well with high-impact regeneration projects.

The remainder of this contribution to the *Handbook* develops these themes and examines how a chief executive can add value to their development.

I will start with the last point, the creating of capacity, managerial and financial, to enable the council to become an effective deliverer of services and become a change agent for economic regeneration. In 2002 the council was at rock bottom in terms of its effectiveness. Performance management was non-existent, financial management was abysmal, and the council lacked clear direction through the absence of well-set corporate plans and strategies. These problems were not due to lack of political direction, which was strong, but it was clear that translation of policy into delivery was weak and needed to change rapidly.

The Leader and I agreed that an external review was required urgently and we commissioned the IDeA to undertake a peer review. The review was a springboard to extensive corporate restructuring with the majority of the senior managers departing in 2003. The first round of CPA in 2004 came too early for the council. We were rated as weak but in all honesty we were lucky to even gain that result.

The CPA result was undoubtedly a strong stimulant to the council to improve, and by 2007/8 we were one of the fastest improving councils. Across the board services have improved – benefits processing moved from 49 to 18 days, planning processing from bottom to top quartile, street cleanliness to top quartile, as just a few examples.

At the same time we were entirely reconstructing the customer focus with the opening of a new one-stop call centre in 2005 and Thanet Gateway Plus – Kent's first genuine one-stop shop – in 2008. Standards of quality had improved so dramatically that the council obtained a Charter Mark for its benefits and customer services provision in 2008. Alongside the front-facing improvements there has been a radical overhaul of IT infrastructure, providing the necessary resilience to deliver consistent levels of service.

Our programme of change also included taking the unusual step of returning services in-house for waste and street cleaning owing to the poor performance of the private contractor. Widespread changes to these services have been introduced, saving millions of pounds and having the added bonus of taking recycling rates from 3 per cent in 2002 to 27 per cent today.

I now turn to the impact of partnerships. In Thanet, four central relationships have grown with partners over the past decade. Each has made a different contribution to economic change.
I start with Kent County Council (KCC). As the UK's largest local authority it was always essential to gain and develop KCC's support for regeneration in Thanet. The council could bring considerable resources, skills and capacity to the table. In the 1990s, KCC had already made two highly crucial transport investment decisions benefiting the area. They constructed the Thanet Way – a dualled road extending the M2 to Thanet and thereby dramatically cutting travel times to London – and then constructed a new harbour approach road at Ramsgate. By the later 1990s under the leadership of the late Sandy Bruce-Lockhart a new approach was emerging from KCC.

The first round of pilot Public Service Agreements in 2002/3 set out convergence targets for key areas of public sector performance in Thanet, such as looked-after children, and other areas of welfare policy. Although targets were missed they provided a platform for the development of more sophisticated objectives in subsequent PSA and LAA rounds. More crucially they signalled the beginnings of an area-based approach within the county.

KCC also were embarking on the plans to build a new contemporary arts gallery on the seafront in Margate. The Turner Contemporary, as it will be known when it opens in 2011, will be a major new regional arts facility built to celebrate J. M. W. Turner who lived and worked in Margate in the eighteenth century. The first iteration of the gallery ended in considerable difficulties as the original cost of building a sea-based structure escalated from £20 million to £48 million. In 2006, new plans were developed and the construction of the gallery is now under way at considerably lower cost, designed by Stirling Prize winner David Chipperfield. The Turner Contemporary has undoubtedly acted as a springboard for a much more comprehensive approach to the regeneration of Margate. In this KCC have been major players in driving forward seafront development that will be complementary to the Turner.

Away from Margate, KCC and TDC formed a joint venture company to develop around 100 acres of employment land. The two councils have also worked together to maximise the educational benefits from the building of a new city academy – the Marlowe Academy – by the construction of a new athletics track and an innovative business centre adjoining the school where pupils can learn business skills in a real environment.

Finally, the two councils are currently co-operating on the delivery of a new employment programme under the Working Neighbourhoods Fund and have recently gained £750,000 to implement the Future Jobs Fund. Plans are also advanced to establish a multi-agency delivery team for Margate and new joint commissioning arrangements for Thanet as part of Kent's Total Place submission. Other partnership arrangements that have been crucial are those with SEEDA, the partners in the East Kent Partnership, and our Primary Care Trust – Eastern and Coastal PCT.

SEEDA has been instrumental in leading the Margate renewal work. Its chief executive, Pam Alexander, has chaired the Margate Renewal Board since its creation in 2005 and grant interventions by SEEDA for both the Turner project and the

development of employment land have been crucial. Other East Kent partners have assisted in providing central mass to wider East Kent regeneration, a key success being the lobby to persuade the government and the rail industry to extend High Speed 1 – the UK's first fast rail service from Ashford to Ramsgate and Dover.

Eastern and Coastal PCT, with the council, is driving forward a new health improvement programme for Thanet called Triple Aim – an idea from America that seeks to tackle the causes of poor health rather than treat their symptoms. With a 17-year difference in life expectancy between Cliftonville and some west Kent wards, we can see why this is welcomed.

The key messages that emerge from these strands are that gaining personal commitment from decision-makers is crucial, and their commitment is greatly aided if it is then within a strategic context that their organisation can support. For KCC it has been the Vision for Kent, for SEEDA the Regional Economic Strategy, for the PCT the World Class Commissioning framework.

The role of the chief executive working with the political leadership can be crucial to securing these commitments, as often I have found good relations can lead to good investment on shared areas of interest.

As we look to the future, my council has just gained a good review with promising prospects for its regeneration activity from the Audit Commission. This would have been an inconceivable outcome a few years ago and reflects the strong base from which we now operate.

Although the current recession has hit our area hard with an almost doubling of unemployment in 18 months, our emerging LDF core strategy maps out a strong future of growth for our area which we are confident we will deliver and which will continue to drive our area towards regional averages of employment and income levels.

East Lindsey by Alison Penn, Assistant Director, East Lindsey District Council

The East Lindsey district in Lincolnshire encapsulates the majority of the Lincolnshire coastline (the bit that sticks out on the right as you look at the map), with its two best known seaside towns of Skegness and Mablethorpe. This has been a favourite holiday destination over the years for visitors from Nottinghamshire, Leicestershire and Yorkshire, as well as further afield. Skegness continues to attract many thousands of visitors in the summer months, who come for a traditional bucket-and-spade holiday. However, the visitor spend is generally low value, and many tourism businesses run on small margins resulting in a lack of development and investment (in property or staff training). Other than tourism (hospitality and retail trades), there is still a reliance on agriculture (though no longer being a big employer), the public sector (probably accounting for a large proportion of our 'knowledge economy' jobs), and a range of small businesses. The result is a low-value economy – low average incomes, a continuation of seasonal work patterns, and a lack of high value-added business.

The peripherality of the area, and its lack of significant transport links (a 720 square mile area with no dual carriageways, so obviously no motorways) can be seen as a curse or blessing depending on your viewpoint! The district is large and rural – the coastal towns are relatively small, Skegness being the largest at around 21,000 (out of season). Despite some significantly deprived coastal wards, with obvious social and economic problems, the area has somehow missed out on the type of funding that has gone to places with a similar socioeconomic make-up. We do, however, have access to a very small proportion of European and regional funding ... but we don't have the research-based, high-tech, knowledge economy businesses that have attracted the big bucks over the last three years.

One can see why we are not a prime businesses location. We cannot deny that physical access in and out of the district is not easy. However, we do offer companies lower wages and a cohort of well-educated people in a rural hinterland that has a high quality of life (safe, clean and uncongested). In terms of 'access', one of the biggest problems these days is the poor broadband access, a barrier to attracting small, creative and knowledge industries that we might otherwise look to offer an ideal location.

We do, of course, see many opportunities for our coastal towns, especially as part of a wider package with inland market towns and countryside. We want to work with our businesses to raise the overall quality of our tourism product. We are clearly offering something for the budget-conscious family who want a traditional seaside holiday (though that offer could still benefit from further investment and development), but there is a lot of potential for the tourist who wants to get away from it all, visit the nature reserves, and have a mix of coastal and inland experiences. We also believe that we should continue to find ways to meet the technical needs of those creative industries and businesses that don't need a motorway to distribute their goods, and provide a place for people to live and work that fulfils their quality of life requirements (thousands of people still choose to move from large urban centres to small towns).

We are also aiming to take economic advantage of having large numbers of older people in the district – much higher than average because of the generally ageing population, but also because of inward migration. There are plans to become a 'centre of excellence' for care and hospitality, creating real expertise and best practice at the same time as meeting resident needs.

To achieve all this, we need to focus on ramping up the skills of the population. There is something of a polarisation in educational attainment, with some schools achieving very high levels of GCSEs, and some still pretty low. This results in lower than average numbers with higher level qualifications, as better qualified young people move out to study and stay away. This is obviously not a unique position – well qualified young people gravitate to cities everywhere, and often don't return for many years. However, East Lindsey – population 130,000 and growing – does not have a further education college or any noticeable higher education provision. FE is delivered in the area, but through a plethora of different training providers in generally small-scale ventures. This makes it feel low-key and not always appealing, much less exciting. Accessing a broader range of choice means travelling significant distances on poor and infrequent transport (some young people have a 65-hour week, with three or four hours of travelling each day).

Aspirations are often low for those who stay, with low-paid seasonal jobs on offer. The area also attracts people with low skills, and other social problems, into the costal area, in the same way that many seaside towns do; and we have a steady supply of older people moving to the coast, often in poor health, who are creating an imbalance in the population.

Our difficulty in recruiting to specialist roles – planners, teachers, engineers, health specialists etc. – also suggests that we are not able to encourage people back to the area. We think that really focusing on a specialism we can be proud of will be good for all – young people, employees and businesses.

One of the biggest issues for East Lindsey's coastal area is the equivalent of a town-sized population that is essentially 'under the radar', and contributes nothing to local service provider coffers. We have around 23,000 static caravans, apparently the largest area of caravans in Europe (not counting mobile holiday caravans that move in and out). While many of these will be rented to holidaymakers, we believe a large proportion provide semi-permanent homes, some on six-month sites, some on 10-month sites. These people do not pay council tax, and it is difficult to assess their contribution to the local economy.

We collect something in the region of £4 million in business rates from the site owners, and we are currently lobbying the government through the Sustainable Communities Act to retain a percentage of those rates to meet service needs, and to help regenerate the towns.

We would like to audit our caravans – to find out who lives there, their health (we think many older people have poor health), how long they stay, how many use caravans as alternatives to other accommodation, how many rely on caravans to be able to work in seasonal jobs, and so on. But it's a big job that will require a significant resource. Neither are we sure of the implications of what we find. The biggest long-term issue for our coast can be seen in the recent flood-risk maps, which have confirmed that much of our coastline is the third most 'at risk' area in the country. We don't have crumbling cliffs (we don't have cliffs!), but identified risk is increased breach and overtopping if we

don't keep building the flood defences higher and higher, which we think will be viewed as unsustainable. We must be one of the only areas with 'minimum' housing growth numbers at the moment, as we await the outcome of a large coastal study as part of the Regional Spatial Strategy partial review. The results of this study will inform whether we can (or cannot) build any more housing on our coast, despite a 5,500-strong housing waiting list, with most people wanting to live on the coast – and figures which show us as having one of the fastest growing population. This is going to require some tough

decisions in relation to spatial planning into the future, not just for the coast itself, but for the rest of this very rural district. So we need to start supporting the adaptation of our communities, both coastal and inland.

Perhaps we can, again, take advantage. The development of highly flood resilient buildings and developments will begin to be imperative for us soon. So we should get ahead of the game, and start to encourage innovative and imaginative solutions that we can share with others in the future. As in many places, we always need to try to see that potentiality!

Scarborough by David Archer, Strategic Director, Scarborough Borough Council

Managing risks remains critical if local government is to be instrumental in driving economic and cultural change in their communities. In Scarborough we appear, so far, to have got the balance between risk and reward just right, but it's a constant challenge.

Seven years into an 18-year project to transform Scarborough, the North Yorkshire town and its council are picking up awards for the work done so far. These include winning the Enterprising

Britain Award 2008, European Enterprise Award 2008/9, Core Value Awards 2009, and most recently the Academy of Urbanism Great Town Award beating off stiff competition

from Cambridge and Chester. The council's regeneration service also picked up an 'excellent' rating from the Audit Commission early in 2009, the first in the UK since 2002.

But, Scarborough at the turn of the twenty-first century century was a place grappling with changing business and tourist trends, economic decline and structurally inherent low expectations and aspirations. Perceived as isolated and with an outdated economy over-dependent on tourism and few major local employers, something had to change.

The catalyst for change happened with the designation of Scarborough as an urban renaissance town which led to a Community Planning weekend in 2002. Over 1,000 local people from all sectors of the community who were passionate and committed to their town attended the event and took up the call to change Scarborough for the better. The enterprise shown by everyone at this event provided the spark for the renaissance of Scarborough, and from this beginning the Scarborough Renaissance Partnership was formed.

The challenge to transform Scarborough from a coastal town with a seasonal economy to one with an all-year economy and an enterprise culture has not been easy to meet. When councils embark on place-changing projects, we are all conscious of trying to avoid promising too much and delivering too little, or of delivering something that does not necessarily fulfill the expectations of local people and businesses. The weekend was critical in helping everyone agree on a long-term agenda for the town.

Since then, the social and economic prospects of the area have been radically transformed through the strands of community involvement, the council's direct input into regeneration projects and business support, together with private sector investment in long-term strategic projects. Community partnerships tackling serious antisocial behaviour problems, creating public realm improvements and giving pride back to the local community have been key in several run-down areas of the town. Public realm improvements at the harbour have inspired local businesses to invest in new cafes and restaurants, creating new jobs and bringing derelict and under-used buildings back into use.

One of the key economic challenges has been to unlock the underlying enterprise of the town by supporting, encouraging and developing the creative, cultural and digital industries. This sector is the fastest growing sector within the town and its contribution to the local economy is fast overtaking tourism. This has been achieved so far through the development of a state-of-the-art creative industries centre, Woodend Creative Workspace, containing 52 office units, nine artist studios, a public exhibition space, conference and meeting rooms, together with a new 83-acre business park.

The business park brought another accolade for the town when it won the government's Business Regeneration Project Award. The introduction of a high-capacity broadband service through NYnet, a local government-backed delivery vehicle, has given the town one of the fastest broadband services in Europe (100Mb/s). NYnet was driven primarily by North Yorkshire County Council, and the fusion with Scarborough Borough Council's flair for innovation and enterprise is an excellent example of local government working together to drive change.

The revitalisation process has acted as a catalyst for an unprecedented level of new private sector investment and confidence in Scarborough. The Sands leisure development is the borough's flagship project and will ultimately bring in £200 million of private sector investment, in apartments, shops and leisure facilities, which will potentially create up to 1,000 new jobs. The town has also seen its first purpose-built hotel for over 80 years.

While development work has slowed owing to the 'credit crunch', the Sands project remains very much on track. The council has just committed £3.5 million to the construction of Europe's largest open-air theatre, seating 6,500, with completion due late in 2010.

The open-air theatre project is the sort of risk that we feel local government should be taking in order to support the private sector and ensure community and economic change continues to happen during these difficult times. It's an iconic project, highly visible and with a limited financial downside.
However, not everything goes according to plan – but that's the nature of risk-taking. The council's approach is about being risk aware and not risk averse; lasting change can only be achieved by bold and decisive decision-making that recognises opportunity and seeks to break new ground. We took a risk in seeking to attract Legoland to the Sands and ultimately it didn't come off. It knocked us back initially, but no place-changing scheme should rely on one project for its long-term success. So we bounced back quickly and moved on to the next opportunity.

Generating community involvement, increased council economic support and private sector investment have seen the town begin to change from a seasonal economy to an all-year economy. In 2000, unemployment was 50 per cent higher in the winter months compared with the summer. By 2008, the difference was little more than 10 per cent.

A raft of enterprising projects has also been completed, including 60 new berths in the Marina, and the first-phase refurbishment of Scarborough's Spa Complex into a modern conference and entertainment venue. There is a new cultural offer being spearheaded by the recently refurbished Rotunda Museum, an internationally renowned centre for geology, and the Stephen Joseph Theatre, home to the playwright Sir Alan Ayckbourn. Hotels are moving upmarket with the Crown Spa Hotel becoming the first Scarborough hotel to achieve four-star status for over 15 years, and new hotels are planned – a sure sign of the increasing confidence in the town.

The momentum produced through the first seven years of the Renaissance programme is set to continue. Next stages under way include: attracting casino operators to the town; creation of a multiplex cinema (the nearest one is 40 miles away); transformation of the Futurist, Scarborough's largest theatre complex, which is now seriously outdated; further modernisation of the Spa Complex; and upgrading of the surrounding public realm.

Despite this being a long-term project, the challenge has been to deliver community-based projects that can win the hearts, minds and backing of local people in a short space of time. We have been able to follow up with medium-term projects, which have only become visible when nearing completion. We have tried where possible to avoid raising public awareness and expectations too soon. This has also taken the short-term pressure off long-term projects like the Sands, allowing them to evolve as market conditions dictate. This ability to engage communities resulted in the council receiving the International Association of Public Participation (IAP2) Award in San Diego in September 2009.

The coastal MP's view

In developing the *Handbook* we invited coastal MPs to offer their views on coastal regeneration. One MP answered all the questions with the same one-word answer. What was that word? Below is a more comprehensive response from **Hugo Swire MP, member for East Devon.**

What coastal resort issues are raised by your constituents?

- Planning and development.
- Coastal erosion and coastal flooding.
- Furnished holiday lets.
- Fire regulations in B & Bs.
- Water charges as a result of investment in clean bathing water and beaches.
- Poor infrastructure (rail links to London).
- Provision for parking of mobile homes.
- Legislation relating to coastal access and marine protection.

What are your priorities for coastal resort regeneration in your area?

- Maintaining and protecting the landscape, coastline and cultural heritage.
- Improving quality and competitiveness for East Devon's tourism industry.
- Addressing coastal erosion and climate change issues.
- Addressing employment, housing and deprivation problems.

What do you consider to be the barriers to coastal regeneration in your area?

- Physical distance from

main markets.
- Pockets of deprivation, particularly in Exmouth (the town has two of the most deprived wards in Devon – Littleham and Town. They are in the upper quartile of social deprivation in the country, with 46.9 per cent of households on an annual income of less than £20,000.)
- Outflow of young adults.
- Low average earnings.
- Underemployment due to seasonality.
- A traditional image that may deter investment.
- Large numbers of pensioners.
- Cheaper overseas travel and introduction of holiday packages.

What are required to reduce the barriers to coastal regeneration in your area?

- Improvement of transport infrastructure within the constituency and to and from it – both rail and road routes for commuters and tourists.
- Addressing the issue of seasonal employment – ensuring the area is seen as a year-round destination.
- Improving the quality of the tourism offer and making the industry more productive and more sustainable.
- Improving housing and

housing conditions.
- Enhancing employment prospects, education and skills.
- Addressing social exclusion and enhancing opportunities for the disadvantaged.
- Enhancing the quality of life and capacity of local people.
- Encouraging local authorities to take a real interest in, and ownership of, the promotion of tourism for East Devon/ Devon.

Given a no/low growth future, how can we reduce deprivation in our resort areas?

- Channel any money (as opposed to more) that is allocated to coastal resorts in a more effective, coordinated way, particularly prioritising and targeting areas that suffer the most deprivation.
- Increase opportunities for apprenticeships and other means of employment for young people.
- Focus on environmental quality as this is a key driver for the economy.
- Focus on improving skills that will be valuable to the local area (e.g. tourism, fishing and agriculture), thus encouraging greater numbers of young people

to stay.

- Promote and enhance the landscape, coastline and cultural heritage.
- Reduce the effect of seasonality with other attractions such as the conference industry.

- Create a clearer structure for marketing domestic tourism.
- Invest in training and keeping skills up to date to ensure continually high levels of service.

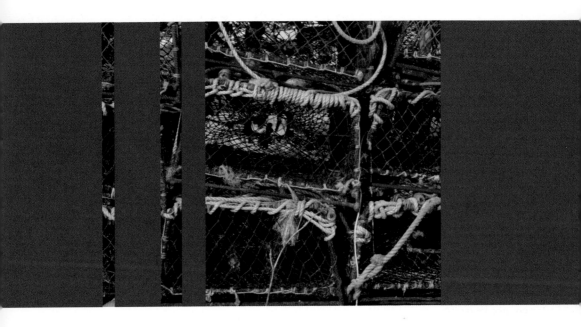

Chapter 6

Enterprising the coast

by Leigh Sear and Jo Lee

This chapter explores the challenges and opportunities faced by coastal towns in stimulating enterprise and entrepreneurial activity, and the policy and practice context for the delivery of business support to assist individuals and communities in starting and sustaining a business.

Rather than facing different challenges and problems, a number of policy reviews have suggested that there is a need for coastal towns to foster greater levels of innovativeness in developing responses within current policy and support environments. While there are examples of good practice within coastal towns in supporting enterprise development, there is a striking degree of similarity in the responses of the practitioner community.

In a recent review of developments within the 20 Local Enterprise Growth Initiative (LEGI) areas, Regeneris Consulting highlights very few differences in the enterprise development programmes introduced between areas such as South Tyneside, Blackpool, St Helens and Hastings.[1] As outlined within the government's response to the Communities and Local Government Committee on coastal towns, such evidence somewhat undermines claims of 'difference' – and hence the need for different sources of funding and targeted regeneration policies and programmes.

There is a general lack of evidence and insights by which to review the authenticity of such claims in terms of the development and promotion of enterprise in coastal towns. A number of recent studies have highlighted a relatively limited evidence base around the specific nature of the challenges and opportunities facing coastal towns. Fothergill notes that:[2]

The present evidence base is also patchy with a distinct dearth of reliable information on some key issues ... Some of the existing information (on population and employment for example) could also do with up-dating.

Within the context of understanding and supporting enterprise development, there is a lack of insights related to the dynamics and trends in coastal towns and the ways in which enterprise can be effectively supported. This chapter will address this gap.

In this chapter, *enterprise* will refer to a set of personal tendencies (including creativity, responsiveness, and need for autonomy) and behaviours that can be manifested in a variety of different contexts, while *entrepreneurship* refers to the process by which an individual or group of individuals start and manage a new venture that involves risk-taking, originality, spotting gaps in the market or new productive processes.

In terms of a coastal town, this *Handbook* is concerned with the socioeconomic conditions of our English seaside resorts; that is to say, towns on the coast that came into being to provide accommodation and leisure and still contain a large tourism infrastructure.

Unpacking patterns of enterprise in coastal towns

While there are a number of ongoing debates about the barriers and challenges faced by coastal towns in supporting enterprise and entrepreneurship, there are no specific overviews within the academic literature of enterprise development in coastal towns.

There are a number of policy statements, strategic overviews and action plans from local authorities and regional development agencies which provide a descriptive overview of the state of business and enterprise in the area, and sometimes its role in tackling the challenges and opportunities faced by coastal towns.

This gap in understanding and the issues with publicly available data are important for practitioners, such as the audience for this *Handbook*, in developing a picture of the challenges faced by smaller enterprises and the responses required to support the development of enterprise. Without access to such evidence, there is a danger that programmes are supply-led rather than demand-led.[3] In part, this accounts for the similarity in approaches among the 20 LEGI areas.[4]

This diversity reflects the interplay between a set of complex local conditions and dynamics that can result in pockets of deprivation within relatively buoyant economies. These will include:

- lack of an enterprise culture in a community;
- historical reliance on a legacy of an employee culture and large business dependency;
- a low number of enterprising role models;
- low levels of mobility;
- limited networking between businesses;
- restricted local business markets.

Certain bundles of these conditions and factors will be present in the less well performing coastal towns. While certain commentators have challenged whether such issues are specific to coastal towns, it is the interplay of these types of factor that may account for the patterns of enterprise observed. On closer inspection, a number of specific themes emerge from the data on changes in the business stock.

- First, there are differences in performance of the coastal towns within the regions.
- Second, at a regional level, there is evidence of a north–south divide in changes to the business stock. Despite evidence of the gap in entrepreneurial activity closing, VAT registration data for 2003 to 2008 shows that coastal towns in the southern regions did perform slightly better than coastal towns in northern regions.

- Third, there is a group of coastal towns that are performing relatively well. Within this group, rates of net change in the business stock are higher than the overall group of coastal towns and national averages. A number of these were identified by Fothergill in 2009 as

towns with the strongest local economies, including Whitley Bay, Bournemouth, Brighton and Whitstable/ Herne Bay.[5] There are a number of characteristics of these towns that support enterprising activity, such as: proximity to a major town or large centre of population; good transport and communication links to these towns and population centres; access to business opportunities and markets; and an awareness of trends in the wider external environment. These are frequently identified as important elements in the development of an enterprising culture.[6]

In comparison, there is a group of coastal towns with net changes in the business stock that are somewhat lower than both the coastal group and national averages. This group includes Clacton, Great Yarmouth, Torbay and Whitby. Again, a number of these were identified by Fothergill and the Local Futures group as towns with the weakest local economies. These areas face a number of structural barriers to encouraging enterprise and entrepreneurial activity, not least reflecting their geographical peripherality and isolation. Poor connectivity and/or a lack of investment in transport and communication infrastructure hinder access to employment opportunities and other business services in towns and cities in the surrounding region. This position is summarised by Shared Intelligence, who note that:[7]

[there is] *a set of shared economic, physical and demographic problems in struggling seaside towns which prevent them growing economically and create concentrations of need which local services are struggling to manage.*

Such challenges provide a barrier to attracting individuals and business investment, stifling the introduction of news ideas and opportunities into the economy and the development of networks to exploit these opportunities.

There is also a need for creativity and innovation from support organisations in addressing these challenges, as traditional forms of business support – such as advice and guidance, grants and loans, and incubation facilities – have generally failed in developing enterprise in such areas.[8]

If a more creative or innovative approach is adopted, a number of these issues can be tackled. In Scarborough, for instance, investment has been targeted at addressing issues related to transport links, enhancing communication links and connectivity (e.g. providing good wireless coverage across the town), developing incubation facilities, supporting the development of businesses in the creative and cultural sector, and public realm improvements at the harbour to attract business investment.

According to the Scarborough Renaissance Partnership, this focus on enterprising the economy has produced results:[9]

Over the past six years we have effectively changed from a seasonal economy to an all-year-round economy. In 2000, unemployment was 50 per cent higher in the winter months compared to the summer. By 2008, the difference was little more than 10 per cent, a dramatic change and one which is the envy of many other seaside resorts.

Finally, over the last five years, 'rural' coastal towns have under-performed in comparison with more urban coastal towns. This reinforces wider trends in the performance of urban and rural areas in rates of business formation and change.

Again, available evidence on this geography of enterprise highlights the importance of access to transport and communication links, connectivity and openness to business networks as key factors in accounting for some of the difference between urban and rural areas.[10] Indeed, the group of traditional seaside 'resorts' have not performed better as a group than other types of coastal town. For example, the net change in the business stock in Brighton and Bournemouth (14 per cent) was double the net change in Blackpool and Great Yarmouth. This difference is reflected in the recent allocation of LEGI and Working Neighbourhood Fund (WNF) monies to areas such as Blackpool, Great Yarmouth and North East Lincolnshire.

The narrative or 'script' within the funding applications submitted by these towns attached a primary role for enterprise development and entrepreneurship in assisting individuals and communities within the most deprived super-output areas in moving out of unemployment and worklessness into more positive outcomes and tackling the key issues related to regenerating the town. The nature of these challenges and opportunities is explored next.

Developing enterprise: challenges and opportunities

The above review of the limited data highlights a somewhat uneven geography of enterprise development across the group of coastal towns in England, with a net change in the business stock varying from 14 per cent in towns such as Brighton and Bournemouth, at a rate well above the national average, to 4 per cent in places such as East Lindsey and Clacton and a net decrease in Southend.

This pattern of enterprise further reinforces the proposition that coastal towns are not a homogeneous group, with similar experiences in coping (or struggling) with enterprising and regenerating the area. But there is evidence of a degree of similarity in the responses of the supply side in supporting enterprise across this group of towns. On the one hand, this may be because they face the same challenges and opportunities in supporting enterprise. On the other hand, it may reflect a lack of innovation in enterprise support and provision.[11]

There are a number of well-rehearsed debates surrounding the challenges and opportunities currently faced by coastal towns in regenerating the coastline of England. Such challenges can be grouped into a number of bundles related to:

- a lack of opportunities for economic diversification;
- a weak local labour market;
- above-average levels of worklessness;
- high levels of incapacity in the population;
- a deteriorating physical infrastructure;
- an unbalanced housing market;
- an ageing and transient population;
- a lack of capacity building and leadership in public services.

A number of these challenges and opportunities are reinforced by a recent survey undertaken by the Coastal Communities Alliance. There are a bundle of explicit challenges related to encouraging and supporting business development, particularly around attracting investment and support from the business community in regenerating resorts. In part, this is rooted within wider concerns about the lack of funding and attracting public and private investment in the light of negative perceptions of coastal towns. This is related to a perceived image problem and subsequent unattractiveness as a place to work, live and learn.[12]

Experiences from elsewhere highlight the role of enterprise development in addressing the set of challenges and opportunities outlined above. For example, a number of the local authorities who were successful in gaining LEGI funding have developed programmes that provide opportunities for a degree of innovation and new thinking in delivery of enterprise support – such as around enterprise coaching – which has enabled

different approaches to be tested. Therefore, there may be benefits from using emerging structures such as the Coastal Communities Alliance as a route to exchanging experiences around the development of enterprise and entrepreneurial activity as a regenerative tool in coastal towns.

A number of studies have explored the challenges and opportunities faced by localities in developing enterprise and entrepreneurial activity, reviewed in 2003 by Bridge

and Associates.[13] These range from a lack of aspirations and attitudes of the community towards enterprising activity, to minimal accessible role models and a lack of awareness of business opportunities in the wider external environment, to a lack of finance and people with the right abilities and skills to support in starting and managing the business. A number of these themes are supported by the outcomes from the CCA survey of local authorities.

Developing enterprise: challenges and opportunities

- *Lack of business development and growth*

About one in three of the surveyed local authorities noted that a lack of business development and growth was a barrier to regeneration. There were a number of aspects to this barrier, including traditionally low levels of business start-ups and development activity, which the analysis of patterns of enterprise above suggests is a key characteristic of a specific group of coastal towns – *but not all of them*. There was also a lack of commitment and low levels of investment from the business community in the area. One local authority noted that a barrier to regenerating the area

was 'insufficient commitment, enthusiasm and active involvement from local private enterprises'.

The experiences of areas such as Scarborough and North Tyneside suggest that there is a need for key stakeholders to adopt a proactive or entrepreneurial approach in

understanding the needs of aspiring entrepreneurs around starting a business in a coastal town, the challenges and opportunities and the associated responses required from business support organisations and other regeneration agencies.

- **The economic performance of the area**

The level of business start-up and change in the business community will be influenced by the opportunities available within the external environment. Two-thirds of the surveyed local authorities identified some element of the performance of the economy as a barrier to enterprising and regenerating the coast.

Specific issues related to the low level of wages offered by businesses, the commercial viability and sustainability of new businesses (particularly in tourism-related sectors), peaks and troughs in demand reflecting the seasonality of coastal towns, and the reliance on tourism-related activity. A number of studies have highlighted that this reliance and the subsequent lack of diversification of economic activity is a key barrier to regeneration.[14] Support to assist individuals in managing the journey into self-employment in different sectors, thereby reducing reliance on specific

sectors such as tourism in coastal towns, will have a role to play here in improving the performance of the local economy. Gibb has noted that this will require an investment in education and training in order to broaden horizons around the opportunities in the external environment which can underpin sustainable enterprise activity, whether on an individual or community basis.[15]

- **A lack of employment opportunities and investment in skills development**

About half of the surveyed local authorities identified a set of issues related to the lack of employment opportunities and skills development. One respondent commented:

In many towns the run-down nature of the resort needs to be addressed at the same time as creating hard employment opportunities by capturing opportunities to respond to tourism trends towards activity and short-break holidays, web-

based businesses, etc.

There were a number of factors at play here including:

- a decline in traditional industries such as fishing, engineering and manufacturing;
- a lack of aspirations and resistance to change among the population;
- a lack of – or limited awareness of – opportunities outside the immediate area;
- a mismatch between the demand and supply in education and training provision and low levels of educational attainment in comparison to national averages.

Archer and Davison note that a number of these challenges require structural changes in the priorities of education and training providers in order to meet the changing requirements of employers.[16]

Hartshorn and Sear suggest that there is scope to encourage greater levels of employer engagement with 14 to 19 year-old employment and learning opportunities, and to support businesses in contributing to the development of people and skills which effectively address business development needs.[17]

- *Transport and communication links*

The survey reinforced challenges identified by other studies related to issues of transport and communication linkages. There were a number of comments from the surveyed local authorities related to 'lack of transport infrastructure investment' and 'poor transport links'. The survey identified a set of specific issues including investment in transport linkages, levels of car ownership and the communications connectivity of coastal towns.

However, there are opportunities for promoting entrepreneurial responses to the issue of transport and communication linkages which may develop greater levels of connectivity. For example, a number of areas have successfully supported community-owned transport businesses to plug gaps in routes, while a number of the local authorities noted that there may be opportunities arising from the development of businesses within the cultural and creative sector, particularly around digital and media technologies, which would enhance the connectivity of coastal towns.
The development of new forms of economic activity not reliant on demand from the local area will be a key tool in enhancing

the linkages and connectivity, through exploiting ties and relationships with other national markets. This need to develop the market scope of existing and new businesses in coastal towns will be critical in the sustainability of entrepreneurial activity as well as providing points of exposure to new ideas and ways of running and managing businesses.[18]

- *A lack of access to finance and funding*

A number of the surveyed local authorities highlighted that a lack of finance and funding from central government and regional development agencies was hindering attempts to regenerate coastal towns. One authority noted:

The remoteness of many resorts and their distance from main centres of population and business has resulted in a lack of private sector investment in basic employment infrastructure. This market failure has to be addressed by public sector investment in these facilities, but many small resorts have found this challenging.

This lack of investment resulted in local authorities either not implementing anticipated plans and priorities and/or introducing activity on a smaller scale. In addition, it was noted that there was an emphasis on funding innovative as opposed

to existing activity. This pattern is characteristic of the system's failure in the provision of small business and enterprise support.[19]

Such experiences raise a couple of issues. First, a large number of non-coastal towns and cities would highlight a lack of funding and investment as a barrier to regeneration, which raises an issue as to the funding priorities attached to regeneration vis-à-vis other policy areas by government departments and agencies.[20] Second, there may be a need for local authorities to adopt a more enterprising or proactive posture in sourcing funding to address some of the challenges and opportunities.[21]

A number of coastal towns have been successful in gaining additional funds from programmes such as LEGI and WNF to support enterprise development and regeneration. If coastal towns do face specific challenges and opportunities in regenerating their areas, in comparison to other types of localities, it is unlikely that they will be able to access monies from targeted funding streams. Given the current national financial situation, the possibility of providing such targeted funding is somewhat limited existing commitments under the truncated SeaChange initiative.[22]

A key issue here is the ability of the local authority and key stakeholders to develop an entrepreneurial posture and mindset in exploring ways of funding planned programmes of business support and regeneration. Therefore, there may be opportunities for coastal towns to exchange experiences around how such a posture can be developed.

Supporting enterprise development and entrepreneurship

What have been the experiences of coastal towns in overcoming the sort of challenges and opportunities outlined above in supporting enterprise development? While there are a number of descriptive 'how to' guides and case studies of 'good' practice, there is a lack of publicly available studies that have explicitly assessed the effectiveness and impact of business and enterprise support programmes in coastal towns.

In reviewing the wider literature, it is notable that an industry has developed around supporting small business and enterprise development over the last 20 years. Over this time, a multitude of policies, organisations and programmes of support have been introduced, some of which have come and gone while others have survived and evolved over a number of years.

The Local Enterprise Growth Initiative is the latest approach by central government to foster an enterprise culture within a range of disadvantaged communities and groups across England, alongside which a number of local authorities have re-packaged enterprise support using Working Neighbourhood Fund monies.

The key trend underpinning LEGI was the devolution of decision-making to the local level as it suggested that devolved decision-making has the greatest impact. This differs from previous government attempts to boost enterprise in deprived areas as it provides local institutions and communities with the authority and freedom to best determine local needs, options and targeted solutions in their area:[23]

By encouraging local authorities to devise plans to suit their specific local areas, it is hoped the initiative will be more effective at creating new enterprise.

Within this context, the programme guidance suggested that local authorities and their stakeholders were best placed to develop programmes of support to reflect local needs and requirements. However, despite this different emphasis in the decision-making, Chitty suggests that these areas have experienced the same issues as before:[24]

More enterprising communities are stronger, wealthier, happier and sustainable. Aren't they? The advantages are obvious. So why, when we've explained the benefits of enterprise so carefully, and offered all the help and support any budding entrepreneur could possibly need, are we not mowed down in the rush as enthused and energised communities respond to the call?

Bennett suggests that this lack of take-up is indicative of a systems failure in the provision of enterprise support:[25]

- There is an array of different providers of support that deliver a wide range of different schemes. These schemes tend to be funded from a variety of sources.
- There is a lack of networking between support agencies. Agencies say that they refer clients between each other, but research has indicated that the extent of networking and referral activity is often limited.
- There is confusion among small businesses as to who to approach from the formal support network for advice and guidance.
- There are overlaps and gaps in support provision. In 1988, this was summarised by the Audit Commission as 'programme overkill within a strategic vacuum'.
- There are clear variations in the quality of business support within and between areas. The level and quality of staffing, the emphasis on training and development of staff and the level of funding varies significantly among agencies in the small business policy community. This influences the quality of service that can be provided to the small business sector.

Underpinning a number of these characteristics is the need for more enterprising or more innovative approaches. What types of business and enterprise support are available within coastal towns? The survey of local authorities and the case studies highlight a wide range of interventions, including programmes of business advice and guidance, mentoring and enterprise coaching, financial assistance, incubation space and training. While the specific configuration of provision is different between coastal towns, reflecting local differences in needs and requirements, there is a large degree of similarity in the 'offer' across the group. For example, the majority of coastal towns offer some form of business incubation or managed workspace for start-ups and growth-orientated businesses. There is also an increasing institutionalisation of enterprise coaching as an offer to supporting individuals in managing the enterprise journey. These patterns are not unique to coastal towns and imply a degree of similarity in the barriers and challenges faced in starting and growing a business.[26]

On the other hand, the survey and case studies highlighted an emphasis on the need for innovation and creativity, and doing things differently, within the guidance surrounding

programmes such as LEGI and WNF. This leads to pockets of good or effective practice among the group of coastal towns. This picture of provision will be driven by the interplay between specific local conditions and factors such as:

- the proactiveness of the local business community;
- the posture of the voluntary and community sectors;
- levels of awareness of opportunities for starting and managing a business;
- the strength of the relationship between the local authority and its partners.

These factors will influence the environment in which different approaches and programmes can be piloted and tested. Again, such experiences provide further evidence of the relationship between the entrepreneurial posture of the providers of business and enterprise support and the difference in performance of enterprise in the area. To this end, it would be interesting to explore whether a key determinant of the patterns of enterprise evident in Figures 6-1 and 6-2 reflect the entrepreneurial posture or approach of the supply side.

- *Start-up support*

As with the majority of localities across England, the survey

information services, financial assistance (e.g. loan and equity financing), follow-on workspace, and training and skills provision (funded via Train to Gain) provided by a combination of quasi-public and private sector providers.

and case studies highlighted that coastal towns provide a plethora of start-up provision. This includes: business advice and guidance; information and signposting; coaching and mentoring; financial assistance (e.g. grants and micro-finance); incubation space; and training and networking. To this extent, there is very little difference in start-up support between coastal and non-coastal towns.

Given recent changes in the Business Link network, this tends to be provided by local enterprise agencies, welfare-to-work providers (e.g. Inbiz, Action for Employment) and other targeted providers (e.g. Prince's Trust, PRIME, Prowess, ethnic minority business groups). The majority of such provision is underpinned by public funding.[27]

Provision across the group of coastal towns varies, reflecting the ability to access funding to offer particular types of support (e.g. access to finance packages), the needs of different groups interested in starting a business, and local priorities

and targets. Therefore, some areas may be able to provide a range of grants to aspiring entrepreneurs, while others can provide only vouchers or a basic training subsidy. This leads to a 'patchwork' of start-up provision which the government is attempting to manage through the ongoing business support simplification programme in England.

• **Business development and growth**

The second key bundle of provision is focused on supporting businesses to develop and grow on a sustainable basis. The publicly funded element of this market is now shaped by the Business Link information, diagnostic and brokerage (IDB) model. Business Link advisers work with a portfolio of businesses to support them in assessing their development needs and brokering access to other sources of support to address these needs. Therefore, across a number of the coastal towns, there were mentoring and coaching services, business

Given that 50–60 per cent of businesses started in the United Kingdom do not survive more than 12 months, such provision has a key role in enhancing business survival and sustainability rates. Bearing in mind the challenges and opportunities discussed above, there is a need to map the balance between start-up and business development and growth provision in coastal towns, as surveys and case studies provide anecdotal evidence that there is a current emphasis on getting individuals into business, as opposed to ensuring long-term sustainability. This is important given the need within coastal towns to diversify local economic activity and reduce the reliance on the tourism sector and associated services.[28]

• **Attracting inward investment**

The promotion of enterprise can play a part in changing attitudes and images of coastal towns. To this end, a number of the towns have developed enterprise marketing campaigns as a way of attracting private sector investment. This manifests itself in TV and radio advertising, extensive coverage of success stories in local press and media, organising inward missions, and attending conferences and networking events.

There are two key customers here: businesses looking to invest, and potential funders. In terms of the former, the marketing campaigns provide a cost-effective route of tapping into businesses outside the area which may be interested in relocating. The marketing campaigns are part of a wider offer which unlocks specific sources of financial assistance and training to assist in embedding the business within the area. In terms of potential funders, the campaigns are targeted at maintaining awareness and reinforcing a commitment to supporting enterprise development and entrepreneurship.

However, there are a number of questions surrounding the effectiveness of enterprise marketing campaigns in targeting individuals within deprived areas, particularly around the focus on generating business ideas. Atherton and Chitty have suggested that such campaigns reinforce perceptions about enterprise as starting business, not enterprise as a skills set which can be applied within different contexts.[29] Again, this different mindset will be critical in the efforts of coastal towns addressing the challenges outlined above related to developing skills in local young people.

Resorting to the Atlantic Coast of Ghana: European Heritage and Tourism of the Seaside - Edward Addo, Memorial University of Newfoundland, Corner Brook, Canada

Beginning in 1471, the Portuguese, Dutch, Danes, English, Swedes, French and Germans visited and settled in Ghana for nearly five centuries. The voyages and settlements involved trans-Atlantic trade in commodities and slaves. To facilitate the trans-Atlantic trade, forts and castles were built to serve as trading posts, lodges, and strategic defense. In 1807 Britain abolished the slave trade but colonized Ghana between 1874 and 1957. The European legacies of forts and castles which still characterize Ghana's Atlantic coast are important tourist attractions. In 1979 some of the forts and castles were designated UNESCO World Heritage sites. The significance of the forts and castles in tourism of the seaside is accentuated by three festivals, namely, Panafest, Emancipation Day, and Joseph's Project which attract tourists in the Diaspora, especially USA. In the past two decades, beach tourism has become quite popular on public holidays, especially on Independence Day. Resort/hotel operations have also become ubiquitous and lucrative on the Atlantic coast. The most popular operations are the 5-star Labadi Beach Hotel in Accra, the capital city of Ghana, the 4 and 3-star Golden Beach Hotels, namely, La Palm Royal Beach Hotel in the Greater Accra Region, Elmina Beach Resort in the Central Region, and Busua Beach Resort in the Western Region, and the 3-star Coconut Grove

for further information on this paper, please visit: www.tourism-culture.com

Conclusion

A number of issues emerge in terms of the 'so what?' question surrounding understanding and supporting enterprise and entrepreneurial activity in coastal towns. First, there is a need to develop the evidence base. The current evidence is either highly descriptive and/or explored as part of other issues faced in regenerating the coast. Despite definitional ambiguities, the analysis of changes in the net business stock of businesses provides a starting point for exploring the specific interplay of factors underpinning the observed patterns and whether these are different from non-coastal towns.

Second, there is evidence in the patterns of enterprise that these are different from inland settlements, but the configuration of business and enterprise support is somewhat similar to other areas. The current policy context is moving away from providing funding targeted at coastal towns 'given that the problems found in seaside towns ... are found in many other kinds of struggling areas'.[30] The gap in our current understanding of enterprise in coastal towns hinders making a detailed assessment of the specificity of the conditions and problems outlined above to coastal towns.

While more case study research will help in generating such evidence, there are indications that issues related to location, seasonality and changing demographics create a set of challenges and opportunities in supporting enterprise development and entrepreneurial activity (e.g. accessing business opportunities and markets) that are not faced by non-coastal towns. According to the Select Committee Inquiry of 2007, these challenges may 'warrant government action'.

Finally, there is a need for more structures by which agencies in coastal areas can exchange experiences, particularly in terms of how they can develop an entrepreneurial posture

Innovating and generating coastal enterprise *by Jo Finlow, Local Action Group Manager, Rural Development Programme for England*

The £2 million of RDPE funding will support Lincolnshire's coastal community in developing new and alternative opportunities for tourism and enterprise while positively encouraging the need to raise quality standards and build sustainability through realising the cultural, historic and natural assets of an undervalued coast.

Innovating and generating coastal enterprise needs the right balance of ingredients. If one is missing, the law of limiting factors comes into play. Just as a plant needs the right balance of light, heat and energy to grow, if one element is in poor supply, growth will be limited by the deficient element.

The ingredient that is usually in shortest supply for the many businesses and people seeking to diversify or evolve their businesses is ideas. Too many coastal businesses get 'stuck in a rut' and 'lulled by the seasonal routines' to explore new opportunities and new income streams. It is only the energetic and risk-defying few that have

the ability to be stimulated by stagnation and rise above routine and move forward their enterprise in new directions. Many businesses and individuals, however, need support, encouragement and the sharing of skills by 'having to work at it, together!'

A helping hand can be particularly useful for sectors that are traditional. Businesses in coastal areas are traditional. For such businesses to expand and serve the changing and different needs of businesses and the public, many coastal businesses need to embrace change and to react positively and creatively. To stimulate business activity, the ingredients needed are:

- innovation and ideas;
- a supportive environment for new businesses from organisations and agencies;
- funding to start or to develop businesses, such as the RDPE.

Business support organisations and funding streams can stimulate ideas and encourage new business thinking by bringing examples of different

ideas and approaches to the coast or take people out to see the alternatives in action, elsewhere in the UK, or even in Europe.

Businesses seeking capital building work in coastal areas need not view planning regulations and coastal flood risks as blocks, but be encouraged to think about other options that would be acceptable and which may achieve their goals by more creative routes. For example, if holiday accommodation is a no-go for your outbuildings, what else could they be used for that would be acceptable and achieve the same income aims?

Once ideas are stimulated they need to be nurtured. Support in the form of funding and advice must be in place. For example, Business Link and RDPE funding, working together, should adjust services to fit with the needs of the types of rural/coastal businesses likely to come forward. This will require understanding and knowledge of the nature of coastal economies and linkages (if any!), the needs of the private sector for flexibility, and responsiveness when applying to access funding.

Sustainability now is paramount and must be considered in funding applications, despite the unique but unfortunate position of possibly seeing a drastically changed coastline in 20 years! Sustainability therefore needs to be built into the activities of businesses being publicly funded. Notwithstanding the need to develop and diversify coastal business now, there is also the need to get the next generation interested in enterprise by encouraging innovation and business awareness in schools. Young people are naturally creative thinkers and adults should encourage and engage with their ideas. There are organisations already in existence. Young Enterprise is an example that has been around for some time, but it requires greater emphasis and support to enable it to do more to generate enterprising and innovative ideas among free-thinking youth.

Art and Representation by the Seaside: Jaywick, Nathan Coley, David Cotterrell, and Alex Murdin - Matthew Bowman, University of Essex, UKUniversity UK

Jaywick, an Essex coastal village located to the west of Clacton-on-Sea, was founded in the 1920s, and its original intention was to provide temporary seaside holiday chalets for Londoners wishing to briefly escape city life. The chalets were cheaply built, small, basic in their amenities but well-suited for the needs of occasional tenants, and offered a striking view upon the North Sea. In the aftermath of the Second World War, however, the character of Jaywick changed dramatically. The chalets began to serve as permanent homes rather than as holiday residences; the East Anglian floods of 1953 swept across the land and damaged many of the chalets; and the decline of the seaside holiday industry had a dire effect upon Jaywick. Since the 1970s, these events and others have had considerable negative impact upon Jaywick, with the consequence that the village has experienced severe social decline and poverty. A tight-knit community has come to feel increasingly sidelined, both socially and economically, from modern Britain.
In the autumn of 2008, two artistic projects became part of Jaywick life. Firstsite, a Colchester-based arts organization, invited Turner Prize nominated artist Nathan Coley to work with the local community to fabricate a temporary architectural artwork; meanwhile Jaywick Martello Tower, an arts centre in Jaywick, asked artists David Cotterrell and Alex Murdin to work independently but interconnectedly to produce works that speak for and to Jaywick residents. Murdin created a multi-media artwork, The Jaywick Tourist Board, that featured contributions from the locals, and Cotterrell made an interactive map of Jaywick

upon which memories and locations could be recorded. This paper will look closely at the works produced, the difficult social situation they entered into dialogue with, and their reception. But especially insofar as all three artists weren't local to Jaywick, this paper will consider the issue of representation - not simply artistic representation but social representation as well. Perhaps most importantly, this paper will examine the difficult balancing act the artists had to perform: a balance between "the indignity of speaking for others" and the possibility of community representation by outside parties.

for further information on this paper, please visit: www.tourism-culture.com

Chapter 7

Culture-led regeneration in seaside towns[1]

by Lesa Dryburgh

In recent years, initiatives to commission art and cultural projects and programmes in regeneration plans have escalated, but there has not necessarily been a shared understanding of the process or possible impacts for seaside resorts. 'We want an Angel of the North, but we don't want anything controversial!' is a summary of the sentiments of many commissioners. This chapter aims to share the potential benefits and inevitable challenges that can arise from such ambition.

Millions of pounds are being invested in coastal initiatives based on 'arts' or 'culture-led' regeneration schemes, designed to improve the visitor image and quality of life in some of the most deprived coastal areas of England. What contribution can such schemes make, what are the barriers to successful commissioning and implementation, and what is being learned about the role of arts and culture in coastal regeneration?

Key findings emerging in arts and culture-led approaches to the regeneration of some of England's seaside resorts are outlined here. While there is no 'one size fits all' approach, there are some overarching common themes contributing to the changing perceptions, challenging processes and emerging successes.

In cases where culture-led regeneration is showing emerging success, three underpinning themes are present. These are:

- strong leadership at local political level;
- a specific artistic vision for an area connected with its distinctiveness;
- a genuine and broad engagement process.

Often commissioners want bold, iconic work – but what does that involve or mean? Where does the process begin? What might be the pitfalls? What could success look like?

What is the role of culture and its link with regeneration?

The first part of the process is to question what you want to achieve and at what level? A report compiled for the Department for Culture, Media and Sport (DCMS), *The Contribution of Culture to Regeneration in the UK*,[2] which looked for evidence of culture as a donor (a contributor), as a catalyst or – at the very least – a key player in the process of regeneration or renewal across the UK, identified three predominant roles for culture in regeneration:

- **Culture-led regeneration.**
  In this model, cultural activity is seen as the catalyst and engine of regeneration. The activity is likely to have a high public profile and frequently to be cited as the sign of regeneration. The activity might be the design and construction (or re-use) of a building or buildings for public or business use; the reclamation of open space; or the introduction of a programme of activity that is then used to rebrand a place.

- **Cultural regeneration.**
  In this model, cultural activity is fully integrated into an area strategy alongside other activities in the environmental, social and economic sphere. This model is closely allied to the 'cultural planning' approach to cultural policy and city regeneration.

- **Culture and regeneration.**
  In this model, cultural activity is not fully integrated at the strategic development or master planning stage (often because the responsibilities for cultural

provision and for regeneration sit within different departments or because there is no 'champion'). The intervention is often small-scale, such as a mini-festival (a public art programme for a business park, once the buildings have been designed), or a heritage interpretation or local history museum tucked away in the corner of a reclaimed industrial site. In some cases, where no planned provision has been made, residents (individuals or businesses) and cultural organisations may respond to the vacuum and make their own interventions.

This chapter focuses on culture-led regeneration as described in the above definition, and cites case studies in relation to different approaches being undertaken in seaside resorts in England's South East, North West and East Midlands.

What might success look like?

What might successful culture-led regeneration look like? Success may be evaluated in many ways: through increased visitor numbers (and tourism spend); communities engaged in cultural activity; skills development; job creation; community sustainability; increased national and international profile; inward investment; renewal of cultural heritage and population increase (or sustainability of existing population). Success may link to myriad cultural, economic or social strategies, initiatives or agendas.

Success may also be viewed in terms of excellence and innovation, such as an international-class artwork or iconic or original project that captures the imagination and touches people's lives – changing the way we view the world, raising aspirations. It could be that the work appears in arts, culture, news and tourism publications and becomes an icon of the place, boosting perception and tourism. It might be that the work makes people feel good, gives people a new perspective, a place to reflect, gather together, make friendships or share opinions, a focal point for the town or the catalyst for annual events in the calendar year. And these qualitative reflections are equally essential to consider in measuring success.

It is vital from the outset that you are clear about what you want to achieve from culture-led regeneration, and that the policies, procedures and people support the implementation.

What might be the barriers to culture-led regeneration?

Potential barriers can include a lack of clarity (about the purpose), understanding (about the possibilities and challenges), positive engagement and ownership (by professionals and public) and an under-resourced or under-represented positive professional support infrastructure (within arts, culture, education, planning, community and political leadership). Positive public relations internally (and cross-departmentally) and externally (with the local press) are vital to support constructive processes. Further barriers to 'perceived success' can include short-term planning and quick-fix solutions. Strategic longer-term partnership approaches marked with investment and resources to truly embed and maintain the potential for positive impact are vital. This includes maintenance and sustainability (of artworks or initiatives), which may take more time to set up and demonstrate success but should, in the long term, bring greater value to commissions and initiatives.

Many of the potential barriers can be overcome by considering what the challenges of the culture-led regeneration approach might be, then developing plans to address them through a strategic communications approach and identifying the right people to influence and engage in the plans. For example, potentially controversial work may offend the local public, innovative installations may be a planning challenge, or maintaining a commission over its lifetime (e.g. 10–20 years) could take financial and human resources.

National and international recognition of innovative art and cultural projects can increase attention on a place or destination, increase tourism and increase awareness of issues faced by small seaside towns.

Case study 1 England's North West: Crosby

Acceptance among local people and businesses can take time to win over, and it is often the case that arts and cultural projects need, somehow, to 'prove their place', to 'justify their worth' in gaining local respect. In small towns, large art projects can cause controversy.

One such example is Antony Gormley's *Another Place*, which was installed in Crosby in 2005.[3] Over the first 18 months, the installation attracted an estimated 600,000 visitors to the coast, but despite this it generated a lot of local controversy. Initially a temporary installation brought to Crosby Beach by Liverpool Biennial in partnership with South Sefton Partnership in 2005, local public opinion was split between some who considered that the work was beautiful and poignant and others who claimed it was ugly, dangerous and even pornographic (owing to the simplified genitalia on the statues).

Local concerns over safety issues caused by the statues included claims that they created a hazard for people involved in sailing, windsurfing and watersports, and that visitors were at risk from incoming tides. Despite these strongly raised concerns, other local pressure groups wanted the work to stay. The case for the work to remain was won and, in 2006, *Another Place* was secured by Sefton Metropolitan Borough Council to be permanently located on the beach and maintained by them. This recognition of the power of culture-led regeneration, and the need for long-term sustainability both in terms of ownership and maintenance plus promotion through partnerships, has significantly increased profile for the region.

The installation was honoured in the waterside regeneration category of the 2006 Northwest Business Environment Awards, and has also been recognised as best tourism experience of the year in the Mersey Partnership Tourism Awards and as one of the best examples of regeneration in the region by the RENEW Northwest Exemplar Learning Programme. Professor John K. Walton comments:

How much regeneration is actually going on at (what has become) Gormley's Crosby?

One could ask, does there need to be? What is the 'measurement of success'? The work has been hailed as one of the best examples of culture-led

regeneration anywhere in the North West and artist Antony Gormley credited with the 'democratisation' of art. A visitor to the work comments:

We've been several times to see this in Crosby. We love it. It looks different each time, depending on the time of year and the tide. At Christmas, we've seen people dress them up in tinsel, Santa hats and foam reindeer antlers. There's nothing else here though!

This example is not untypical of many culture-led initiatives in seaside towns which, although perhaps not as widely known, receive initial strong local opposition, generate outstanding international recognition and ultimately become owned and locally loved! The example is included here to share knowledge and expertise amongst readers who are looking to innovate, take risks and ride the waves to support bold initiatives in seaside resorts.

Case study 2 England's South East: Folkestone

Folkestone Triennial[4] includes headline artists and mixes temporary and permanent art in a deliberately small geographic area of Shepway. The Triennial is one part of a larger culture-led regeneration programme led by the Creative Foundation,[5] which includes property acquisition and letting for creative and cultural industries and links with education and communities.

Focusing on a small geographical area, concentrating attention at the core of a problem and nurturing the solution within a defined physical area is key. Conducting rigorous analysis and then having the courage in resulting convictions to initiate and grow innovative solutions is essential. And, while ensuring stakeholder support, being bold enough to keep strong attention on 'the big idea' and not dilute it ought, ultimately,

to enhance civic pride and build stronger communities. Measuring impact is complex and a longitudinal study will be necessary to assess the effect on local communities and people's decisions to remain, leave or indeed move to the area. Commissioned impact and evaluation reports are in progress, but not available at the time of publishing this research.

Case study 3 England's South East: Margate

Turner Contemporary[6] is a visual arts organisation that celebrates J. M. W. Turner's association with Margate and, through a varied programme

of exhibitions and events, promotes understanding and enjoyment of historical and contemporary art. Work is underway to build a permanent

gallery which is due to open in Margate in 2011. As many readers will know, the project has not been without its complications over the past several years and lessons learned are generously shared. James Kennell, Senior Lecturer in Tourism and Regeneration, University of Greenwich suggests:[7]

What Turner Contemporary can't do is address all the factors that have contributed to the decline of tourism in the South East and in seaside towns the the UK generally. What it can do is act as a catalyst and, over a period of time, attract other investment, attract tourists and really make a change in the town but the success factors for that are very complicated and very long term.... Historically, seaside towns always innovated with culture, with piers, winter gardens, pleasure beaches. What's new is that everybody is doing a similar thing at a similar time, so the real challenge for cultural regeneration in seaside towns in the South East is to work together; to collaborate, strengthen local partnerships, strengthen transport infrastructure, so it's easier for

tourists to move between these different destinations and not have to just pick one, but to be able to put together destinations that constitute a meaningful long-term trip.

This example is included here to indicate how art alone cannot be the magic bullet. It is a component of wider initiatives and requires joined-up thinking with tourism and transport strategies and community engagement and participation.

This is the case of an iconic physical building as a catalyst for renewal. A summary of key findings is as follows. It is essential to embed culture in strategic thinking, vital that directors of cultural projects have significant time to develop key partnerships locally and regionally with communities and policymakers, and essential to share joined-up thinking in relation to the cultural tourist offer. Ultimately, 'the building is the backdrop' to culture-led regeneration which requires

strong political leadership and community ownership and engagement to support success.

A tentative conclusion might be drawn in the differences between approaches in Folkestone and Margate. Folkestone's culture-led regeneration is business-driven, very rooted and strong on governance and, as such, had a competitive advantage from the outset. Margate's culture-led regeneration appears to have commenced with poor leadership and was icon-driven but with little substance from the beginning. At the outset, it did not have an opportunity to engage with local communities or potential local opposition. As such and with the benefit of hindsight, Margate's culture-led regeneration has struggled through difficult years to reach its current position, which now appears to have strengthened leadership and community engagement and may therefore have succeed in turning the place around.

Case study 4 England's North West: Blackpool

The Great Promenade Show[8] is a permanent outdoor linear public art gallery – ten permanent installations over two kilometres, commissioned and curated between 2000 and 2003 by a small team of north-western artists as part of a culture and regeneration

scheme in the development of Blackpool's South Shore Promenade. Artist and co-curator Michael Trainor conceived They Shoot Horses Don't They?, a 20-feet diameter rotating mirrorball as part of the project.[9] He comments:

The Great Promenade Show obliquely references aspects of Blackpool's special culture and history without being literal. 'They Shoot Horses, Don't They?' was initially treated rather coolly and is now featured on everything from the Blackpool train timetable to the opening sequence of the BBC nightly regional news. The work was recently selected by Blackpool residents as an icon for the town second only to Blackpool tower (which, to be fair, has been there since 1894).

The initiative was part of Blackpool's coastal protection scheme which included space allocation for art in the public realm. It was also intended to diversify the visitor audience for Blackpool with public art as a cultural attraction. The iconographic nature of the rotating mirrorball has become a Blackpool landmark and a twenty-first century symbolic image for the region, as well as an example of 'art as visual representation of place'.

A more recent initiative is the temporary attraction Art Car Parade.[10] Produced by Walk The Plank in Manchester in 2007, and in Blackpool and Newcastle in 2008, Art Car Parade invites professional artists, individuals and groups to 'make transportable artworks from vehicles' for procession. It is an example of the potential for capacity building in culture-led regeneration. Anthony Preston, Head of Resource Development, Arts Council England North West, comments:

The illuminated Art Car Parade has the potential to grow to become an innovative addition to the illuminations attraction. When it took place on Blackpool's promenade in 2008, it achieved community involvement and developed a new relationship with tourism. In fact the tourism department paid towards Art Cars 2008. The next stage is to begin to explore how the producers, Walk The Plank, together with the council, can put in place the building blocks for developing local skills and the capacity of communities in Blackpool to sustain this activity into the future and balance real meaningful participation alongside a high calibre, quality artistic offer.

There are some possible conclusions to draw. Blackpool's regeneration has struggled for several years with the role of 'culture', initially through pursuing a culture and regeneration model. It has had deeper structural problems, a lack of inherent creative industries or at least the profile, recognition and development of such industries to meet the demands of a twenty-first century market, audiences and contemporary tastes, or strong links with higher skills or knowledge economies. Instead, strategies have for decades focused on engagement with spectacle. Now, more than ever, opportunities for culture-led regeneration, brought about by strengthened partnerships, financial investment and visionary leadership, can steer Blackpool's fortunes with deeper rooted impact for long-term economic, cultural and community growth.

Case study 5 England's East Midlands: Lincolnshire

Bathing Beauties®[11] was conceived by Michael Trainor in response to his appointment as lead artist on the Lincolnshire coast from 2005 to 2008 and part of a series of coastal environmental improvement projects commissioned by Lincolnshire County Council, part funded by the European Regional Development Fund. Bathing Beauties® – 'Re-imagining the British Beach Hut for the 21st Century' – was initiated after identifying the potential based on an already existing 15-kilometre stretch of over 500 beach huts in varying states of repair. The project launched one of the most popular international art and architecture competitions in the UK this century – attracting 240 scale model entries from 15 different countries, gaining over 400,000 visitors to the website, and welcoming more than

10,000 additional visitors to the Lincolnshire coast in its first two-day festival in 2007. It has resulted in the commissioning of eight permanent small structures on the coast and additional strands, including a UK touring scale model exhibition and local annual festival. Additional European and other funding is being sought for a second phase.

The project, over its three-year span, included many successes and challenges. Positive outcomes have included world-wide attention on the tiny towns of Mablethorpe, Sutton-on-Sea, Chapel St Leonards and Anderby Creek, global media coverage and thousands of new visitors to the region. Challenging elements have been at a local level and included lack of professional infrastructural support (arts, education), outright rejection from one of the parish councils to permanently site one of the series of commissioned beach huts in their town (it will be located elsewhere on the Lincolnshire coast), and ownership regarding ongoing cost and maintenance of the work.

While positive global recognition of a culture-led regeneration and increased tourist visitor numbers may exist, local level leadership, ownership and support is essential. Revenue costs as well as capital costs for ongoing maintenance of permanent installations is critical in long-term sustainability. Positive public relations at local level, knowledge sharing and capacity building are crucial to embed long-term success.

Advice to artists and those responsible for commissioning art

Artist Michael Trainor, who has led projects on England's North West and East Midlands coasts, offers five key recommendations to artists involved in culture-led regeneration schemes, or those responsible for commissioning or supporting them:

It is never going to go all swimmingly, but if I had to summarise general advice it would be:

(1) *Have or support a great idea.*

(2) *Talk to and engage with everyone you can about it from the outset – even if they end up not liking it at least they may understand it.*

(3) *Try to get a small team in the local authority to help support the work thorough the various stages. This is what should be in place and provided for the artist from the outset but rarely is and is one of the fundamental failings of public art schemes.*

(4) *If the budget or practicalities allow, try a 'temporary' on-site experiment to gauge opinion and garner engagement and support.*

(5) *Keep the media informed at key stages (but only when ready) and invite them to events and openings, give them nice hospitality and never release images of the work before it is fully designed or ready to be issued – thus avoiding mis-interpretation or objection not based on reality.*

Finally what is vital for the artist – and it is their sole responsibility that no-one can help with – is to ensure that the art that comes out at the end is worthwhile and not a confection of compromises based on fears and constraints.

Key findings from the research

Findings emerging from this research project include the following factors in relation to developing successful art and culture-led regeneration initiatives in English seaside resorts. While it is clear that there is no single solution, there are generic components to success.

- Understanding, respecting and incorporating the history of a place in its culture (although not always in a literal way) is vital both in developing uniqueness and building long-term impact. Each place is its own place.
- Community engagement, ownership and participation is essential but this does not necessarily mean community involvement in the design process.
- Strong governance, leadership and a broad strategic approach to innovation, partnership working, education and skills development and local authority structures are critical.

- The art alone is not the magic bullet. Good infrastructure including transport links, a strong cultural tourism offer and joined-up place marketing are significant factors to success.
- Commissioned artists need support at every level from local residents to regional political level to make international-class art with and within communities.
- Revenue budgets for maintenance of permanent public artworks must be considered at the outset for project sustainability. This may also include human as well as financial resources.
- Careful marketing and positive local media relations have a direct influence on aspiration and success of the project from day one.
- Agency and departmental flexibility for innovation and entrepreneurialism in business planning and funding models should be inherent.
- Business and funding models for the acquisition of property, and skills development to support and nurture artists and creative practitioners, are critical in contributing to the long-term success of place-making.
- Culture-led regeneration strategies don't work when they are seen as decoration around the edges of renewal. They work only when they are seen as a central component of both a wider physical and social design strategy with quality and creativity at its core.

Resorts of the world: Estoril Coast, Portugal's first summer resort,

Cristina Carvalho, Estoril Higher Institute for Tourism and Hotel Studies

Coastal tourism reached Portugal in 1870 when the court started spending the end of summer in Cascais. Later, the early 1900s witnessed the widespread scientific belief in the therapeutical benefits of sea and sunbaths for the improvement of conditions like consumption, and bone and skin diseases. Overnight, Parede's natural conditions (sunlight and iodine beaches) led to the transformation of a village into a therapeutical resort with facilities like sanatoria, solaria and a heliotherapy clinic. In 1915, Fausto Figueiredo turned Estoril into Portugal's first coastal resort based on its maritime, climatic, thermal and sporting potentialities. His daring project included the construction of first-class facilities, the recovery of the already existing thermal complex, and technological improvements like the electrical train connection to Lisbon. Figueiredo's vision proved worthy when, during the Second World War, Portugal's neutrality and the natural and manufactured conditions around Estoril allowed European refugees and spies to seek shelter or information in Estoril, a town which inspired Ian Fleming to become the birthplace of James Bond.

However, despite the 1948 plan for the urban development of the then 'Costa do Sol' (Sun Coast), the political and social commotions that marred Portugal from the 1950s to the 1980s led to the loss of both tourist amenities and quality image.

Since the 1990s, many have been the promotional strategies, international mega-events, amenities and facilities that have been implemented for the recovery of Estoril's image – including the foundation of a Higher Institute to upgrade the education level of professionals, and the development of products directed to different niche markets, as a means to fighting seasonality on Portugal's fourth largest tourist destination. But not without controversy.

☞ further information on this paper, please visit: www.tourism-culture.com

Chapter 8

Researching the coast

by John K. Walton

How can we arrive at, and make readily available, a body of evidence on the full spectrum of information that might be relevant to optimizing coastal regeneration? We have firm foundations, recently updated, from the Beatty and Fothergill reports, from the English Heritage architectural survey, and from the British Resorts and Destinations Association's evidence on seaside entertainment. We should be able to pull together extensive databases, in one form or another, on such matters as erosion, sea defences and global warming, or traffic and transport flows to and from coasts and along coastlines. We have ways of measuring seasonal fluctuations and bed occupancy, and we can chart the relationships between tourism and other kinds of economic activity on coastlines, and examine the relationships between them and the viability of alternative options and mixes.

Crucial to all this is making decisions about what to measure, *how* to measure it, how to compare, and how to take account of what is *not susceptible to measurement* and even what is *too important to measure.*

There is a growing literature on the limitations of cost–benefit analysis.[1] Definitions are always a problem in coastal settlement analysis, and once we have resolved these issues our choice of methodologies will be crucial to the outcomes of our deliberations and recommendations. It will be important to agree on the values that underpin our choices, or at least to be transparent about the nature of such values and choices. This is therefore an important, demanding and potentially contentious chapter.

To begin with, we must decide what we need in the way of contextual material, identifying trends and patterns at national and regional levels, and across particular coastlines. Within such a framework, what kinds of local research are appropriate to the needs and opportunities of specific places or kinds of place? Can we identify clusters or systems of coastal towns that would benefit from complementary development, and how might we make this work? Clearly, untrammelled competition between destinations is not the best way forward, resulting as it does in over-development, surplus capacity, waste and decay. The British seaside has always flourished best on the basis of complementary development, the creation of niche markets, the sharing of complementary assets, and an understanding that attractions within resorts are more complementary than competitive: having two piers rather than one, for example, makes a coastal destination more attractive, offers choices to visitors, and brings in a larger pool of visitors for each attraction. This is not always understood by private companies, which are likely to take a narrow, instrumental and short-term view in the current climate of economic expectation. Taking a wider view would add an extra dimension to their need to identify markets and compete for their share of them.

This should also remind us that coastal destinations depend on attractions and amenities that may not be profitable in themselves without subsidy, but are essential to sustainability and success for the resort economy as a whole. The most obvious examples involve sea defences, bathing water quality control, promenades, parks and gardens. But the questions of to what extent and under what conditions subsidy may be valid on these terms, and the legality and practical politics of providing such assistance, is of longstanding and continuing relevance.

These themes are brought together when a regeneration scheme involves providing support from the public purse for attractions that may be thought to be competing with existing private companies, and these issues need to be carefully managed.[2] An excellent illustration might be found in the endemic and enduring conflicts at Bexhill over the De La Warr pavilion, which began with the original proposal, pitting residential against resort interests, the public purse against the private, and (at least in origins) the xenophobic against the international.[3] There are lessons to be learnt, too, from the unhappy saga of Brighton's West Pier, and the shifting conflicts between sectors and interest-groups that have accompanied the pier's demise and proposed revival in a new form.[4] Examples could be multiplied endlessly.

We all know that there is a *politics of regeneration* – who makes decisions? how should income, expenditure, subsidy and profit be allocated? how are conflicts managed? Managers of interventions need to keep this constantly in mind at the research and planning stage as well as in day-to-day operation, by which time – for better or worse – the rules of the game will have been established.[5] And beyond all this, how do we assess the potential and actual impact of interventions, and how should we incorporate qualitative dimensions that take us beyond 'things that can be counted', or at least that appear susceptible to counting?

A lot of the quantitative groundwork has been laid in the academic field by the Sheffield Hallam studies of coastal town economies, demographics and social problems, which have already been discussed extensively. Fred Gray has also emphasised the importance, as a resource, of league tables of indices of multiple deprivation, and of aggregating social analysis from the smallest units of statistical capture. This draws attention to the scope for detailed local studies that might probe more deeply into particularly problematic locations, seeking the roots of problems and the potential levers of positive change, providing scope for identifying patches of deprivation and disorder that have been shifted elsewhere rather than rectified, and offering insights that may be transferable as well as being of local relevance . Here as elsewhere, access to contextual and background information becomes important, to assist in identifying what is unusual and where the most promising comparators are.

This is where the discussion of definitions of coastal towns, and of which sub-set of the wider category we are concerned with, becomes important. The Sheffield Hallam studies enable us to focus on a particular group of towns, and it will be dangerous to stray too far

beyond their categories. Some of the evidence available to us is rendered unusable for most statistical purposes by the extent to which its coverage diverges from our central dataset.

For example, we cannot incorporate the findings of surveys of 130 'coastal places', or of coastal 'marginal seats', or even the North-West Coastal Forum's interesting recent analysis of coastal settlements in that part of England, into quantitative analyses based on the Beatty and Fothergill projects.[6] The categories employed are widely divergent, and some of the places concerned are barely recognisable as coastal towns of any kind, although some of this material is of course usable as supplementary evidence.

- The list of 'coastal places' seems to include everywhere with an administrative boundary that touches tidal waters, a category that apparently includes Sherwood in Nottinghamshire, one of England's most obviously 'inland' constituencies.
- The 'coastal marginals' are a very diverse group, from which it is impossible to generate useful generalisations. The fact that they include Westmorland and Lonsdale, whose coastal

strip is completely swamped by rural and inland small-town settlements, or old industrial Camborne and Redruth, or rural and suburban Beverley and Holderness, illustrates that very few coastal towns, or even stretches of coastline, have sufficient population concentrations to dominate the character of a parliamentary constituency.

- The north-west survey recognised this problem at one level, by looking at coastal 'places' rather than local government units. But its categorisations are sometimes eccentric (putting Silloth and Barrow-in-Furness in the same box as 'maritime towns', for example), while grouping the places into counties is contradictory and unhelpful on the NWCF's own terms. Meanwhile, any attempt at averaging, or even aggregating, would fall foul of the numerical predominance of Liverpool, whose size and distinctive characteristics present a longstanding problem of distortion for attempts to provide statistical portrayals of the region.

Such problems underline the utility of the Sheffield Hallam studies in providing a clearly articulated national baseline.

But even the solid-looking economic and demographic evidence pulled together by the Sheffield Hallam and similar studies runs up against the endemic and deep-rooted problems presented by the seaside economy. For example, the populations of coastal resorts vary widely through the year, owing to seasonal migration as well as to the ebb and flow of visitors. So what should our base figure be for making local calculations?

This problem became apparent to me as a historical researcher when looking at the impact of changes in the census date on apparent population trends in resorts. When the census date was moved from early April to early June in 1841 and 1921, the population returns for resorts were considerably inflated by seasonal workers and residents as well as visitors, and this affected apparent inter-censal population trends, to such an extent that in 1921 attempts were made to adjust the official census figures to take account of the problem.[7]

So the question of when and how to count resort populations needs to be taken seriously. Their structures, as well as their numbers, will change considerably during the year, as those local authorities who complain about the failure of central government financial allocations to recognise this are well aware. The taking of a census on a single day is highly problematic when we are examining seasonal economies: the historic 'Spanish' system of combining a New Year's Day census with a record of regular and transient residents has provided one way of reducing this problem.[8]

We need to be aware more generally of the problems entailed in using census-type statistical evidence as a direct record of reality. By defining the classifications used for localities, occupations and even ages, the census-takers influence in advance the versions of reality they present to us.[9] It is quite clear that 'official' figures of all kinds underestimate the complexity of real economies,

especially in seasonal industries with extensive intermittent opportunities for female, child and indeed pensioner employment, often in the 'black economy'. Any exercise in information gathering that assumes that individuals have one, stable occupation – if only as a heuristic device to make a kind of provisional sense of complex data – will miss out on fundamental insights into how things 'really' work.

High levels of mobility in coastal populations, which are recognised as generating such problems as 'churn' in school enrolments, are also likely to be imperfectly grasped by the existing statistically driven methodologies. This is where qualitative disciplines such as anthropology, ethnography and some kinds of sociology – using survey, interview and participant observation methodologies – should come into their own. Phenomena such as 'dovetailing', where people move between occupations on a seasonal basis, and different family members becoming dominant earners

at different times, are well established in coastal settings. This applies to fishing, trade, building and manufacturing as well as tourism, which also provides large numbers of ill-paid but flexible and part-time opportunities for women and young people.

All these are well-established and persisting phenomena for which there is a good deal of historical evidence, and we need to be able to take them into account when assessing the nature of coastal employment, under-employment, migration and demography.[10] These and other questions of definition will also affect the gathering, classification and assessment of issues relating to health, disability, access to services, and problems of educational outcomes, antisocial behaviour, addiction and self-harm. Therefore it is essential that researchers look critically and analytically at the statistics they mull over, and try to situate them within the wider picture.[11]

Our understanding of coastal tourist economies is hampered

even further by the continuing lack of convincing, or even plausible, statistics of visitor numbers, length of stay and expenditure. This problem is not peculiar to Britain: it is endemic in the nature of tourism itself, which sells experiences rather than tangible products and whose infrastructure is easier to quantify than its customers or consumers. This applies especially to domestic tourism, with its characteristic multitude of small firms, informal arrangements and complex family economies which mix incomes derived from tourism with those from a variety of other sources. This tends to make domestic tourism, which of course predominates overwhelmingly at the British seaside, less visible and susceptible to quantification than its international counterpart, where tour operating companies and formal travel arrangements involving public transport and frontier controls make basic figures and trends easier to establish – though still by no means infallible.[12]

Alarm bells ring immediately when we try to look comparatively at visitor numbers to the English seaside. An obvious approach might be to examine submissions to the Casino Advisory Panel for the allocation of casino licences in 2006, which drew bids from several coastal towns. They, alongside their inland rivals, proffered current estimates of visitor footfall. In fact, such an exercise immediately brings out the scale and scope of the problems. Some of the comparative evidence presented on visitor numbers is counter-intuitive. North East Lincolnshire (represented by Grimsby and Cleethorpes) reported higher visitor numbers than Bournemouth, while East Lindsey (Skegness and district) was not far behind the big south coast resort. Newquay's staying visitors were ahead of Bournemouth and Torbay, which in turn was only just ahead of Great Yarmouth on overall visitor numbers. Torbay, Great Yarmouth and Blackpool attempted to present trends over time since a 1970s peak, but there is no suggestion that they were all calculating on the same basis.

Even more worrying is the evidence that several inland towns with no pretensions as tourism magnets were claiming similar or greater tourist numbers than major coastal resorts. The industrial town of Dudley, in the West Midlands, recorded visitor totals on a par with Bournemouth, and staying visitor numbers on a par with Folkestone. Coastal tourism in Britain may have declined, but surely not to the extent that Dudley, even with its Merry Hill retail centre, open-air museum, castle and zoo, is as attractive to leisure visitors as Bournemouth.

Some of the bidders were using the widely adopted STEAM model developed by Global Tourism Solutions. This presents itself as a supply-side model that provides only an 'indicative base for modelling trends', and anyway displays vague flexibility about some of its data sources while shrouding many of its assumptions in 'commercial confidentiality'. Others, including Shepway (Folkestone), used the alternative model on the market, the Cambridge Economic Impact Model. This accepts that, just as its sources are of variable quality, so its outcomes are of uncertain accuracy – to the extent that no numerical confidence level (in terms of being accurate to plus or minus x per cent) can be provided.

This display of disarming honesty has not prevented some local authorities from presenting the figures generated by both models as if they were solid, firm and grounded, rather than cloudy and vaporous as (implicitly and sometimes explicitly) admitted by the proprietors. West Sussex, for example, displays the results of the STEAM model (up to 2005) and of Cambridge (after 2006) as 'Tourism facts and figures' to the nearest pound, giving a 'headline' impression of undisputed accuracy, without making clear how the change from one model to another might have affected apparent trends.

Several key inputs to the models are based on remarkably vulnerable assumptions about accuracy of data capture and the scope for extrapolation. An example is the attempt to derive national, regional and county tourism patterns from 1,000 weekly telephone interviews under the auspices of Visit Britain. Another is the UK Occupancy Survey which is based on a sample of occupation providers and relies on the accurate completion of monthly forms. Any attempt to derive remotely plausible local statistics from these highly generalised datasets, or to fine-tune the sub-division of categories such as types of accommodation, becomes highly vulnerable to the magnification of error in small sub-samples.

The remarkable career of the STEAM model, since it was imported from Canada to Scarborough in 1988, has been summarised by its main proponent in an 'overview'.[13] What seems remarkable is the degree of influence that such packages have been able to exert, given their disturbing reliance on 'proxy variables' and admitted lack of precision at the local level.

acknowledged, but the problems are endemic across the board. Comparative tourist expenditure is, of course, even more difficult to measure or model, and the continuing lack of remotely plausible data on tourist numbers and expenditure, especially for individual destinations, is attracting increasing attention.

Generalised models such as Cambridge and STEAM have not swept all before them, and other casino bidders preferred to rely on local surveys organised by tourist boards or local government, which the standard models (as they seem to be) also try to incorporate where available, in ways that are not precisely specified. As Restormel council rightly pointed out with regard to Newquay: 'Day visitors are difficult to categorise and vary according to weather patterns' – and they do so in ways that are unlikely to be picked up by the relevant databases.[14] The STEAM definition of a 'tourist day visit', as one that 'crosses a boundary from one area into another area for a period of at least three hours for non-routine leisure purposes' provides an indication of the problems of both definition and measurement. It is very similar to the Cambridge definition, and seems to be endorsed by the DCMS. But it is clearly highly problematic. If I travel the short distance from Lancaster to Blackpool to watch a football match, crossing

municipal and parliamentary constituency but not county boundaries, arriving three quarters of an hour before the game and leaving half an hour after it, paying at the gate and perhaps buying a pie at half-time, this makes me a tourist. The same would apply if I travelled for the same purpose from Lancaster to a rather marginal 'tourist' destination such as Accrington. What is a 'non-routine' leisure activity? Would it become 'routine' if the match were played, and visited, every year; or would regular attendance at any kind of football match make attendance at this one 'routine', even if it were itself an annual or random event? If I go to Blackpool six times a year to see a show, is this 'routine'? Is this definition sensible? And how can such activities really be captured with any conviction? This raises very difficult issues about how tourism levels and impacts can or should be measured, and existing methods remain unreliable and inconsistent.[15]

Day trips are especially problematic, as is widely

Some of the problems are now being recognised by, for example, the English Tourism Information Partnership, following rather belatedly the unease about the validity of current national, regional and especially local tourism statistics that was articulated in the Allnutt Report in 2004.[16] This was commissioned by government and exposed a general lack of fitness for purpose in national tourism statistics; but four years later Professors John E. Fletcher and Victor Middleton complained to a DCMS Select Committee that the report had still had no positive impact:

There is no other sector in the United Kingdom economy as significant as tourism in which the key strategic and management decisions are so hampered by a lack of adequate data.
They suggested that, if anything, the quality of available tourism statistics had deteriorated over the last quarter of a century, and they singled out five key issues:

- the lack of definition and understanding of the widely used concept of 'visitor economy';
- the misleading precision too often imputed to the use of Tourism Satellite Accounting to assess national and regional value, and the damaging impact of the poor quality statistics that were often used;
- the impossibility of conducting effective destination management in the absence of trustworthy local statistics (with a plethora of improvised local studies that could not be compared with each other);
- the complete impossibility of pursuing the fashionable goal of 'sustainable development' in the absence of usable definitions or methodologies;
- the general lack of timely information of all kinds to feed into rational management decisions.

This was a scathing indictment of current practice and of the absence of any sort of central direction or even advice.[17]

It now seems that this nettle is about to be grasped, although there have been so many false starts that a certain enduring scepticism remains permissible. The establishment of ETIP by the Partners for England Forum at the end of 2007 is a promising initiative, alongside the Tourism Intelligence Unit of the Office of National Statistics. The report it commissioned from The Tourism Company points up a lot of the problems identified above, indicating the lack of available statistical data to inform tourism planners, noting the dangers that arise from undue reliance on modelling from national databases of doubtful validity, and expressing well-founded doubts about the prevalence of proprietary economic impact models.[18] Current attempts to place tourism statistics on a more convincing footing, to enable trends, contexts and local conditions to be assessed in a more plausible manner, are admittedly unlikely to bear much fruit before 2011 or 2012. In the meantime the poverty of existing models, especially at the local level, has been thoroughly exposed. The age of STEAM may well be drawing to its close.[19]

Beyond all this, an unhealthy aspect of the ruling assumptions underlying the collection of tourism statistics is the exclusive focus on businesses that levy charges for the services and experiences they supply. This neglects the importance of free access and the uncommodified enjoyment of views, tranquillity, relaxation or wildlife as part of what draws people to the coast and makes destinations attractive to residents as well as visitors. Attempts to conduct economic modelling on the basis of 'willingness to pay' for such experiences are more disturbing still. It is not only commercial provision that generates 'indirect' or 'induced' employment: so do coastal paths, nature reserves, National Trust or English Heritage sites, or attractive public spaces that draw people in who then make use of commercially provided services.

This is a variant on the recognised importance of local authority infrastructure and amenity provision that does not make a profit itself, but enables others to do so, creating multiplier effects in the process. The development of Blackpool is a classic example of this phenomenon at work.[20] Similar arguments might be applied to public transport. Most railways to resorts, most of the time, probably did not make a profit in their own right, depending on the accounting conventions adopted; but they did enable others to invest successfully in providing goods and services for those who used their facilities.[21] We must not lose sight of this dimension in developing new tourism statistics.

The unreliability of quantitative tourism data is, not surprisingly, also evident in other settings. A current Italian study informs us that:[22]

Data comparison demonstrates that the real volume of tourism reaching the Italian coastal destinations is five times higher than what is measured through the official statistics.

But the British case is, overall, particularly problematic, and there is an urgent and recognised need to improve the quality of British statistics to meet the EU standards that are now required by Eurostat.

Part of the problem at the local level is the very variable quality of the resources provided by consultants' analyses. It might be thought invidious to single out and name coastal examples, but a very recent illustration from personal experience in an inland location may be helpful. A consultant's report on the likely visitor demand for an edge-of-town shopping mall development in a north-western town predicted an annual footfall of eight million. This appeared implausible, not least in the light of data submitted to the Casino Advisory Panel, and the objectors sought clarification of the methodology used. It transpired that the consultants had taken the current annual estimate for Greater Manchester's Trafford Centre, compared the size of that centre with that of the proposed development, and assumed that visitor numbers could be 'read off' *pro rata*:

one-third the area, one-third the visitor numbers. This approach would have predicted eight million visitors even if the proposed development had been on St Kilda or Rockall. The local authority had simply accepted the projection.

That is a reminder that the quality of consultants' work may vary from the excellent to the flimsy, that the nature and expected scope of commissions need to be carefully specified, and that the outcomes should be analysed critically. It may often be better to do the work in-house, if qualified employees with appropriate skills, contacts and a professional ethic of public service are available. The lack of reliable local tourism statistics makes this problem particularly pressing.

But there is a great deal more to the informed, research-led pursuit of coastal regeneration than the accumulation of quantitative economic and demographic data, important as this is to providing basic information if considered properly in context. *Such material can inform policy but should not determine it.*

Evidence on the nature and popularity of live entertainment provision in coastal towns is highly relevant, and Stephen Hayler's assessment of the changing nature of provision and size of audiences, and

the role of local authorities in small and medium-sized resorts in trying to meet visitor expectations, provides essential underpinning.[23] The role of live entertainment in regeneration should be an important dimension wherever a coastal destination has an infrastructure a tradition of provision or a potentially responsive market. Evidence of successful practice and its potential transferability needs to be carefully investigated, as in the case of Blackpool's *Admission All Classes*, which during its 2007/8 season effectively combined the traditional, the innovative and the edgy in a setting that does admittedly boast a uniquely strong and full-flavoured reputation for popular entertainment, with a challengingly large number of seats to fill.[24] Here as elsewhere, the challenges are to attract new generations and visiting publics without alienating existing visitors and residents, and to sustain the momentum after the completion of a single major project.

Admission All Classes is an excellent example of an attempt to regenerate coastal entertainment provision by building on a tradition while transforming and updating it from within, so as to appeal to an array of niche markets nesting in a broad and inclusive cross-section of popular audiences. This seductive combination of living heritage, including that of the 'recent past' and of veteran but still attractive performers, with current technologies, allusions and modes of presentation, contributes to a 'cultural landscape' of the sort UNESCO had in mind when constructing new categories for World Heritage Sites.[25] The necessary research in such areas entails looking at local live entertainment traditions in a broader context over time and space, thinking about what might be distinctively 'seaside' or place-specific about them, becoming aware of what has worked in other places and how its positive outcomes might be transferable, and seeking advice and inputs from people with relevant records of attested achievement in these areas.

Similar points might be made about architectural and town planning heritage, where the relevant expertise is more established and accessible through English Heritage (especially), CABE and campaigning organisations like SAVE Britain's Heritage.[26] Awareness of the distinctiveness, significance and value of seaside architecture as living heritage has increased considerably in accessibility over the last decade, through the expansion of listing and awareness of the 'heritage of the recent past'. It should

form an essential aspect of the necessary research in support of seaside regeneration projects, not least as part of the necessary discouragement of routine, 'could-be-anywhere' developments and urban cloning. Coastal towns need to regenerate in ways that respect and build on their distinctive features, otherwise they will fail to attract visitors, residents and businesses that have an unprecedented range of choices of location in an internationally competitive market.[27] Public art is also part of this picture, as **Chapter 7** in this *Handbook* underlines.

A further aspect that needs to be considered, however, is what might be called the 'informal coast' and the representation of fishing and beach tourism (especially) by artists, photographers and related visual commentators, from Constable and Turner to Paul Martin and Frank Meadow Sutcliffe, in their contrasting idioms, and on to Tony Ray-Jones and Martin Parr.[28] Many resorts have had recent

locally organised exhibitions celebrating 'unofficial' aspects of their recent remembered past, as at the Blott Artist Studios in Blackpool.[29] The tradition of seaside photography has embraced a particularly strong strand of celebrating the untidy, relaxed and spontaneous aspects of 'ordinary people' at leisure and play, often affectionate, sometimes incorporating elements of the voyeuristic or censorious, but always creating and sustaining those shared traditions of nostalgia and self-mockery that keep British coastal tourism alive and inhibit attempts to take it seriously. An understanding of this almost anarchic dimension of coastal pleasures and imagery, evident in the 'plotland' settlements of the inter-war years and attempts to defend their informality against commercial redevelopment (as at Humberston Fitties, Cleethorpes), is essential to underpin the sort of regeneration that will enliven and not sterilise, and that will liberate a sense of fun and frolic.[30] As David Chandler has

observed:[31]

Going to the seaside was like going back in time, in a sense, to a country that was still struggling to become modern. ... There's a sort of abandon about the seaside, you find people performing in a way that they wouldn't do at home and then in that performance they're revealing something of themselves that they wouldn't normally do.

This kind of empathetic understanding, 'from the bottom up', will be an essential part of open, participatory approaches to coastal regeneration.

How should we assess the impact of regeneration interventions? The problems of statistical measurement have been discussed above. Moreover, as the Casino Advisory Panel noted in its report, it would be all too easy to identify positive changes that march in step with regeneration initiatives, and to ascribe the former to the latter through a simple, and tempting, 'post hoc ergo propter hoc' argument.[32] We need to remain aware of the complexity of the interactions between amenity, recreational provision, 'natural' and built environment, security, comfort, tradition, innovation and excitement in creating a 'spirit of place' and a 'place-myth' to generate an ambience that will attract and retain the loyalty and affection of a sustainable and renewable sufficiency of people. Such awareness should inhibit us from the uncritical adoption of mechanistic statistical measures of success or failure. We can witness in other chapters of this *Handbook* that such findings are often at odds with observed reality, and the pitfalls of statistical methodologies are obvious enough to discourage us from discounting the evidence of our own eyes.

This is not to advocate the abandonment of quantitative and classificatory modes of analysis. It is to suggest rather that they are not infallible, and that their terms of reference are often ambiguous and value-laden. We need to be able to look holistically at issues, to take account of the unquantifiable and intangible alongside those phenomena that we can legitimately attempt to count, to be particularly sceptical about surveys based on loaded questions or subjective grading on scales of 1 to 5, and to be creatively critical of whatever expertise we buy in.

Above all, we should talk to each other *across* imagined disciplinary boundaries, liberate ourselves from silo mentalities, and regenerate in fully informed ways that embrace traditions, cultural landscapes, attachment to place and the 'heritage of the recent past' alongside, and in dialogue with, the necessary economic, demographic and social indicators that normally dominate such discourses. This chapter is, then, a plea for the eclectic, the interactive and the open-minded.

Resorts of the world: Development of an Adriatic coastal resort
by Tomi Brezovec, University of Primorska, Slovenia

Portorož is situated on the northern coast of Istria, a peninsula in the northern Adriatic. Until the late nineteenth century, Portorož (or Portorose at the time) was only a name for a scarcely populated area covered with olive trees, vineyards and Mediterranean greenery. The development of tourism has significantly changed the scenery of the place. Investments in the tourism industry have transformed this area into an important regional tourism destination generating over 1.5 million bed-nights.

Development of tourism in Portorož has been strongly influenced by political reality. Since the beginning of tourism development, the Istrian peninsula frequently passed from one authority to another.

Each has distinctly marked its period. Until the First World War, Portorož was a resort in Austria–Hungary. Tourism development was based on climate and spa treatments. The growing elite tourism was stopped by the war. After the war the area found itself under Italian rule and became one of many Italian seaside resort destinations offering classical sun and beach. Despite investments in tourism the number of arrivals could not match pre-war figures.

Immediately after the Second World War, Portorož was included in a Free Triest Territory (FTT), a temporary entity set up to overcome border disputes between Italy and Yugoslavia. Military government of the area did not stimulate tourism, and investments in tourism infrastructure were very limited.

After 1954, Portorož and its surroundings became part of Yugoslavia. Soon after, intense renovation and investments in necessary facilities turned Portorož into a classical mass-tourism destination. The number of arrivals was growing rapidly until the 1980s when tourism needed new investment but the funds were not available. Decline of tourism was further accelerated by the dissolution of Yugoslavia in 1991. The war of independence of Slovenia had a long-term effect on tourism. Repositioning of the destination and large investments in infrastructure renovation have accelerated the destination's recovery process.

further information on this paper, please visit: www.tourism-culture.com

Regenerating coastal towns: balanced housing and sustainable populations? - *Darren P. Smith, University of Brighton, UK*

This paper considers the key housing and population-related challenges for the regeneration of some coastal towns, which have experienced long-term decline. It is contended that there is an urgent need to rebalance local housing markets dominated by Housing in Multiple Occupation (HMOs) – by delivering a more sensitive mix of housing, via the use of enforcement powers and strategic intervention (Use Classes Order). This would involve the de-conversion of HMO and new housebuilding. It is contended that this will realign many coastal towns with the impulsion for mixed, balanced and sustainable communities. It is suggested that the system for the funding of Housing Benefit is a major factor here, which has encouraged irresponsible private landlords to create unsustainable and deprived local populations. It is suggested that placemaking strategies will be vital for the rebalancing of housing and populations in coastal towns by encouraging specific flows of immigration and countering the depopulation of some social groups from coastal towns.

for further information on this paper, please visit: www.tourism-culture.com

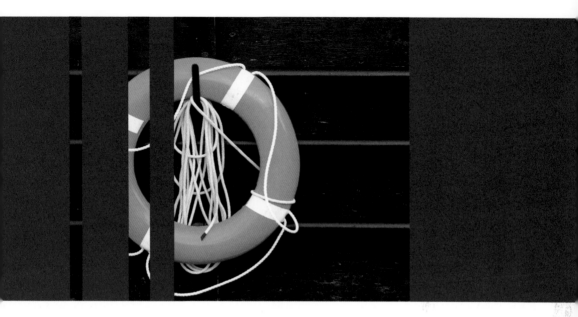

Chapter 9

Cultural regeneration in four South East coastal towns
by Fred Gray and David Powell

Barriers and unintentional consequences
by Tim Brennan

This chapter reports on research conducted in the first six months of 2009 on regeneration programmes in four coastal towns in the South East of England (SECTs) with substantial cultural and higher educational (HE) activity. The research examined how such approaches to regeneration based on cultural and HE interventions might offer practical solutions to the challenges of the recession, and decreasing levels of public and private regeneration funding. Funded by the South East England Development Agency (SEEDA), the research focused on Margate, Folkestone, Bognor Regis and Portsmouth. The central research methods were documentary and statistical analysis and qualitative interviews.[1]

As part of central and regional government's developing focus on coastal regeneration, the role of culture in coastal regeneration is widely acknowledged and has assumed a high profile in some places. The role of higher education is less well understood both in the coastal context, and in terms of universities' and colleges' contributions to the cultural vibrancy and prosperity of their own localities.

Culture, HE and the renewal of the four coastal towns

The research placed the four SECTs in the context of the post-war decline of many coastal towns and the regeneration strategies that have been used in attempting to reverse decline. We recognised the distinctiveness of individual coastal towns, each with its unique geography and history set within a particular locality and sub-region. Many coastal towns see cultural activity as an integral part of their approach to regeneration, and with universities have realised the role of higher education (HE) in transforming local prospects. There is no single model shared between the four towns, in terms of exploiting the optimum benefits from connecting regeneration, culture and HE.

There are significant differences in the way in which culture and regeneration has been approached in each of the four places.

- In Margate there is a strong arts and cultural emphasis in the regeneration programme and a focus on major investment projects with Turner Contemporary art gallery and the Dreamland amusement park.
- There is a broadly based arts, cultural and education approach to regeneration in Folkestone driven by events, festivals and fixed-term projects to develop local capacity, aspiration and new cultural markets, and delivered by an autonomous social enterprise body.
- In Bognor Regis, large-scale investment, with commercial leisure including substantial new investment in the Butlins resort, is building on programme delivery in partnership with the University of Chichester.
- Regeneration in Portsmouth has an established array of naval, maritime and related heritage attractions, and visitor and retail destinations with an established and expanding relationship with the University of Portsmouth and a range of mature cultural producers.

The research identified important positive synergies between cultural regeneration programmes and HE initiatives in coastal towns that hitherto have been often unacknowledged in strategic and policy terms. The clearest differences are in the way in which the contribution of higher education institutions (HEIs) have been planned, and/or in which the roles of the individual universities have been engaged as partners.

- HEIs are not involved yet in Margate as an active regeneration partner, nor with a significant physical presence in the town.
- In Folkestone, HEIs are part of a major education transformation, and help with intensifying the regeneration impact of the creative quarter.
- In Bognor Regis, HEI activity is being rolled out through programmes, but planned investment is not yet in place to integrate higher education in town centre/ cultural quarter regeneration.
- Long-term higher education presence in Portsmouth has enabled the HEI to become a substantial regeneration partner, developing solid relationships and joint projects with cultural partners, and building the capacity and sustainability of the local cultural and creative sector.

We believe that the four SECTs contribute in different and interesting ways to the wider pattern of coastal regeneration practice. However, the value derived from the ways in which they are engaging culture and education in regeneration is under threat from new priorities generated by the economic crisis and imminent and expected constraints in public and private spending. These are challenges both to the four towns in the study and the wider coastal regeneration community.

Major findings

How can this research assist local partnerships to sustain themselves in the face of significant upheavals and continuing great financial stringency? What are the important messages for local government, delivery partnerships, cultural agencies, higher education and for the cultural and creative community? In each of the four towns, the local civic, cultural and educational leadership can take steps better to identify and make use of local strengths and opportunities to support the continued role of culture and education through challenging times.

- *Cultural vitality*

Cultural vitality is as important as business vitality. Each of the coastal towns was looking to develop its own combination of cultural activity for its residents and programmes, events and places which can attract visitors and tourists. This works best through investment in the quality of programmes and on local distinctiveness. Giving residents and visitors the best possible experience is essential. On the coast as in many places, local civic and business leadership recognise that places with vibrant creative and cultural communities help attract and retain talented people and companies across the whole local economy.

Culture, creativity and higher education play a substantial role in place-making. Higher education investment and activity can be harnessed effectively to local regeneration and development processes. Cultural talent, activity and infrastructure are already helping to raise the profile of the place and individuals' aspirations in towns like Folkestone. Cultural, educational and civic bodies need to work together effectively to make their towns work better.

- *Scale and locality*

Some culture and education-led regeneration programmes have large scale projects at their heart. Where this is the case, all partners involved need to do whatever they can to ensure that they are sustainable, and bring the benefits that investment of scale demands. However, there is equal, though different value in encouraging small-scale, autonomous, artist-driven and community-led projects as well as seasonal and occasional activity. The range of artists' studios, galleries, cafés, small music venues and other arts projects help build a rich offer in Margate: Turner Contemporary requires a critical and successful mass of such venues and businesses for its own survival and sustainability as much as it offers these smaller enterprises the benefits of a major attraction.

Events and fixed-term programmes enable local agencies to test markets and ideas. Seasonal events and festivals intensify local cultural experience, and provide the kinds of high-quality programme which small coastal towns could not sustain year round. Ownership, leadership and autonomy are determining factors in seeing projects from idea to actuality, and into the long-term success. Portsmouth's Love Albert Road is just one example of recognising and supporting local champions, and supporting effective grassroots and locally driven, community and business facing regeneration. This approach can provide locally embedded, cost-effective ways of generating commitment and change.

- *Independence of means*

The leadership and delivery role of the Creative Foundation and the Roger De Haan Charitable Trust demonstrate the strength of the social enterprise model, where it is using commercial disciplines in sustainable and socially focused development programmes, and in particular where it can develop an asset-based approach to culture and education-led regeneration. The case of Butlins in Bognor Regis shows the potential of enriching and complementing the investment in high-quality culture and/or education with commercial leisure attractions. In any event, the prognosis for the reduction in public sector funding is both challenge and opportunity: projects will need to work out how best to survive with reduced, little or no dependency on public sector funding.

- *The long view*

You don't turn around a failing seaside town in a few years. The data shows how little relative change has been experienced between these four towns and regional and national benchmarks through the years that preceded the recession. These places are still haunted by embedded poverty. Decades of poverty and low self-esteem take more than a few time-limited projects to remedy.

The long view also commends early and sustained action. The Creative Foundation manages its charitably owned properties on 125-year leases. Early and continued commitment should help secure the value of new projects and investment, paving the way – for example as Turner Contemporary is doing – for new venues and attractions by investing in programmes and capacity building activity and pre-opening programmes. The universities of Chichester and Portsmouth demonstrate a similar sustained commitment to their home places.

Actions

The partners in this research have placed a high value on sharing intelligence and taking concerted action across their local communities. They recognise the local, collective and mutual benefits of partnerships between agencies and simplifying decision-making and delivery processes. They are interested in continued sharing of knowledge and good practice as part of a south-east and national coastal towns' network of leaders, with reliable local intelligence mechanisms and indicators for tracking impacts and opportunities.

In the context of the radical consequences of economic change on the public, not-for-profit and private sectors, the research indicates some important messages and recommendations for action for all those involved in the continued cultural and educational transformation of coastal towns. These may be summarised as follows.

- Local authorities, delivery agencies and partnerships should review their regeneration delivery plans and see how and where less expenditure-intensive approaches might be delivered by increased involvement of cultural and educational bodies, and by sharing resources and joint action.
- Cultural organisations should prepare for involvement in planning and direction of local delivery, identifying where and how they might contribute. Local delivery agencies should rethink ways of involving cultural and education bodies in planning and governance. Higher education institutions need to deliver effective ways of engaging with and supporting local cultural organisations and networks, and of delivering professional development and management support to small cultural businesses.
- Cultural and regeneration leadership are encouraged to work closely with private sector champions and networks to engage business skills in local governance arrangements for cultural and education projects. Cultural and education projects must be encouraged to participate in local business networks.
- National and regional cultural agencies should agree where, at board and senior management level, the ownership of this analysis and these responsibilities will sit in the new institutional arrangements. Leadership in the four coastal towns should work collaboratively in support of this, and the actions that should result.

The substantive recommendation to government is that coastal towns and their challenges and opportunities are a legitimate special interest group. These towns should continue to be regarded as places in need of focused attention. Investment in cultural and educational infrastructure and activity needs to be sustained because it demonstrably contributes to the broad regeneration process, delivering layers of value beyond the primary outputs of cultural and creative activity and teaching, training and research. Excellent practice, nationally and within these four towns, shows how asset-based social enterprise can deliver effective change. The government should continue to encourage these kinds of locally controlled, socially responsive and effective agencies. To enable this to happen, everyone involved must invest in strengthening local civic, cultural, educational and private sector leadership.

English Heritage: barriers and unintended consequences in coastal regeneration!

There now appears to be a national consensus that coastal communities are worthy of significant investment, but that any such initiatives will face major challenges. Most of these are faced by any community seeking to strengthen their economy and enhance their historic character, but some issues are peculiar to coastal communities. From a heritage-sector perspective, our experience tells us that there are two ways to consider the issues that can arise in projects such as these:

- as barriers to achieving regeneration objectives;
- as unintended consequences for the historic environment created by regeneration schemes.

Barriers to achieving regeneration objectives

In many coastal towns, the historic environment (eclectic architecture, colourful gardens, exotic piers, extravagant bandstands, busy promenades, bustling harbours etc.) is a significant element in the original 'unique selling point' that attracted visitors and businesses in the first place. English Heritage's experience suggests that regeneration projects that integrate investment in the historic environment within wider regeneration programmes are those that have the greatest impact and create the most eye-catching and long-lasting results.

Analysis of successful regeneration projects identifies a number of common principles and valuable transferable lessons running through them, and these are set out in *Regeneration and the Historic Environment.* But equally there are a number of common barriers that can delay, disrupt or even ultimately derail the best intentions of heritage-led regeneration. Some of these are perhaps well known and create similar problems in all types of regeneration schemes:

- *Partnership working/ stakeholders.* All types of regeneration projects need the widest possible range of stakeholders to maximise their chances of success. Without establishing links to other departments within the local authority and external stakeholders there is an obvious risk that a project will focus on a single objective without taking account of other issues or ongoing projects in the locality.

- *Leadership.* Strong political leadership is vital to get key decisions made, strategies agreed and funding delivered. Clear reporting lines with straightforward governance structures are also important in terms of ensuring projects continue to reflect corporate priorities and are fully supported by other parts of the local authority. English Heritage's network of elected member 'Heritage Champions' in local authorities (around 80 per cent of English councils have now appointed a Champion) offers an excellent opportunity for political leadership of heritage-led regeneration projects and a direct link to embed 'heritage thinking' in a local authority's future strategy.

- *Challenges.* There is sometimes a short-term view that fails to see beyond the challenges and towards the benefits of the historic environment. There is an often a perception that historic buildings and areas are difficult to deal with – awkward to navigate through the planning system with extra red-tape and expense to deal with. However, historic buildings provide a quality environment to live and work in. Refurbishment and reuse will also ensure the retention of the sense of place and the distinctive coastal character that matters to residents and visitors.

There are also some issues that are peculiar to heritage-led regeneration projects:

- *The balancing act.* Heritage can play a variety of roles in coastal regeneration. It can be the catalyst for local revitalisation (e.g. the refurbishment of Cromer Pier), or it can be complementary to other regeneration strategies that are already some way to achieving their goals, such as the public art focusing on the maritime history of Whitehaven. The historic environment will play some kind of role, even if only as a backdrop, in almost every coastal regeneration project. Ensuring that it is integrated as a prominent, high-quality component to these kinds of project will create an excellent platform for increased confidence in the locality and will reinforce a sense of place and belonging for the community.

- *Using the historic environment to address local circumstances.* There is a risk that the focus of a project on the retention of an historic building will overlook issues about its end-use and revenue costs. However, the reverse of this situation is that heritage assets can be used to address specific local issues, such as the lack of affordable housing. For example, Great Yarmouth Borough Council has created a number of innovative partnerships with housing associations to refurbish and convert vacant historic buildings to address the pressing local need for affordable housing.

- *Measuring impact.* It can be difficult for heritage-led regeneration projects to quantify the effect that they have had on their local area, and in particular the impact they have had in non-monetary terms – for example, attitudes to the local environment or the way that people regard the retail offer. Evidence of such impacts is crucial in demonstrating the benefits of such projects, and benchmarking of the initial situation is important to be able to measure success. Nevertheless, projects such as the evaluation of the Falmouth Heritage Economic Regeneration Scheme have been able to demonstrate the impact and achievements of heritage-focused funding. Similarly, an in-depth analysis by the Heritage Lottery Fund (HLF) of its Townscape Heritage Initiative funding stream has not only focused on economic regeneration and improvements to physical appearance, but has also looked at measuring effects on public perception and the quality of life. These have demonstrated clear benefits, including a 'multiplier' effect where the HLF's funding has been aligned with other regeneration projects.

Unintended consequences for the historic environment created by regeneration schemes

Regeneration projects are, by definition, intended to have a significant impact on the area in question and aim to raise the quality of the local environment. Nevertheless, owing to their scale, major projects can also have unforeseen consequences for local distinctiveness and the character of the historic environment. There is a danger that development designed to regenerate coastal towns could potentially detract from the special character that originally made them attractive. Interventions that are inappropriate can be caused by a number of underlying reasons.

- Physical improvements to the local environment are only one element of comprehensive regeneration and will almost always need to be complemented by efforts to stimulate economic

and social regeneration. As part of an overall programme, regeneration schemes will often have consequent implications for local character and distinctiveness. Undertaking proper research and ensuring it informs the masterplanning of regeneration strategies allows informed decisions to be made about future development. Historic landscape characterisation and historic area assessments are central to establishing such understanding and much work has been done by English Heritage and others that can be filtered into this process. Ensuring that development is both sympathetic and responds to its context is a vital step in ensuring its long-term sustainability. Without starting from this position of understanding, regeneration projects can cause urban design conflicts. Regeneration strategies such as those containing plans for iconic new buildings or large scale retail development can compromise distinctive coastal or maritime character, and careful consideration is needed at an early stage to ensure

that such development does not 'jar' with its surroundings.

- The implications of climate change, such as coastal erosion, potentially higher sea levels and increasing numbers of storms, will endanger historic buildings and archaeology. However, responses to these issues, such as the increasing numbers of sea defence projects, can themselves create problems. Flood defences can impair the character and setting of historic quaysides and waterfront buildings as well as having an impact on archaeology. However, well-designed, large-scale projects such as the new sea wall at Blackpool demonstrate how sea defences can be installed or upgraded without affecting historic character, and potentially can even enhance the historic environment.

- Many historic coastal towns suffer from poor transport links and the perception of being at the 'end of the line'. Regeneration projects involving the improvement of transport links can have obvious implications for heritage assets and local character, while the upgrading of port facilities can damage historic harbour structures and associated archaeology. The increasing popularity of sailing and consequent increase in the number of new marinas also has implications for historic harbours and ports.

- Historic coastal towns often have large numbers of lodging and boarding houses originally built for week-long family holidays, and many have been converted into houses of multiple occupation. Regeneration projects that include the modernisation of accommodation such as this can affect the significance and character of the locality. Innovative schemes, such as that undertaken by Lancaster City Council in the West End of Morecambe, have been able to avoid the incremental erosion of character. The local authority purchased a number of HMOs in the area and converted each property into two or three high-quality flats.

It then entered into a joint ownership agreement with a new purchaser and retained half the ownership. The benefits are twofold: houses in the locality are better maintained so retaining and enhancing local character and attractiveness, while a greater stock of affordable housing is also created.

- Clarity about the end-use of buildings and a clear business plan quantifying costs and income are essential features for the long-term sustainability of a regeneration project. Landmark buildings and structures in coastal towns that have become disused or are at risk, such as theatres or piers, create strong feelings locally and it is not uncommon for campaigns to be started to retain them. Such campaigns need to be clear about the

demand for such buildings (or an alternative use) as few buildings can justify preservation without a clear function or an income.

In seeking to harness the local historic environment's capacity to contribute to economic, social and environmental regeneration, practitioners need to ensure that their projects have a full and proper understanding of local character and distinctiveness. This is the essential first step in ensuring that the vision for the area makes the best use of existing heritage. Celebrating the colourful past of England's coastal towns should help to guarantee that they have a bright future.

Information: For further detail of English Heritage, its activities and guidance publications, see www. english-heritage.org.uk and www.helm.org.uk.

In the Realm of the Raucous. Donald McGill: King of the Saucy Seaside Postcard.

"I want to back the favourite, please. My sweetheart gave me a pound, to do it both ways!"

The risqué, near the knuckle but worth a chuckle, seaside postcard was once an integral part of the holiday routine. But no more. Superseded by technology and changing tastes, the saucy seaside postcard is of another time. Or is it? From pier revue to peer re-view, the paper explores the legacy of Donald McGill – the undisputed doyen of the genre.

The past master of the pithy innuendo and double-entendre he was the King of Seaside Saucy Postcard. And well might he wear his crown. Although his kingdom was extensive, the seaside was his true domain. It was there in the heady atmosphere of the hustle and bustle of the milling crowds that McGill's medium worked its magic. And it was there, in the realm of the raucous, that sales of his cards burgeoned as the visiting hordes took to his humour with gusto. Achieving sales well in excess of 250 million cards, it is the sheer volume, the extraordinary proliferation of his work that astounds.

It is, essentially, English humour: captured and contextualised in time and space – epitomising the English seaside holiday of a by-gone era. Perhaps no single resort is so evocatively captured by, nor representative of, McGill's work as Blackpool of the late 1940's and 1950's. With McGill's life and work as exemplar, and contextualised within the passing of time, the paper focuses on the high culture/ low culture class values that underpin, or rather undermine, much of today's thinking on tourism, notably the charade of ego/ eco/sustainable tourism. As academics we should eschew the absurd notions of objectivity, declare our respective interests and proceed enthusiastically. Here is no exception. Indeed, McGill is the perfect subject with which to embrace another of my long held beliefs....the power of the visual. And the paper draws on an eclectic range of material by way of illustration. Combining the 'personal' with 'visual', the presentation assesses McGill's relevance to the study, and analysis, of contemporary tourism.

Brian Wheeller NHTV Breda, The Netherlands University of Tasmania

for further information on this paper, please visit: www.tourism-culture.com

Chapter 10

Coastal areas and their duty to undertake an economic assessment

by Ivan Annibal

The development of the duty for local authorities to undertake an economic assessment – unveiled in the Sub-National Review of Economic Development and Regeneration – puts economic geography at the heart of local economic development.[1] This is not new, but it is a theme that had lain dormant for most of the 1980s and 90s. The modern origins of the debate go back to the Redcliffe Maud Commission instituted by Prime Minister Ted Heath in 1966.

Broadly, the report recommended the abolition of all the existing county, county borough, borough, urban district and rural district councils, which had been created at the end of the nineteenth century, and replacing them with new *unitary authorities*. These new authorities were largely based on major towns, which acted as regional employment, commercial, social and recreational centres and took into account local transport infrastructure and travel patterns.

The report triggered a debate which, in its watered down form, led to the introduction of the current system and more importantly boundaries of local authorities in 1972. Interestingly, Redcliffe Maud also proposed a regional tier of government based on boundaries similar to those on which Regional Assemblies and RDAs function today.

Unfortunately, somewhere between 1966 and 1972 the wiring got twisted and the pattern of local authorities that came into being lost its focus on functioning economic areas. Instead there came into being a patchwork of authorities based on local lobbying, compromise and tradition. No change there, then! This largely dysfunctional pattern has predominated for a generation, and now we have an *ad hoc* 'pick and mix' approach to boundaries based on incremental changes, with still relatively little focus on the actual functioning of places.

To be fair, in parallel with the evolution of administrative boundaries there has been a debate about how local authorities can be empowered to work across their boundaries to form alliances based on economic geography; and how, if all are willing, these arrangements can be put on a statutory footing through the implementation of the sub-national review referred to above. Perhaps it is the ability to be flexible in creating sense from complexity that is more important than creating simple structures themselves. There is a strong tradition in Britain of hanging on to strange and evolving systems rather than sweeping them away. Compare the rebuilding of London on almost the exact same street pattern after the Great Fire of 1666 to Hausmann's complete remodelling of Paris in the 1860s. Or think about the evolution of our system of government without a written constitution.

If we therefore choose to 'go with the flow' in terms of seeking to make the best of the new powers local authorities have been given in recent years, starting with the Power of Well-Being in the 2000 Local Government Act, and building through Michael Lyons' exhortation to us all to get on and shape our places, what does the requirement to undertake an economic assessment mean for coastal areas?

As evidenced elsewhere in this *Handbook*, coastal places are different. They have a number of generic features that make them different and we can also differentiate between them. Generically they are different for these reasons:

- They are liminal. That is, they exist between two planes – physically and in the mind – being on the cusp of the land and sea and having only an 180-degree hinterland (albeit the sea itself is a resource).
- They have a terminus feel,

all being literally 'at the end of the line'.

- They have a set of special environmental challenges around their relationship with the sea.
- In the context of an island nation they have a fascination for people. This creates sentimental and, in some senses, irrational approaches to investment in them. You only have to take a trip to the theme park at Lands End to get a sense of this.

It is important to begin to draw out some shades of grey – particularly in terms of functionality – when thinking about coastal settlements. We need to distinguish them into more distinct and individual categories based on their economic geographies.

In considering the intersection of economy and geography on our coastline I have come up with a four-fold categorisation of places based on *deprivation* and the ways in which it manifests itself. Of course this is not the only way of considering the matter, but it does drive out some interesting insights. Why is this important in the context of the duty to undertake an economic assessment? The answer is that the duty to undertake an economic assessment is not predicated on the basis of creating something that sits on a shelf. In fact the

actual techniques used to prepare the assessment are largely irrelevant provided it is done technically well. There are any number of consultants offering a 'stop me and buy one' approach to this aspect of the task.

What the creation of the first statutory duty for local authorities in terms of economic development is about – and there are some del who have operated at the margins of local authority discretion for years and who have mixed views about this new statutory status – is the challenge for local authorities to prove they understand what is happening 'on their patch'.

Approaches to monitoring and performance management in the public sector are cyclical, and we seem to be coming to the end of one cycle of micro-recording and management. I foresee new approaches arising very soon that concentrate more on action than measurement. This will be partly driven by the need to respond to recession, and partly by the weight of the current regulatory regime collapsing in on itself. In my view that will be a good thing because there is a tendency in local government for measurement and process to become a proxy for actually doing. This is a feature also of other areas of the public sector. This is not to say that all

measurement is bad – some approaches are underpinned by more reason than others.

The National Performance Indicators introduced for local government are a case in point: top-down; imposed by central government; some hard to measure in technical terms and others based on perception. The jury is still out in terms of their usefulness. They sit alongside school league tables, which recently led a London headteacher to reflect that we should concentrate more on fattening the pig than constantly weighing it. Continuing with this analogy, the economic assessment offers enlightenment and provides the opportunity for local authorities, based on their own analyses, to explain and justify how they have used their discretion to tackle local economic challenges.

There has been a debate within the development of the guidance for the assessment itself about *prescription*. A number of voices have been arguing for a standard approach to assessment. Others, led by the Local Government Association, have argued for a light touch based on the fact that local authorities – and more specifically places – all have unique characteristics and narratives and should not be shoe-horned into some sort of standard template.

Approaches to developing an economic assessment ought to use comparable statistical bases, but it is important that local authorities be allowed the discretion to prepare the assessments in a way that reflects *their understanding* and allows them to *express it freely* rather than requiring them to follow a prescriptive format. These economic assessments also have to find a place within the framework of plans and assessments that exist already in the context of local government – ranging from the regional evidence underpinning Spatial Strategies to the local analysis in development frameworks (LDFs).

The process of considering where the assessment fits in will inevitably cause some tension and debate, but that is a good thing if it challenges established approaches that put land use at the heart of economic thinking. The new proposals for Planning Policy Statement (PPS) 4 point to a positive and more integrated way forward in this context.[2] Matthew Taylor's recent

review of rural economies and housing has raised the level of debate around the need to consider things on a wider basis than the current housing/planning-led dialogue about what makes a settlement sustainable.[3] Interestingly it is proposed that the economic assessment's primary audience should be the Local Strategic Partnership (LSP) – this provides real opportunities to avoid it becoming the technical preserve of a few statisticians within councils.

So at the heart of the assessment is the need to bring out the distinctive nature of places and to demonstrate (notwithstanding some geographically flawed administrative boundaries) the basis on which local authorities use their discretion to work collectively or independently to 'do' economic development.

In rising to this challenge it is important to consider not just quantitative but also qualitative evidence that is based on tradition and informal activities. One key issue to surface in writing the narrative of place

is 'embeddedness', a well-established concept based on describing how patterns and traditions of human interaction in places condition their development. Social and group norms often lead to economic behaviours that appear counter-intuitive but which are conditioned by the history and traditions of a place. For example, Mablethorpe – threatened by rapid inundation from the sea according to the Environment Agency – has a far more vibrant housing market than anyone would imagine. This is based on retirees who have 'always holidayed there' selling their homes in the Midlands and circumventing the normal constraints in the market by coming in as cash buyers. With regard to the technical operation of the assessment, the Local Government Improvement and Development Agency (IDeA) and the Planning Advisory Service (PAS) have commissioned some sector-led guidance. This has been developed by Globe Regeneration and Rocket Science, working with 17 local authorities, and it can be viewed on-line. The sparser and in many senses companion guidance from the Department for Communities and Local Government (DCLG), developed in parallel and with many a useful conversation between the two groups in the process, is also available.[4]

There are *two key components* that are relevant in terms of the sectoral guidance: a list of sources of data, and a cycle that describes how the assessment might be undertaken to squeeze the maximum insights and dynamism out of it. The planning cycle for the assessment is shown in Figure 10-1.

Figure 10-1

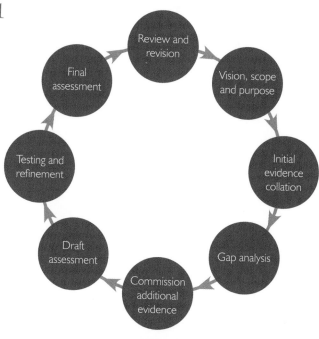

Figure 10-3

This simple cycle is underpinned by ten *key questions* that need to be asked to ensure the assessment works effectively in terms of the collection of data. The questions are set out in Figure 10-2.

Figure 10-2

Ten key questions to ask in developing an economic assessment

1. What do we already know that can be justified with reference to the evidence we hold?

2. Does this enable us to describe both what is going on directly in our area and the global, national, regional and local forces driving it?

3. Can we describe the economic geography of our area in terms of the impact of other places on it and its impact on them?

4. Can we supplement this with forecasting information that will show future trends and developments?

5. In light of the above, how can we best describe our economy in terms of:
   (a) economic sub-areas?
   (b) the key characteristics of those areas in terms of demography, skills, employment and enterprise?
   (c) the drivers for change in terms of each of those factors in each area?
   (d) the relative importance in each area of supplementary contexts around inclusion, environment, housing, planning and connectivity?

6. If this represents a 'factual' description of place, what anecdotal or other impressions exist that challenge or validate it?

7. Do these reveal gaps in data or knowledge, for each of the sub-areas and categories of relevant information set out above, which can/need to be collected/mapped?

8. Can this data be collected easily, can proxies be developed, and can it be accessed on a commercial basis?

9. What other documents, produced by the authority and its partners, can be used to challenge or confirm your analysis?

10. How can we use the evidence within the LEA to support our planning and policy activities?

Other challenges in undertaking the assessment involve building a consensus among partners about its content, and thinking through carefully how it will be used to plan and monitor the economic interventions in an area.

The key categories of data and their sources are set out in Figure 10-3 and Tables 10-1 and 10-2.

Table 10-1 Recommended data sets

Data Set	Main Source	What it tells you	Key sources
Linkages and Flows	Commuting by place of residence and work ONS Nomis ON S commuter view ONS Commuter Flow	The level of self containment and interdependence of your geographies	TTWA data (ONS), Commuting data – 2001 census, Strategic Housing Market Area Assessments (Local Authorities), Forecasting models in Regional Spatial Strategy and Regional Economic Strategy documents. Proprietorial databases
Demography	Population Structure by age, sex and demography and patterns of change ONS Mid year estimates	The economic potential and challenges in terms of the components of your resident population	Age, Ethnic group, Residential population and Sex distribution (ONS), Disability (ONS, nomis), Age structure change over decade, No. Of Households (ONS, NESS)
Skills	Proportion of population with qualifications in the range NVQ 2-4 and no qualifications ONS Nomis from APS Percentage of 16-19 year olds not in Education of Employment with Training DCSF via Connexions	The skills base and "human" potential of your area along with the challenges it faces in terms of employment and skills	Census and Labour Force Survey, Key figures for education, skills and training (ONS), NEET (DCSF and Connexions CCIS)
Employment	Economic Activity, employment and unemployment rates ONS Nomis from APS rolling years figures	The relative level of your employment structure and trends around those in and out of work	Annual Survey of Hours and Earnings workplace income data, Job density data, Unemployment rate 16+ (nomis), Local units by employment size band, (ONS)
Enterprise	ONS: Inter-Departmental Business Register and Business Demography Nomis: Annual Business Inquiry Annual Survey of Hours and Earnings	The level of entrepreneurship in your area its relative dynamism and its structure in terms of sectors and types of business and employment size	Valuation Office Agency (VOA) register, Companies House database, Homeworkers Census, Self-employment (nomis), VAT based businesses by age, employment group and industry group, Floor space & rateable value (ONS, nomis, Commuterview), Proprietorial databases

Productivity	ONS: GVA per head and Gross Fixed Capital Formation – in addition for a really useful discussion see: "Productivity in the UK The Evidence and the Government's Approach" HM Treasury 2007	The economic potential and relative position of your authority's economy	GVA per head, Gross Fixed Capital Formation (GFCF) - (ONS), 5 Drivers: Investment in Physical Capital / Workforce Skills / Innovation / Competition / Enterprise

Table 10-2 Contextual Data

Data Set	What it tells you	Sources of information
Inclusion	You will have a sense from anecdotal perspectives about the relative deprivation and challenges facing your authority in the context of inclusion – this should guide your thinking, in what is an economic assessment about how much of the data from the identified sources of information you should include in this aspect of the context of the assessment	Notifiable offences recorded, Benefits data, Index of Multiple Deprivation, Life expectancy, Infant mortality, All age/all cause mortality rate (NCHOD), Worklessness, Ethnicity (ONS), Active people Sport Survey (Sport England)
Housing, Planning and Connectivity	You should have a sense about the physical configuration of your area, the challenges it faces in terms of its residential characteristics in terms of issues such as affordable housing or housing renewal, the availability and quality of industrial and commercial workspace – this should inform how much attention you pay to these issues in the context of this aspect of the assessment	VOA register, Census, Road Accidents, Household spaces and accommodation type, Vacant dwellings, Tenure (ONS), Annual Business Inquiry (employment changes), House price to income ratios (DCLG), Housing Market Area Assessments, Land Use data (local authorities), LA & RSL Housing stock (local authorities), No. of additional/ affordable homes delivered (local authorities), Core national accessibility indicators (Dept. for Transport
Environment	The National Performance Indicators for Local Government bracket Environment and Economy together. Whilst this is not the only way to consider the importance of environmental indicators, pulling out the relationship between environmental issues and your economy is very important to provide a rounded picture.	Agricultural Census (Defra), Domestic Energy consumption (ONS), Land use database (CLG), Land use change statistics (CLG LUCS), CO2 consumption (Defra), Shoreline Management Plans (Environment Agency), Strategic Flood Risk Assessments (Local Authorities), Household waste collected per head (Defra), Waste recycling rates (Defra), Biodiversity/Habitat Inventory (MAGIC), SSSIs/AONB (NE), Joint Character Areas & LA Landscape Character Assessments (CQC)
Spatial Definitions	The development of the 2004 Rural_Urban definitions has enabled those authorities outside of urban cores to map the functionality of their areas far more effectively and is a boon to the process of rural proofing. This may be more relevant the the majority of coastal resorts.	Rural_urban definitions: Commission for Rural Communities

• *Linkages and flows*

Economic forces do not follow administrative boundaries. This dataset is really important in helping you to determine the economic geography of your area and to map how it relates to the areas surrounding it. The most robust data for this area of analysis is based on the Census and is therefore somewhat out of date. However, using Census data in conjunction with Travel to Work Area data and Housing Market Area Assessments is a good starting point for the process of mapping out where your residents live, work and play and how this affects the overall functioning of the sub-economies in your area. It is important to note that there are no formally agreed areas when using this approach.

• *Demography*

This is particularly important for understanding the economic potential of your area. It should not be seen just as an indicator around the age profile of the workforce (and therefore the productive potential of your area). In addition, particularly in those areas with a high proportion of more elderly populations, the potential for the development of economic activities and approaches that maximise the volunteering, spending potential and adult social care opportunities should also be examined. This should

also help to examine the role of the authority in supporting the economy as an employer.

• *Skills*

This will set out, more clearly than any other element of the assessment, the supply-side strength of your economy. It is also very important for scoping out the speed with which your economy might make the transition out of recession. It will also put into clear perspective the real challenges facing your area in terms of responding to the worklessness agenda. The national Regeneration Framework[5] and the Houghton Review[6] have set out the importance of local authorities undertaking a worklessness assessment.

An important aspect of the development of your economic assessment is that it should provide all the key elements of analysis to ensure this can be effectively achieved. It should be integral to the assessment rather than a stand-alone exercise. According to the

prevalence of worklessness issues in your area, the assessment itself should identify key areas of need to inform the Work and Skills Plan – a key outcome requirement from the worklessness assessment. Taking this a step further, this plan could also inform a 'commissioning blueprint' for your authority which you could use to ensure that skills and employment commissioning within the authority and with partners at local and regional level reflects local needs.

• *Economic inclusion*

This category of information will again play an important role in helping to sketch out the worklessness issues facing your economy. It will also identify key issues and opportunities around how the social and economic cohesion of your area impacts on its sustainability and economic viability.

• *Employment*

This will further build the profile of the supply-side of your

economy, informing the view of demand and indicate how your economy compares with the national picture in terms of its relative strengths and weaknesses as an employment environment. It is important in this area of analysis to draw out the sectoral nature of your employment base to get a sense of how diverse (and therefore relatively vulnerable or robust) your economy is. It is also important to look at employment structures and issues alongside the flows and linkages section.

It is useful in considering the sustainability of your economy in this context to consider how self-contained it is. How high is the proportion of those who live and work in the area compared with those who live in it and work elsewhere, or vice versa?

• *Enterprise and business*

With enterprise we enter the demand side of the economy. It is important in developing a profile of enterprise in your area to take account of the fact that self-employment and businesses not VAT-registered are important alongside the more standard and easy to access data around VAT-registered businesses. Sectoral analysis is also important, as is a concentration on the distribution of knowledge-intensive businesses that many

economists feel underpin the dynamism of local economies. Rather than just concentrating on data around companies, it is also very useful to consider the inferences that can be drawn from business premises and Valuation Office area data as a means of developing further information on the dynamics of the enterprise agenda in your area. This includes the percentage of self-employed in the workforce.

• *Housing, planning and connectivity*

This is a crucial area of analysis. The data sources we have identified are a good starting point for considering how the requirements for the development of the economic development components of Local Development Frameworks in terms of Planning Policy Statement 4 (PPS4) can be brought together with the economic indicators that describe another key element of the supply side of economies. Bringing together an analysis of

(a) the location and densities of non domestic properties
(b) the relationship of the skills base which sits alongside, and
(c) a consideration of its relative accessibility or remoteness is really important in scoping out its economic strengths and weaknesses.

There are a significant number of sources of data available. Many of them, such as the Valuation Office area database, are very current and up to date. Not enough use is made within economic analyses of this range of data, considering that it provides real insights that should not be missed. Housing completions, trajectories and targets are also very important in assessing the economic vibrancy and sustainability of key places within your area, particularly in terms of the relationship between housing and jobs. An analysis of these issues should form a key part of your local economic assessment.

• *Environment*

There has been considerable debate about whether the issues in this category should be a cross-cutting or discrete theme within the local economic assessment. Ultimately it is up to you to decide how best to introduce these to draw out the most compelling and authentic narrative of your area. You should definitely be able to show that your assessment has covered the evidence sources set out in Table 10-2, as a minimum.

• *Spatial definitions*

The rural and urban definitions set out effectively how rural or urban each component part of your area is. They provide real insights into the relationships between key service centres and their hinterlands. When used to underpin the analysis on linkages and flows, these provide a powerful means of understanding the interdependency of different smaller and larger settlements within and outside of your administrative boundaries. They help flesh out the challenges of achieving the same level of service delivery across rural and urban areas, and they provide an excellent context for the development of rural proofing approaches.

- **Productivity**

This continues to sit at the heart of regional policy in terms of the RDA Tasking Framework. It is important to scope out the contribution your area makes to the productive capacity of the region. It is useful to bear in mind that the principal indicator of productivity, gross value-added (GVA), only really works at county levels of geography and above. There are now

datasets which enable GVA to be measured at more local levels; however there are real challenges in being able to attribute productive capacity to specific work sites and plants. This is because productivity is measured at the workplace but takes no account of the home locations of the individuals who work in those plants.

There are also reporting distinctions between head and sub-office locations of companies and the actual places where the companies produce the goods concerned. This further affects the story arising from the evidence, particularly below the NUTS3 picture.[7] In addition to mapping the productive capacity of your area by taking these issues into account, it is important to think about how the individual components of productivity, its five drivers, manifest themselves in your area. There is an ongoing debate about how best to manage each element, so no prescriptive approaches are suggested here. I have instead just raised the importance of seeking to

measure these indicators and listed them Table 10-1.

- *Local government national performance indicators*

In addition to the key areas of analysis set out above, a number of local authorities will have committed themselves to economic development, environmental and inclusion targets as part of the development of their assessment. It is clearly important to cross-reference these targets and the rationale for choosing them with the development of the economic assessment. It is also important to look at these in terms of how the assessment will be judged as part of the Comprehensive Area Assessment (CAA) process. The economic assessment itself is unlikely to be checked and verified by a government agency; however the process by which the LEA is used to inform how your authority responds appropriately to the area will be judged through the CAA. Therefore making these distinct links will be very important.

Why are coasts special?

Returning to the theme of coasts, it is clear that they have a unique narrative that needs to be drawn out by the assessment. In a number of local authorities they are

different from their surrounding hinterlands. They also do not always fit straightforwardly into the regional mindset for economic interventions. Skegness, for example,

has more in common with Hunstanton and Bridlington – regionally removed to the south and north respectively – than it does with Mansfield or Corby or Glossop in its own

region. We have to be careful in making simple statements like this, however, as with seasonal patterns of tourism it is possible to buy the *Nottingham Evening Post* and *Leicester Mercury* in the town, demonstrating deep seasonal links with other settlements in the East Midlands.

Nevertheless it is possible to begin thinking about patterns of how places work using some of the approaches relevant to both coasts and the economic assessment process. I shall seek to demonstrate this here with reference to the work I did recently on coasts and rural deprivation. This work was prepared for evidence I gave to an All Party Parliamentary Inquiry into rural coastal deprivation.[8]

The work was based on looking at the East of England coastline, which is very significant in size and scale. It comprises:

- 1.6 million people and a GVA of £24 billion (greater than Northern Ireland);
- significant ports from Haven Gateway southwards, influenced in terms of transport, migration and employment by Greater London;
- an internationally significant coast subject, in a number of areas, to significant coastal erosion and sea-flood risk challenging the viability of a number of settlements along with significant areas of grade 1 agricultural land;
- an underperforming economy on most measures of economic vitality when compared to the East of England as a whole;
- particular challenges around deprivation and worklessness in Yarmouth, Lowestoft and Tendring.

In thinking about how *deprivation* manifests itself in rural settlements on this coastline, and what drives it, I formed the following views.

- Everywhere is different, and it is difficult – perhaps even dangerous – to have a simple view of what a rural coastal area is. However, there is a way of homing in on the issues which is straightforward but which embraces some of the complexity.
- There are *four stages of evidence* to consider: (a) the depth to which places are urban or rural using the rural–urban definitions; (b) how places link to each other by looking at the flows of people, goods and services between them; (c) how environmental/climate change impacts upon them; and (d) how traditional patterns of economic activity, particularly tourism, have affected them.

This led me to an approach based on considering the distribution of disadvantage and the factors that condition it in terms of rural settlements, with respect to the space where they sit, how things move around within that space, how the environment is changing the context of that space, and how traditions and ways of doing business have and continue to condition the nature of that space.

- **The space where a place sits**

It is now a straightforward process to determine the gradations of rurality in any given place using the rural–

urban definitions developed by Professor John Shepherd for the 2004 Rural Strategy.[9] This helps us to determine how sparsely populated places are, and to think about how their connectedness might impact both on their economic potential and the deprivation they experience.

In a recent study, *Productivity, Peripherality and Place*, John Bibby at the University of Sheffield argues that the vast majority of the variation of productivity in any place is determined by 'economic mass'.[10] In simple terms this means how densely populated and built up it is. This raises a really interesting connection between economic mass and connectedness which suggests that economic potential – or lack of it and consequent levels of deprivation – are strongly affected in rural coastal settlements by their density of population and their level of connectedness to other major settlements.

- *How things move around within the space*

Looking in more detail at how things move around in terms of connectivity and patterns of commuting, based on linkages between settlements and flows of people, goods and services, it is possible to suggest that those places with poor connections and poor economic mass may well suffer deprivation driven principally by their location. This can be characterised by looking at the linkages and flows of rural places and their consequences on the basis of Figure 10-4.

Figure 10-4

Linkage and flow issues

Mapping how people move for work in and out of places brings out their true economic character

We need to understand the inter-relation of places to truly understand the issues around deprivation they manifest

Linkage and flow consequences

The seasonal nature of all coasts conditions their viability and deprivation

Whilst bigger and better connected rural coasts may have distinctive deprivation features, the reasons for the nature of their deprivation and strategies for tackling it need to be based in part on the external major settlements that drive them

Isolated small rural settlements have distinctive, not always common, but more difficult to tackle deprivation and mainstreaming approaches may work less well in them

The relationship between connectedness and economic mass is further affected by environmental and custom-and-practice issues unique to each place. In considering these issues in relation to rural coastal settlements, following the same 'issues and consequences' approach modelled above, I developed inferences by looking at the policy and data issues around each of these themes (see Figures 10-5 and 10-6).

Figure 10-5

Environment issues		Environment consequences
Flood risk affects the viability of coastal settlements irrespective of their size and connectedness	→	Settlements with greater critical mass will have higher priority in terms of flood protection
Flood protection issues focus in a major way on economic value	→	A number of unique features that don't have straightforwardly measurable economic values are not adequately recognised in less well connected and peripheral rural areas
Flood protection strategies focusing on larger settlements run the risk of creating a 'cuspate' coast	→	Peripheral and smaller rural settlements are not only more at risk but larger settlement flood protection can exacerbate the position

Figure 10-6

Tradition issues		Tradition consequences
Many coastal settlements were developed as holiday locations in the nineteenth century	→	The principal rationale for the development of coastal settlements has in many cases been superceded **Clacton**
Patterns of visitors and settlement have often significantly changed over the last 30 years		Larger coastal settlements have had more scope to diversify. **Southend** is a city by the sea, others with good connections or attractive landscapes have re-invented themselves **Southwold**
		Other, less well connected locations have deteriorated through reduced connectivity and changing habits **Leiston**

The schematic in Figure 10-6 demonstrates how the post-Victorian evolution of coastal settlements has conditioned their role and function and has an impact on the issues underpinning their deprivation.

Looking at these four issues in combination, we are able to draw out the interrelations between connectedness and economic mass as a means of categorising rural coastal places in terms of their deprivation.

To summarise: Bringing together the spatial context of rural coastal settlements and considering their wider context around linkages and flows, environment and customs/ traditions enables us to make inferences about the factors underpinning deprivation in them, categorise them in groups, and then begin to think through the issues linked to how we might intervene in them.

In big-picture terms, the outcome in relation to this particular area of analysis is that policy interventions need to be based on a two-fold approach.

- For connected or larger rural settlements the solution lies in traditional approaches to tackling deprivation and focusing on the key settlements with which they interact.

- For less connected smaller settlements, focused policy interventions, taking account of the market failure which sits at their heart arising from their low economic mass, requires more innovative and individual settlement by settlement thinking.

In Figure 10-7 I have set out my thinking on how the four categories of settlement, in terms of the relationship between economic mass and connectedness, experience deprivation – referenced by real places. Figure 10-8 shows how deprivation in each of the four categories of rural coastal settlement manifests itself.

Figure 10-7

Deprivation driven by links with other settlements having a seasonal character linked to flows of visitors and workers - complex issues around flood protection where they are outside the envelope of bigger places close by.	Complex and varied deprivation not linked solely to rural or coast less likely to face flood protection issues have scope for re-invention and development.
Unique deprivation linked to former roles as visitor locations, often shrinking in terms of function and viability, market failure and not able to justify significant flood protection.	Settlements likely to be in transition or no longer to a tourism rationale in need of significant re-invention and development.

ctedness

Economic mass

Figure 10-8

Migrant workers, high proportions of caravans some in long-term oocupation, 'turned off' in winter, low-skill low-value jobs, seasonal visitors with 'urban' deprivation	Urban style deprivation, high incapacity benefit, low economic activity rates, low skills, low wages, often, 'resort driven' negative demography, houses in multiple occupation
Devalued properties, poor access to services, dormant declining economies, market failure restricting investment	Poor employment prospects (high unemployment), market failure in terms of investment, attracts incapacity benefit claimants and early retirees because of low property prices

Connectedness

Economic mass

The duty to undertake an economic assessment provides local authorities with the opportunity to develop a unique narrative about how their coast works. This has the potential to provide a new impetus to joined-up thinking by the council and its partners, and could re-energise commitments to coastal regeneration from the national tier downwards. There are many ways of looking at coasts and I have provided just one example in this part of the *Handbook*. What is important is that local authorities seize the opportunity to renew and refocus their discretion and engage others in the coastal regeneration agenda, rather than letting their economic assessment sit on the shelf and gather dust.

Tramore by the Sea: the 'Margate of Ireland'
by Irene Furlong, Ireland

From its metamorphosis from a pleasant retreat for those who assembled there for the benefit of the salt water in the mid-eighteenth century, to its present incarnation as the leading holiday resort in the south-east of Ireland, Tramore has consistently reinvented itself to adapt to changing holiday patterns.

Once the resort of the 'dournawns', the hobnailed visitors from Kilkenny who stayed in local farmhouses and fishermen's cottages, it has experienced innumerable reincarnations in its efforts to continue to exploit its beautiful beach and surroundings.

The first amenities were provided in the eighteenth century by local landowners such as Lord Doneraile, who laid out private access for the gentry to its secluded coves, while resident entrepreneurs such as Bartholomew Rivers built hotels and houses for letting, assembly rooms and bathing lodges. Rivers also founded local industries, initiated horse races on the beach, obtained a charter for the holding of fairs, and developed a spa outside the town in the 1780s.

The most important event in the expansion of Tramore as a holiday resort was the opening of the railway line to Waterford in 1853 and a racecourse and golf links were established in the 1880s, by which time the town boasted seven hotels. A pier, sea wall and promenade were completed in 1915, and a cinema which also provided a stage for concerts and boxing tournaments was built in 1918.

Thus was set the scene for almost a century of ups and downs as Tramore experienced the vicissitudes of the Irish seaside resort in the modern age.

For further information on this paper, please visit: www.tourism-culture.com

Coastal areas and their duty to undertake an economic assessment 158

Chapter 11

Health, wellbeing and regeneration in coastal resorts

by Ben Cave[1]

Enjoyment of the highest attainable standard of health is one of the fundamental rights of every human being without distinction of race, religion, political belief, economic or social condition.[2]

Coastal town needs tend to be intense ... The isolation of coastal towns reinforces limited outlooks and poverty of ambition.[3]

Much of what affects our health lies outside the domain of the health sector. Local authorities are responsible for the maintenance and creation of healthy environments for everyone. They occupy a vital role in our democracy, providing governance, coordination and strategic leadership. Public health explicitly recognises the role played by the state in preventing disease, prolonging life and promoting health. Public health professionals reach outside the usual National Health Service structures and work in partnership with different agencies. This chapter aspires to be the start of a dialogue between coastal public health professionals, regeneration practitioners and spatial planners in coastal resorts.

Local neighbourhood renewal and other regeneration initiatives are in a particularly good position to address health inequalities because they have responsibility for dealing with the wider determinants that have impact on people's physical and mental health.[4]

In this chapter, the terms 'health and wellbeing', 'coastal resort', 'inequality' and 'regeneration' are defined with reference to coastal communities. It looks at examples of good practice, and draws on the results of a survey of coastal health issues conducted with directors of public health in primary care trusts having coastline in their area.[5] Above all, we invite readers to use this chapter as a basis for local discussion on an agenda for coastal public health, and to contribute further examples on health and wellbeing in coastal resorts to support the work of the Coastal Communities Alliance.

Health and wellbeing are central to most people's understanding of, and relationship with, the coast. The coast is seen as being good for your health: a review of coastal towns found that one of the most important reasons for moving to the coast was simply that respondents wanted to live there.[6]

Spatial planners, regeneration practitioners and public health professionals in coastal resorts have similar strategic agendas in terms of creating sustainable environments, improving people's life experiences and addressing social exclusion. These are reflected in the range of issues that respondents to our survey cited as affecting the health of coastal communities: joint top were alcohol and in-migration of older people, followed by houses in multiple occupation (HMOs) and opportunities for younger people. Note that these issues are outside NHS control. Table 11-1 highlights the shared relevance of these issues to public health and regeneration professionals.

Table 11-1: Key issues for public health and regeneration in coastal resorts

Key coastal issue	Relevance to public health and regeneration
Alcohol	Recent gains made by NHS through clinical improvements in interventions for cancers and heart disease have been almost cancelled out by the continuing steep rise in alcohol related morbidity and mortality over the past five to ten years. This reflects increases in alcohol consumption across the whole population and is driven by increased availability and reduced cost of alcohol relative to disposable income. Economic regeneration policies focused on alcohol and the night-time economy are a major driver (4).
In-migration of older people / demographic change	Can create additional pressures on social care and NHS services Poor mental health eg older people becoming isolated and requiring support following bereavement Prevention agenda becomes key: this may require regeneration policies to provide relevant opportunities/services.
Houses in multiple occupation	HMOs may attract vulnerable groups or those already receiving benefit, requiring specific support and long term collaborative planning that reduces HMOs numbers overall and supports homeless and vulnerably housed.
Opportunities for young people	Limited opportunities may lead to low self-esteem, poor mental health, harmful behaviours, and difficulties in providing a stable workforce.

Coastal resorts have been noted for in-migration of older people, many arriving with no family support and some with pre-existing health conditions (see case study 2). Housing is an issue as in-migrants may live in poor accommodation such as caravan parks (case study 3) or HMOs, creating a population hidden from primary care and other services (case study 5). Some coastal resorts have a preponderance of second homes which reduces the housing stock available to permanent residents. Smaller coastal resorts can be geographically isolated, making access to services, to education and to employment difficult (case study 2). Coastal populations tend to be more deprived than their counterparts living inland: 21 of the 88 most deprived authorities are in coastal areas.[8] Looked-after children from urban areas are moved to seaside towns for care. Opportunities for young people are limited: employment opportunities centre on tourism, they are thus seasonal and tend to be low-paid. Tourists also create particular public health issues: they may indulge in risky behaviour ranging from too much sun to excess alcohol or unprotected sex. The emphasis on entertainment and the night-time economy does not always benefit residents of coastal resorts (case studies 4 and 5).

Public health has a broad remit and we would expect priorities for action to vary between areas and resorts. A recent independent review lists public health priorities in England as: cardiovascular disease and cancer; obesity; risk-taking behaviours in younger adults (alcohol, drugs, violence); mental ill-health throughout life; and the threats to wellbeing in older people.[9] Minimising, and adapting to, climate change is so a critical issue for public health.[10] Our case studies show how some coastal resorts have identified and then sought to address public health priorities, and how local government plays a central role in this work.

Definitions

Coastal resorts are defined as having one or more of the following features:[11]

tourism as the dominant industry;
a specialist tourist infrastructure (promenades, piers, parks etc.);
housing stock that includes HMOs and caravan sites.

Regeneration has been defined as the broad process of reversing physical, economic and social decline in an area where market forces will not do this without intervention.[12] In seaside resorts this means a focus on the specific shared challenges for coastal public policy and regeneration, such as:[13]

in-migration;
decline of the traditional tourist industry;[14]
failure to diversify from traditional tourism;
traditional building stock that is highly suitable for single-resident occupancy dwellings.

In 1946 the World Health Organization defined health as being not just the absence of sickness but the attainment of a complete state of mental and physical wellbeing. This broad definition continues to be relevant and challenging. Figure 11-1 shows how healthy public policy looks beyond health services, which help people once they are ill, and emphasises factors that maintain health. When we realise that core functions of local and regional government such as employment, transport, access to green spaces, social support, education and housing are all components of a healthy community,[15] we recognise the importance of regeneration and public policy in improving and protecting health and wellbeing. Mental health, which ranges from anxiety to more severe conditions, is very much a part of this picture and was a recurring theme in our survey responses. Poor mental health is believed to cost the economy £77 billion a year and the cost in terms of GDP is expected to double to over 10 per cent by 2026. The indirect costs of poor mental health include poor educational attainment, unemployment and increased crime and antisocial behaviour.[16]

Reducing inequalities in health and improving the health of the most deprived people in society is a main driver for public health policy.[19] A look at the national picture shows that inequalities have persisted even though average measures have improved. For example, if we compare life expectancy between the 'routine and manual' groups and the population as a whole we see that, for men in the period 2005–7, the gap between these social groups was 4 per cent wider than it was in 1995–7; for women this gap was 11 per cent wider.[20] The case studies repeatedly show that populations in coastal resorts are older and more likely to be materially deprived than their counterparts inland. Since 1997, nationally there has been a 2.2 per cent increase in the number of people claiming incapacity benefit, special disability allowance or income support for disability, compared with a 12.3 per cent rise in the number of claimants in coastal towns.[21]

Community health profiles provide data on a local authority basis on a number of health outcomes and indicators of deprivation.[22] These are a good introduction to local health concerns and help to highlight where health is poorest. Pooling this information with relevant economic and regeneration indicators creates a richer understanding of life in a coastal resort. This gives us part of the picture, but one of the problems with using routine data is that many indicators are not readily available below local authority level and so issues in smaller coastal resorts can be masked by the rest of the area.[23] This can mean that the needs of small coastal resorts get overlooked. The case studies show how NHS organisations have commissioned studies and Health Impact Assessments to investigate specific concerns of small areas in coastal resorts.

Whitehead offers a useful typology of policies and interventions through which health inequalities can be reduced.[24] Table 11-2 shows how our case studies can be grouped under Whitehead's typologies and illustrate the variety of issues faced by coastal communities and the ways in which local authorities can influence health. There are six case studies presented in this chapter and two on the IDeA website.[25]

Figure 11-1

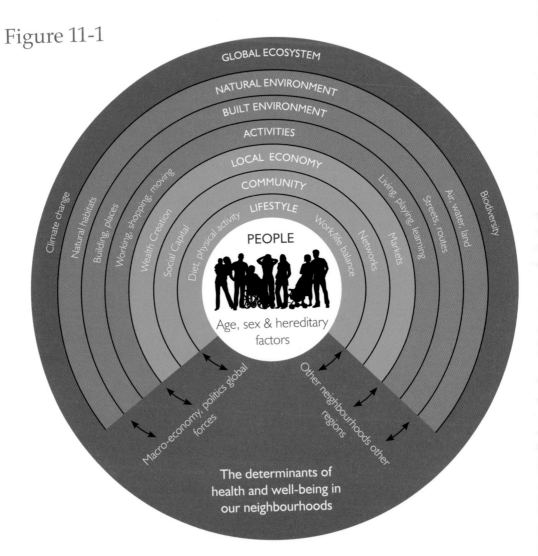

The determinants of health and well-being in our neighbourhoods

Table 11-2 : typology of actions to reduce health inequalities

Category 1: strengthening individuals. Developing an individual's knowledge, beliefs, self-esteem, practical competence in life skills or powerlessness.	**Figure 3** shows how access to good and sympathetic primary care, as well as to exercise classes and green gyms, improves people's confidence and sense of wellbeing. **Figure 4** reports how NHS East Riding of Yorkshire and East Riding of Yorkshire Council conducted specific research into the needs of people on caravan sites. This has lead to a programme with people in caravan sites that are tailored to individual needs.
Category 2: strengthening communities. Covers a wide spectrum of interventions aimed at strengthening communities through building social cohesion and mutual support and addressing social exclusion / isolation experienced by some deprived communities	**Figure 2** describes key messages from a Health Impact Assessment (HIA) of an Area Action Plan in Herne Bay. **Figure 4** reports how NHS East Riding of Yorkshire and East Riding of Yorkshire Council conducted specific research into the needs of people on caravan sites and how this work has informed service delivery. A case study on the IDeA website looks at work with HMOs and vulnerably housed in Central St Leonards.[3]
Category 3: improving living and working conditions and associated access to essential services. Reducing exposure to health-damaging environments, both at home and at work, and ensuring access to essential goods and services.	**Figure 3** looks at some of the challenges faced, and achievements of, Mablethorpe Health Centre in East Lindsey District Council. **Figure 5** reports on some of the adverse health effects of the night-time economy and steps taken to mitigate these effects. **Figure 6** shows how Blackpool Council is co-ordinating efforts to increase living and working conditions. A case study on the IDeA website shows how the Environment Agency and local authorities work with the emergency services to protect health.[3]
Category 4: promoting healthy macro-policies. The interventions in this category aim to alter the macroeconomic or cultural environment to reduce poverty and the wider adverse effects of inequality on society.	**Figure 7** looks at how partnership working is developing a shared and a sustainable vision for the coast in the South West.

Case study 1 Health Impact Assessment, planning and regeneration[26]

In 2008, Canterbury City Council issued a draft Area Action Plan (AAP) that set out a number of preferred options for the regeneration of Herne Bay.[27] AAPs are part of the Local Development Framework (LDF) which is, in turn, the spatial expression of a local authority's Sustainable Community Strategy. LDFs set the framework for planning and development in a local authority for 15–20 years.

AAPs provide a specific focus on a particular area: the majority of the Herne Bay AAP is in Heron ward which is one of five wards in Herne Bay.

NHS Eastern and Coastal Kent commissioned a Health Impact Assessment (HIA) of the Herne Bay AAP.[28] The HIA had three objectives:

- appraise the potential positive and negative health and wellbeing impacts of the AAP on people who live and work in Herne Bay and those who visit the town;
- highlight potential differential distribution effects of health and wellbeing impacts among population groups by asking 'who is affected';
- suggest actions that aim to minimise potential negative health and wellbeing impacts and maximise potential

positive health and wellbeing impacts of the AAP.

The HIA included policy analysis, a review of relevant literature, community profile and workshops and interviews with people living and working in Herne Bay. The HIA concludes with a Public Health Management Plan that lists the suggested actions and identifies the agencies with a potential role in delivering the actions. This was presented to the Local Strategic Partnership, the Canterbury Health and Wellbeing Partnership and the Neighbourhood Development Team.

Herne Bay is characterised by marked age polarization and relatively low numbers of people of working age. The AAP has a strong focus on business growth and local employment. The HIA concludes that this may help to encourage more people of working age to stay in the community, with social, economic and subsequently health benefits. The HIA emphasises the importance of local skills development and signposting in relation to new employment opportunities, including higher quality jobs for local people.

Some of the key findings include concerns that new employment may be of low quality and that any benefits may bypass local people and lower income groups, and that inter-group tensions could develop between those favouring conservation and those seeking innovation. The tensions would be inter-generational or between residents and tourists.

The HIA suggests using community development to determine an inclusive image and identity for Herne Bay. Integrating healthy lifestyle interventions with this work may contribute to mitigating potential impacts on health-related behaviour.

Since some of the recommendations concern education and training, the HIA has been shared with the Local Children's Services Partnership, the Head and Senior Management Team of the main secondary school for the town, and other stakeholders. As a result of the HIA it is now accepted that the AAP is mainly directed towards the physical environment. Social issues have since been introduced and consolidated by an action plan that cuts across directorates. This was developed by the city council with full participation of the Primary Care Trust (PCT). This is long-term work. Progress will be monitored by the PCT's Health and Wellbeing group (a partnership of city council, social services, voluntary sector and PCT representatives). The work-plan envisages a timescale of some years, as does the AAP

Case study 2 Providing primary health care to a coastal resort[29]

Mablethorpe is one of three seaside resorts in East Lindsey District where the main industries are agriculture and tourism.[30] The 2001 Census lists the Mablethorpe and Sutton Parish as having a population of 11,780. The resident population of the parish is older than the national average and has high levels of long-term limiting illness. This resident population is swollen each year by people visiting on holiday. These are made up of three groups.

- An older population typically come from ex-mining communities in South Yorkshire. They may have been coming to the resort all their lives, as children, as young adults and now as retired people. They come because it is familiar and because they love it. This group tend to spend about 3–4 months of the year in Mablethorpe and live in the caravan parks and rented accommodation.
- Holidaymakers come for 2–3 weeks, during the school holidays, often with young children.
- Day-trippers arrive by coach or by car and come for the sea and the sand.

As with many rural, isolated communities there are relatively few activities and opportunities for young people. Local organisations and businesses want positive change in Mablethorpe through developing new markets and branding to reflect their aspirations for Mablethorpe as a place to live, work[31] and visit.

The Mablethorpe Health Centre is part of this new vision. It has come up with ingenious ways in which to offer care to residents and visitors alike. The Practice Manager explains that their patient list has approximately 40 per cent who are over 65 and the list has three times the national average for conditions such as obesity, hypertension, coronary heart disease and diabetes. This means that, although the patient list is 14,000, they are operating as though they had a list size of 21,000 patients. This is not currently recognised in the funding allocations.

Success is hard to come by and is a result of continuing dedication and hard work from staff and care providers alike. Holiday times are busy for staff and this creates difficulty with annual leave. There are two other secrets to their success:

- the building out of which they operate;
- the services they provide. In April 2000, the Practice Manager began discussions with organisations providing care in the town. The GPs and nurses, the ambulance service, the primary care trust and the district council all agreed that services would be improved if they were located under a single roof. The district council provided the land and the primary care trust funded the private finance initiative (PFI) build. The new practice building opened in 2007.

The Mablethorpe Health Centre is an impressive new build in which the design of the building is integral to the way in which staff are able to offer services. The Health Centre plays an important part in contributing to the regeneration of Mablethorpe.

is set up so that patients can get all they need in one visit, creating a 'one stop shop'. Staff at the Centre provide fitness classes and green gyms which boost people's confidence. They provide care to everyone in Mablethorpe, including the resident population and the visitor populations. The Mablethorpe Health Centre aims to bring services to their elderly patients, avoiding them travelling long distances to hospitals for outpatient appointments, countering the coastal isolation of communities.

The Health Centre helps to attract staff. There are currently eight GP partners and two trainees. The Health Centre offers many services including community nurses, health visitors, district nurses, Macmillan nurses, podiatry, physiotherapy and dentistry. They have a minor operating suite and an independent pharmacy. The ambulance service also operates from the site. Everything, from the design of the building to the way in which services are provided,

Case study 3 Assessing hidden need: the caravan park population[32]

Caravan parks are popular along the British coastline, and a considerable proportion of people in parts of the UK reside in static caravans for much of the year. Residents in caravan parks can be a group hard to reach, and they may have an ambiguous legal status (caravans are often used as permanent homes irrespective of whether the caravan park has a license for long-term residential use). Residents of caravan parks are less likely to be registered with a GP and less likely to be represented on the Census.

In South East Holderness, on the Yorkshire coast, there are more than 2,500 caravans. The PCT had anecdotal evidence that residents in the caravan park communities experienced greater socioeconomic and health problems than the general population in South East Holderness, which is itself a deprived coastal area. A substantial proportion of the caravan park community was understood to be elderly, frail and materially deprived. Many of the caravan park community were understood to have migrated to the area, perhaps to escape financial hardship.

The predecessor organisation for the NHS East Riding of Yorkshire commissioned a survey of the caravan park community. This was done jointly with East Riding of Yorkshire Council. After exploratory discussions with caravan park residents it was decided to administer a postal health and lifestyle questionnaire to GP-registered caravan residents. Basing the sample on the GP-registered population was acknowledged to risk excluding people, but it allowed comparison with a recent survey of the general population. Data was gathered on respiratory problems, falls, smoking, alcohol, body mass index (BMI) and service utilisation and compared to national and regional information. The authors state that to avoid intrusion and to achieve reasonable response rates the survey deliberately omitted questions on mental and sexual health, domestic violence or suicide. These were noted as topics for future consideration.

Residents in caravan park communities reported greater levels of poor health than in England. Compared with the local population survey, caravan respondents over 55 years of age were almost twice as likely to report poor health. Three lifestyle areas were addressed: alcohol consumption, smoking and BMI. Caravan park residents drank alcoholic drinks less often, they drank smaller amounts, and were less likely to exceed safe weekly limits than their regional and national counterparts, but they were also less likely to be non-drinkers. Caravan respondents over 55 years of age were more than twice as likely as their counterparts in the local population to be current smokers and 2.3 times as likely to be obese. The survey found rates of chronic cough and rates of wheezing which exceeded twice the national average. Asthma and other chest problems were also frequently reported.

NHS East Riding of Yorkshire have used the results to inform resource allocation and service delivery. These include:

- continued caravan research linked with health promotion;
- health trainers in coastal areas;
- a health improvement programme covering anxiety and depression, healthy eating, confidence building, relaxation, eating to a budget, and living a healthy lifestyle;
- future plans (e.g. a Health Bus);
- development of new health interventions, accelerated by linking up with local economic regeneration resources.

A special East Riding of Yorkshire council overview and scrutiny review has recently focused on coastal health.

Case study 4 The night-time economy[33]

Brighton and Hove has a thriving tourist economy. By night it is a popular destination for stag and hen parties and its restaurants, nightclubs and bars make up a bustling centre of entertainment. Pubs and clubs play an important role in our city's culture and economy but alcohol is a factor in at least 40 per cent of violent crime ... Brighton and Hove is known as a good place to enjoy pubs and clubs but people want to be confident drunken behaviour won't spoil their enjoyment.[34]

Residents in Brighton and Hove also have a worse profile for alcohol-related harm than the national and regional averages. Compared with the England population, there are greater alcohol-specific mortality and hospital admission rates among men; among women, hospital admission rates are higher.[35] Compared with regional averages, residents of Brighton and Hove have:

- greater alcohol-specific mortality, alcohol attributable mortality and mortality from chronic liver disease;
- been admitted to hospital more frequently due to alcohol-related harm or other alcohol-specific or alcohol-attributable reasons;
- committed more alcohol-related crimes, including violent crimes and sexual offences;
- more frequently made alcohol-related claims for incapacity benefits among working-age people.

As part of their ongoing work to manage the public health effects of alcohol use, Brighton and Hove City Council and the PCT conducted a Health Impact Assessment on the provisions for flexible alcohol licensing.[36]

These provisions are contained in the Licensing Act 2003 and they enable premises to apply for a licence to serve alcohol at any time.[37]

The HIA involved data analysis to look at health outcomes before and after the introduction of the Act and wide consultation.

Is there a discernible pattern before and after the introduction of the Act? Early results suggest that if knowledge of alcohol consumption is relevant to services, for example specialist health care treatments or hostels, data about alcohol consumption is perceived to be recorded well and may bear closer inspection. It is harder to draw conclusions about the health effects of the Act from data relating to services which deal with the indirect effects of the night-time economy such as street cleaning. The data analysis is ongoing. Results will be presented to Brighton and Hove later.

The HIA team consulted widely with residents, licensees, service providers and elected members. All stakeholder groups expressed concerns about antisocial behaviour, particularly the increase in antisocial behaviour since the introduction of flexible alcohol hours and the increase in the length of time over which such behaviour takes place. In addition, service providers were concerned about difficulties in managing alcohol-related antisocial behaviour. Residents, licensees and service providers were concerned about noise, in particular the level of noise in residential areas and the length of time during which that noise is generated (it carries on into the early morning) since the introduction of flexible alcohol hours. Residents described the impacts on their health and wellbeing arising from loss of sleep, inability to sleep and sleep deprivation as a result of disturbances due to noise and/or antisocial behaviour. Both residents and service providers were particularly concerned about the adverse effects of such disturbances on vulnerable groups in the community such as children, older people and families.

The city council as licensing authority intends to use the HIA to inform its statement of licensing policy. It needs to be careful as public health protection is not a statutory licensing objective; however, access to alcohol is dependent on licensing. The HIA would be used to inform other corporate strategies such as planning documents and guidance, the local transport plan and tourism strategy. It was proposed to report the study to the Licensing Committee so that licensing members would have the opportunity to comment, discuss and make recommendations that in turn may be used to inform licensing policy, including matters such as cumulative impact, special stress areas, dealing with off-licences and high-volume vertical drinking, current practices in terms of local crime prevention strategies and enforcement pathways, and ensuring community safety, particularly around licensed premises, late-night transport and large events.

Tackling alcohol issues is one of the PCT's World Class Commissioning priorities and specifically reducing alcohol-related hospital admissions is a priority health outcome against which the PCT has committed to measure itself. This work is an important part of that overall approach and will inform the interventions that the PCT will be seeking to see implemented across the city with the support of local authority, private sector and voluntary sector colleagues.

Case study 5 Blackpool[38]

Blackpool has more than 10 million visitors a year, seven miles of beaches, many tourist attractions, hotels and guest houses.[39] The health profile of its 142,500 residents shows that their health is generally worse than the England average, with higher rates of violent crime, hospital stays for alcohol-related harm and drug misuse. There are inequalities in life expectancy by both deprivation and gender. And while there have been decreases in death rates from all causes and in early death rates from heart disease and stroke, and cancer, these rates remain well above the England average.[40]

We look below at two examples whereby agencies in Blackpool are working with each other to enforce standards and improve living conditions for Blackpool's residents and visitors. With the support of elected members, council officers in Blackpool have been able to send out a message that standards across the town will be robustly enforced.

Over recent years the number of visitors to Blackpool has fallen. This decline set in train a grim cycle whereby some of the struggling hotels gradually became permanent accommodation, often as HMOs. Blackpool then

became known as having a plentiful supply of cheap rented accommodation, and agencies such as probation and youth services across the region began to advise their clients to go to Blackpool to find housing. The number of HMOs grew and the lifestyles of the HMO residents, often chaotic and damaging, proved incompatible with families and holidaymakers. HMOs in the main holiday areas were beginning to affect the main tourist economy. In some wards the numbers of young people and care-leavers, ex-offenders and homeless people spiralled. The concentration of HMOs meant that the volume of work for the fire brigade and the police, probation services and council services such as quality standards and adult social care and housing also began to grow. Each agency knew about the problems but responses were dealt with individually. Enforcement was long and drawn-out and sometimes was

unintentionally prolonged the life of unwanted properties.

Towards the end of 2008, Blackpool issued a clear policy statement that there would be no permanent accommodation in the holiday area; agencies began to take action in partnership. Instead of the previous piecemeal approach agencies now moved straight to action and pursued all possible options for enforcement. Attention was given to the three Ps: property, place and people. People had traditionally dropped out of the equation. This partnership approach to dealing with people was the culmination of many years' work and drew on housing options assessments and lessons from previous projects in the town whereby intensive support had been offered to families and to people in need. Council officers are spreading the word that Blackpool no longer has a plentiful supply of cheap accommodation: new

arrivals are counselled and offered practical help to return home.

The council, NHS Blackpool and the police all recognise that alcohol is a priority and since 2005 have been developing joint approaches. The Night-time Economy Strategy is a multisectoral group that meets bi-monthly: approaches include ensuring that the town centre includes restaurants and alternative entertainment such as ten-pin bowling; marshals assist the police and work at taxi-ranks to avoid fights and conflict; and entertainment is provided throughout the town centre to keep the atmosphere light. ALTN8 is a public health campaign that encourages alcohol awareness including advising people to drink soft drinks in between alcoholic drinks.[41] The police strongly favour polycarbonate glasses as these reduce the incidence of facial injuries. As part of ALTN8, NHS Blackpool distributed 20,000 polycarbonate glasses to licensed premises. These glasses were also marked with the units of alcohol.[42]

Blackpool is working with licensed premises to improve standards: the council offers subsidised training in all aspects of running licensed premises. The council also has an important policy of robust and repeated interventions for premises that transgress standards. During the financial year 2007/8, Trading Standards initiated 170 prosecutions. Over the same period the total number of prosecutions for the 30 other unitary authorities in England that submitted returns was 258.[43]

There are common threads between these two examples:

- There is support from the elected members and senior management for council officers to take bold steps to improve standards in Blackpool.
- Officers are empowered to prosecute for all transgressions and to take careful and calculated risks. This means that some losses are inevitable but also that Blackpool becomes known for its robust approach and high standards.
- Innovative approaches to enforcement mean that officers visit hotels, HMOs and licensed premises when conditions are most likely to be broken (e.g. at 3 o'clock on a Saturday or Sunday morning) rather than at a prearranged appointment in the middle of the day.
- There is a focus on protecting the residents of, and visitors to, Blackpool and on enhancing the quality of life in Blackpool.

Case study 6 Regional planning for a sustainable coast[44]

The South West of England has 62 per cent of the region's 5.2 million population residing in the coastal area, and living within 10 kilometres of the sea.[45] With a 700 mile coastline that includes more than 60 per cent of England's heritage coast, it has good reason to concentrate on the sustainability and vitality of its coastal communities.

The conference 'Our Coast and Public Health' has been held every two years since 2004. The conference is organised by the South West Regional Public Health Group and is now drawing together a wide range of partners to take stock of the challenges to sustainable living in the south-western coastal areas. Sustainable development is all about achieving a balance between social, economic and environmental considerations in any decision.

Tourism is one of the key planks in the south-west's coastal economy. It also creates an environmental footprint and imposes a growing demand on infrastructure. People holidaying, as well as people who live and work, at the coast need roads, healthcare, power, waste disposal facilities, water supplies and sewage treatment etc. Providing this infrastructure can come into conflict with the qualities of attractive coastal resorts. For example 40–50 million people walk along the SW Coast Path every year. The people who travel to the region contribute to the local economy, and over 89 per cent of these walks are over an hour[46] so good for body and soul. Wherever possible this path needs to be sheltered from all the infrastructure needed to support the walkers.

How can we characterise the population? Two key facts are that, of the nine English regions, the South West has

- the highest life expectancy for women (82.0 years compared with 80.9 for England) and for men (77.8 years versus 76.6);
- the highest percentage of people of retirement age and above (21.7 per cent compared with 18.5 per cent for England; males 65+, females 60+).

The regional average of people who have reached retirement age is even more noticeable in some of the counties and towns. For example, the 2004 mid-year population estimates showed Dorset county and Torbay as each having more than a quarter of their populations of retirement age and above. The combination of longevity and a high ratio of elderly to general population will increase the burden of both primary and domiciliary healthcare.

In 2008, the conference agreed to work towards an action plan with, and for, all coastal communities in the South West to ensure an ongoing, cohesive, inter-sectoral approach to sustainable development. The Regional Spatial Strategy (RSS) has been identified as the key policy document as this sets the spatial planning framework for the South West for the next 20 years.

As preparation for the 2010 conference, the Health Protection Agency (HPA) set up groups to look at tourism, infrastructure, environment and health. The groups enjoy

a wide membership including the Environment Agency, Department of Health South West, South West Strategic Health Authority, Plymouth Marine Laboratory, South West Public Health Observatory, South West Tourism, Chartered Institute of Environmental Health, academia and government. These groups will shape the conference as they consider and report on what is going to be required over the next two decades, by which time the population of the South West is expected to have grown by approximately 900,000 people. It is projected the region will have 6.1 million residents by 2026, twenty per cent more than in 2006. This is higher than the projected UK increase of 14 per cent.

The RSS will now become a single regional strategy and have regional objectives for economic growth. This moves the goalposts in favour of economic policies. The current challenge is to demonstrate how social and environmental policies for coastal communities are integral to economic stability in the South West of England.

Conclusion

Survey respondents demonstrate the breadth of the agenda that public health covers. They were clear that regeneration contributes to improved health.

Physical improvements to [the] built environment [have had an effect on the] wider determinants [of health]. Impact on mental health [and] community cohesion; improvement in

access to training/life skills; access to affordable/improved accommodation, improved access to facilities eg leisure; working closer with faith sector to engage with communities

(spiritual health)
... regeneration has been directly linked to the development of new health services and there are indications of improved perceptions of wellbeing among local people.

Local government and NHS colleagues have a range of mechanisms available to improve public health. For example:

- Local government has powers to promote the wellbeing of its citizens.[47]
- Local authorities lead a range of local partners through Local Strategic Partnerships.
- Joint Overview and Scrutiny Committees police health outcomes/services and the extent to which inequalities are being tackled.
- Local Area Agreements (LAAs) bring local authorities and the NHS together to develop and deliver health targets.
- Joint Strategic Needs Assessments are a responsibility of the directors of public health, adult social services and children's services, designed to inform long-term planning and commissioning for health and wellbeing. These should draw on a wide range of information and drive the local vision for health improvement.

Planning and health are also beginning to develop closer links. The Royal Town Planning Institute and the NHS Healthy Urban Development Unit have each issued good practice guidance on delivering healthy communities.[48] The National Heart Forum and the National Institute for Health and Clinical Excellence (NICE) have prepared guidance for physical activity and the environment.[49] Health Impact Assessments are cited in several case studies as ways in which public health considers, and presents, the potential effects of planning and regeneration policy. Strategic Environmental Assessments (SEAs) apply to a range of strategic plans including Local Development Frameworks and Shoreline Management Plans. The Department of Health has issued draft guidance as SEAs are legally required to identify effects on human health.[50] This is a big opportunity for health professionals to take on a greater role in influencing planning and regeneration policy. NHS colleagues and joint processes such as the Joint Strategic Needs Assessment (JSNA) can play a key role in enabling regeneration and planning colleagues to better understand the health needs of local communities and support appropriate planning to meet these.

The current economic situation is focusing attention

on economic factors. The challenge will be to show how social and environmental factors, including health, contribute to economic security (see case study 6). How should planning and regeneration work with public health? We are not talking about full-time hand-in-hand work but about partnership work that might be time-specific and designed to achieve particular outcomes. Whitehead's typology is useful for framing an agenda.[51]

A note of caution. Much of the work described above will contribute to improving health, but it is hard to link improved health outcomes directly to regeneration activities.[52] If we are to see improvement in health and reduced health inequalities we must be clear about the aims and objectives of regeneration programmes and they must be properly monitored and evaluated.[53] Local knowledge and the experience of health professionals, regeneration practitioners and community members are key to charting the best course in each coastal community.

There is much excellent work in coastal communities across England that is not cited here. This chapter could be the start of a dialogue and we look forward to continuing this discussion with readers via IDeA's Health Community of Practice: this is an online community that brings together local government and public health colleagues from across the country to share activity and work collaboratively on improving health and reducing inequalities.[54]

We leave readers with some key questions for effective partnerships between local authorities and the NHS.

- What are the five or six key health issues in your area and how can regeneration and planning help to address them?
- Who is your local director of public health and his/ her team? Have you met to discuss the health impact of regeneration and planning?
- Who, in your council, holds the portfolio for health services, health improvement and health inequalities?
- How can regeneration and planning contribute to meeting needs identified in the local Joint Strategic Needs Assessment (JSNA)?
- Can health impact assessment be used within regeneration and planning to ensure positive health outcomes?

Improvement and Development Agency for local government (IDeA): support for healthy communities

The Healthy Communities Programme is funded by the Department of Health and managed by the IDeA. The programme aims to build the capacity of local authorities to:

- tackle local health inequalities;
- provide leadership to promote wellbeing;
- work in partnership to improve health locally. The programme provides a range of support to local authorities and their health partners. This includes:
- the healthy communities

peer review process;
- a health, care and wellbeing leadership academy for elected members;
- a wide variety of good practice examples from around the country via the Knowledge website (www.idea.gov.uk/health);
- opportunities to build networks, collaborate on challenges and debate topical issues (www. communities.idea.gov.uk);

IDeA also undertakes specific activities on issues like the

social determinants of health, partnership working for health and workforce health.

Recent publications from the programme include Valuing Health: *Developing a Business Case for Health* (www.idea.gov.uk/idk/core/ page.do?pageId=15246382) and *Leading Together Better* (www.idea.gov.uk/idk/core/ page.do?pageId=15727555).

Contact: Julia Sherfield (julia. sherfield@idea.gov.uk).

Chapter 12

Ageing and coastal communities

by Jane Atterton

Advances in medicine, education, diet, living conditions and material wealth throughout the last century contributed to increased longevity, falling mortality and a falling birth rate among the populations of most advanced societies. This led to a changing population age profile, so that older age groups now outnumber younger age groups – a situation described as *demographic ageing*.

Populations are ageing in both the developed and developing worlds, although at varying rates in different countries. In the United Kingdom, the proportion of the population aged under 16 years fell from 25 to 19 per cent between 1971 and 2004. In contrast, the proportion aged 65 and over increased from 13 to 16 per cent. The most marked increase has been in the proportion of the population aged over 85, due largely to people living longer.[1] In August 2009, it was reported that there were 1.3 million people aged over 85 in the UK, a record number, making up 2 per cent of the total population.[2] This ageing trend is expected to continue to increase in future as those born in the 'baby boom' after the Second World War reach retirement and as the number of people in the younger age groups continues to decline.

In common with other sections of the population, the older generation of today is increasingly diverse in terms of its cultural background, skills, lifetime experiences, health, mobility and geographical location. Some older people are wealthy, whereas others live in poverty – and evidence suggests that the gap is increasing. This heterogeneity is an important aspect of the policy context around age.[3]

In the UK's rural areas the ageing population trend is particularly marked. This is a result of the out-migration of younger age groups and selective migration into rural and coastal areas by older age groups – especially those aged over 35 who then age *in situ*.[4] In 2006, the median age of the rural population in England was 44.4, compared to 38.5 for the urban population.[5] This median figure is rising faster in rural than urban areas, and particularly in the sparse areas.[6] Compared to urban areas, rural communities, especially the smaller ones, now have a higher proportion of people in the age groups 40–64 and 65 and over. Conversely, in the last 20 years, the proportion of people aged 15–24 in rural areas has fallen from 21 to 15 per cent.[7] Despite a common perception of 'retirement to the countryside' in the UK, generally speaking, retirement in-migration makes only a minor contribution to the greying countryside, with only around 10 per cent of rural in-migrants being retired.[8]

Behind the headline median age figures are marked geographic variations in the age structure of the population. Britain's coasts have long been popular destinations for in-migrants in older age groups. Data presented by the Commission for Rural Communities in 2007 shows a concentration of older people in the population of coastal locations of England, including Lincolnshire, East Anglia, the South East and the South West (with the latter being particularly striking).[9]

Daniel Vickers and colleagues at the University of Leeds produced a classification of UK local authorities. In the classification there are nine classes within the category 'Family B, Rural UK', three of which make up 'Group B2 – Coastal Britain' which includes a total of 44 local authorities. The 44 local authorities in 'Coastal Britain' account for 7.6 per cent of the UK population and are generally characterised by a large number of retired people, many of whom live alone. There are also many couples without children, women working on a part-time basis, below average health and some holiday/second home accommodation.[10]

Within 'Coastal Britain' there are three classifications that were used as the basis for analysing demographic data from the 2001 Census:

- **Coastal resorts** – local authorities that contain large towns/cities that are holiday centres (mostly beach resorts), a high proportion of very old people many of whom live alone, below average health (linked to the older population), and a significant number of households with two adults and no children.
- **Aged coastal extremities** – local authorities that are all on the coast with no urban areas of any great size, an aged population with below average health, few women working full-time, a higher than average proportion of the workforce employed in agriculture, many pensioners living alone, and a higher than expected number of homes with no central heating.
- **Aged coastal resorts** – local authorities that all have a coastal location and contain several small towns but no major urban areas, many areas contain coastal resorts that are in decline, a very old population structure with a high proportion of pensioners living alone, many households with two adults

and no children, low full-time female employment and a higher than expected number of people in self-employment.

The median age of residents in 2001 was found to be highest in 'aged coastal resorts' (48 years), although 'coastal resorts' (41) and 'aged coastal extremities' (42) also had median ages higher than those in Great Britain (38) and in urban England (36). 'Aged coastal resorts' also had the highest proportion of their population aged over 65 (26.4 per cent), although the proportions in 'aged coastal extremities' and 'coastal resorts' (20.2 and 21.1 per cent, respectively) were again higher than the Great Britain average (16 per cent).

'Aged coastal resorts' had 13.7 per cent of their population aged 75 and over in 2001, compared to 11.3 per cent in 'coastal resorts' and 9.8 per cent in 'aged coastal extremities' (and 7.5 per cent in Great Britain). In terms of the proportion of people aged 85 and over, it was again highest in 'aged coastal resorts' (3.9 per cent), compared to 'coastal resorts' (3.4 per cent), 'aged coastal extremities' (2.6 per cent) and Great Britain as a whole (1.9 per cent).

Retirees made up the highest proportion of the population aged 16–74 in 'aged coastal

resorts' in 2001 (21.5 per cent), compared to 17.4 per cent in 'aged coastal extremities' and 16.1 per cent in 'coastal resorts' (13.6 per cent in Great Britain as a whole).

Looking at trends over time reveals a complex and variable pattern in the age structures of these areas. The general pattern is that 'aged coastal extremities' experienced an increase in the proportion of their population aged over 65 between 1981 and 2001. As a whole, 'aged coastal resorts' experienced a slight fluctuation in the proportion of their population aged 65 and over between 1981 and 2001, while 'coastal resorts' have seen a decrease in the proportion. It is important to note that these changes reflect somewhat lower birth rates during the inter-war years, so they are not necessarily a good indication of likely patterns over the next 20 years as baby-boomers reach later working age and retirement.

Beatty and Fothergill's work revealed substantial net in-migration to seaside towns amongst both men and women during the last few decades.[11] The authors note the importance of this in-migration as a driver for economic development as most of these 'pre-retired' are not wanting to give up work and may be keen to take local jobs. It can also drive employment growth in consumer and public services such as education and health, and generate extra spending.

Before moving on to talk about the implications of demographic ageing for coastal locations, it is interesting to note that the Rural Evidence Research Centre (RERC) at Birkbeck has recently developed a typology of the 1,353 settlements in England and Wales with populations between 1,500 and 40,000 (in 2001). Eight groupings of towns have been developed based on the demographic, economic and social characteristics of the people who live in them (48 variables from the 2001 Census were used). Although small coastal towns feature in a number of the groups, Group 3 (older persons, leisure jobs) has an overwhelmingly coastal geography. In terms of their characteristics, towns in this group are characterised by older people, single pensioners, hotel and restaurant workers, part-time and home workers, and second-home owners. The average size of the 123 towns in this group is 4,950 (the total population is 0.61 million) and they saw an average growth in population of 3.8 per cent between 2001 and 2006. More information about the RERC work is available on-line,[12] and this typology may be useful in future as a means of analysing the changing characteristics of coastal towns.

Tourism and sea turtles: the "Zakynthos Saga" - Lily Venizelos, MEDASSET-Mediterranean Association to Save the Sea Turtles, Greece

The first footsteps of man had little impact on the sand of the world's beaches. It is only in very recent times that human activities are showing their disastrous effects on the planet's shores. With the aid of modern means of travel, the formalised annual migration we call tourism, burst out towards the coasts. Endangered sea turtle species are now in direct conflict with tourists, their nesting coinciding with the tourism high season.

This paper examines the socio-political and environmental interaction between tourism and sea turtles, focusing on the way tourism has affected the very significant loggerhead (Caretta caretta) nesting rookery at Laganas Bay on the Greek island of Zakynthos, drawing on a 25-year history of environmental nongovernmental campaigning, monitoring and study. Since the early 1980's, local economic motives started to clash with ecological protection, leading to rampant illegal tourist development and culminating in legal action against Greece by the European Court of Justice in 2002.

To sustainably manage tourism it is necessary to fully understand all the varying facets of the industry and the very diverse types of tourists, ranging from educational or eco-tourism to mass tourism. It is vitally important that authorities, local communities and also tour operators are made responsible to clearly define which sector they are aiming at, if protected areas and fragile ecosystems are to be preserved.

further information on this paper, please visit: www.tourism-culture.com

Up until now, demographic ageing has tended to be seen as a 'pensions and care' issue in the UK, with older people viewed as dependent and as a growing burden on society. Stereotypes of older people as 'takers' rather than 'givers' can contribute to discrimination, social exclusion and isolation.[13] Ageing has profound implications for wider economic and social policymaking and is critical for policies related to economic growth, employment, productivity and social cohesion.[14] However, it is increasingly recognised that older people, while bringing challenges for local and regional infrastructure, can also provide a potential driver for a regional economy. A recent survey by Saga (as reported in the *Guardian*) revealed the aspirational nature of older people: they didn't see retirement as something that comes at the end of life, but rather as something that marked a new life.[15]

A growing body of research shows that older people, including those approaching or over state pensionable age, want to remain economically and socially active. While some wish to remain in full or part-time employment, others may wish to start up their own business, work on a flexible basis from home, provide care for grandchildren, elderly parents and friends, or engage in learning opportunities. Levels of participation in voluntary and social enterprise activities are increasing among those in later life, and many older people are active in community groups, churches and schemes such as Neighbourhood Watch. Many older people are more wealthy than ever before and do not wish to save money 'for a rainy day' or to pass an inheritance to family. They are increasingly discerning consumers who demand choice and quality.

Rural areas, and particularly rural areas along Britain's coast, are at the forefront of demographic ageing, which will become more marked in future. This represents a tremendous opportunity for these areas to develop innovative, cutting-edge and proactive approaches to dealing with the implications of this trend. Two possible models may be pursued, which can be termed the *pre-retirement model* and the *retirement industry model*. Both represent progressive approaches focusing on deliberately drawing in more people in the pre-retired and retired age groups. The key is to make the most of the resources that both the indigenous population and the in-migrants in these age groups have to offer as a catalyst for future economic development.

An approach that simply tries to deal with an increasingly elderly population restricts the process of demographic ageing to too much of a problem: instead the focus is on enhancing the capacity of coastal areas to develop economically and socially by operating models that are based on seeing the opportunities provided by demographic ageing.

Analysis suggests that coastal areas are attracting large numbers of people who have reached later working age. The pre-retirement model draws on the positive resources and benefits that these individuals can bring, not least in terms of continuing economic activity and employment (be it full-time, part-time, self-employment or flexible work from home). Evidence suggests that older people are more successful in starting and sustaining a new business than their younger counterparts,[16] and Atherton and Frith suggest that the pre-retired may have a crucial role to play in raising productivity and the rate of new business starts in Lincolnshire, for example.[17] Evidence also suggests that in-migrating pre-retirees have a high level of educational and vocational qualifications,[18] and many wish to further their qualifications. The pre-retired also make a sizeable contribution through their spending patterns, and Baker and Speakman suggest that people in their fifties are more likely than their predecessors to try new ideas and approaches in consumer products and behaviour.[19] The pre-retired can also make a substantial contribution to the vitality of their local communities through their engagement in social enterprises and voluntary and community sector activities, including caring responsibilities for family members, friends or neighbours.[20]

Analysis also suggests that coastal locations are home to substantial numbers of people who have reached retirement age. As with the pre-retired, many of these individuals are more active, healthy and wealthy than ever before. Many wish to remain economically active beyond the state retirement age, and thus will undergo a transition out of the labour market rather than taking an abrupt step into retirement and 'old age'. Other retirees wish to spend time engaged in voluntary activities. Work by the Office for National Statistics in 1997 revealed that 45 per cent of those aged 65–74 and 35 per cent of those aged over 75 engaged in some form of organised voluntary work. Wenger, in her 1992 study of the over-65s in rural areas, found that most older people continued to lead social and domestic lives as usual and many more gave help than received it, particularly in supporting adult children and grandchildren.[21]

At the same time, some older people will require a range of health, transport and retail services, and the increasing demand may result in improvements in the current infrastructure and the creation of new employment opportunities that may help to stem the out-migration of young people. Evidence also suggests that planned retirement villages, which are a relatively new phenomenon in the UK, bring positive impacts for local communities as well as for older people themselves.[22] Much of the income of retirees comes from transfer payments and pensions, and these sources provide high employment multipliers in local economies since evidence suggests that older people tend to use local services.[23] While the idea of attracting retirees to a locality in the UK is somewhat new, evidence from the United States suggests that rural places benefit from retirement in-migration, not least through the stimulation of local markets, raising the standard of existing local services and creating a demand for new services and through the influx of new skills and knowledge.[24]

There are many examples of initiatives and strategies adopted elsewhere in the European Union and in the United States to deal with demographic ageing from which coastal locations in the UK can learn. Such strategies may be based on ensuring older people have access to vital health services, or they may be broader, encouraging a change in attitudes towards older people and ageing among government bodies and the public, helping enterprises to respond to the opportunities offered by ageing, and running conferences and pilot projects. In the USA, a number of states actively pursue retiree in-migration as an economic development strategy.[25]

While these two suggested models are based on a recognition of the benefits and opportunities provided by demographic ageing, it is important not to lose sight of the challenges that ageing brings. Many older people do not enjoy good health, are reliant on low incomes, live in inadequate housing, lack access to essential services, and do not have good social networks – and thus find themselves excluded from society. It is important that these positive strategies do not overlook, or further contribute to, the isolation and exclusion of these individuals. Moreover, it is important to acknowledge the long-term implications of drawing in more older people as they age *in situ* and place ever-growing demands on local services.

One of the most important features of today's older population is its diversity. While coastal locations have long been regarded as popular places in which to spend later life, a series of articles in the *Sunday Times* in April 2006 noted an increasing preference among older people to move to non-coastal rural and small town locations. These towns are seen to be offering better services in the form of restaurants, art galleries and theatres and a stronger sense of community as they are less affected by seasonal changes in population.[26] However, in contrast a recent study of 14,000 people in the UK commissioned by Saga revealed Devon as the best county for retired people to live in, as chosen by one in ten survey respondents. The survey revealed that for many of the older generation, raised in an island nation with a strong bond with its seaside resorts and bucket-and-spade days out, the sea is still a major draw. In the survey people rated the sea over the countryside as their aspirational retirement destination.[27] Policymakers and planners in coastal locations will need to respond to the diversity of the older population by offering a range of activities and services.

A new trend which has been reported in the British media recently is return migration of older British ex-pats from countries such as Spain and Portugal.[28] There has long been a outflow of British people to the warmer climates of Mediterranean countries in search of a better quality of life at lower cost.[29] However, the falling value of the pound against the euro during the current economic downturn has meant that many retirees (who receive their pension in sterling) have faced massive increases in the cost of living. Emerging evidence suggests that some older ex-pats are being forced to return to the UK, and it will be interesting to observe the locations that these individuals choose to settle in on their return.

Policymakers and decision-makers looking for ways to boost the economic and social development of coastal communities could do worse than build strategies based on the wealth, skills, energy and time that older people have to devote to starting new businesses and social enterprises, or to participating in voluntary and community sector activities. However, there are a number of issues that policymakers should consider when adopting such strategies. These include:

- the need to change negative perceptions of ageing;
- the need to take a broad approach beyond pensions and care to address the economic, social and civic aspects of ageing;
- the need for better research and information on older people;
- the need to recognise the diversity of older people;
- the need for a more strategic approach to encourage older people to remain economically active or to take up voluntary roles;
- the need to ensure both compatibility with other local objectives and local community buy-in.

First Contact supports 'Sure Start to Later Life'

Lincolnshire is pioneering a project to ensure people enjoy a full, independent, healthy life as they enter old age.

Sure Start to Later Life recognises that older people want services delivered not as isolated elements but as joined-up provision. The Sure Start to Later Life programme has been put together to:

- encourage agencies to work together;
- help the over-sixties navigate public and third sector services;
- avoid agencies duplicating work;
- help the over-sixties receive the services they may be entitled to;
- work preventatively rather than reactively.

The building block for this Sure Start approach is a signposting and referral scheme called First Contact for people aged 60 and over who require low-level preventative services from a range of public and third sector partners.

First Contact works as a simple checklist that customers can complete to access services from different agencies. Coordinators use it to address any concerns they may have for the safety and wellbeing of customers.

The scheme is simple to use. Partner agencies and scheme coordinators complete a checklist with an older person or speak to them on the phone. First Contact volunteers living in local communities offer advice and support to vulnerable adults and people aged 60 and over. Leaflets containing the checklist are also available around the county for customers to complete on their own. Referrals are made to relevant listed agencies if the answers to the checklist show that help and support is needed.

This prompts agencies to contact the customer within 28 days and provide information and advice on their services. Jointly managed by Lincolnshire County Council's adult social care and Age Concern, it is delivered in partnership with Lincolnshire Fire and Rescue, district council housing teams, Lincolnshire Affordable Warmth Partnership, Lincolnshire Police, Local Pension Scheme, Accessibility Policy Unit and voluntary centre services.

Mrs Clark (73) from Mablethorpe is a fine example of how the scheme can provide valuable support. She is the main carer for her husband who was in hospital at the time of her referral. Her family lives hundreds of miles away so they were not able to provide much practical support. She says; 'I used the voluntary car schemes to visit my husband in hospital which halved the cost. It was a lifeline as I felt I couldn't ask friends and neighbours to help in the long-term. ... First Contact was a great help to me at a time I needed it the most. I had no idea there was such a range of help and support. It's great to know that someone can visit you at home and take some of the strain of caring for a loved one.'

Graham Marsh, Lincolnshire County Council's executive councillor for adult social care, says: 'We are proud of the scheme we have set up to help support our older residents. First Contact has proved itself to our customers, providing a quick and easy way to access I I services and providing them with support they are entitled to. Older people feel more valued, it helps them remain safe and independent, and they can easily ask for help while maintaining dignity.

... Partners benefit by strengthening relationships and the scheme provides them with a quick and easy tool for signposting to give customers guaranteed contact from the agency they are referred to.'

Contact: John.Giblin@lincolnshire.gov.uk.

The Pursuit of Health and the Origins of the English Seaside Resort - *Gary Winter, English Heritage, UK*

This paper explores the fundamental importance of the pursuit of health to the creation and development of the seaside resort in England, and is based on extensive documentary research undertaken by Gary Winter and Allan Brodie as part of English Heritage's recent Seaside Resorts project.

The pursuit of health was the principal motivation for those with the disposable time and income to resort to the coast, and it was this health culture that led to the creation and early development of England's seaside resorts. It was a culture that had been established at the inland spa resorts, and was arguably exported to the seaside following the discovery of a fresh-water spring in the cliffs at Scarborough in circa 1626. However, in order for Scarborough and other coastal settlements to evolve into seaside resorts, they required their own health-related selling points to distinguish them from the inland freshwater spas. This was provided through the publication of numerous papers and treatises by physicians and others who, through their own historical research, medical observations and analysis, had begun to advocate the seaside environment, and the unique elements it could provide, not only as a place in which health could be sustained, but also one that could provide remedies to scores of medical conditions.

Ultimately, the medical 'evidence' was robust enough to give credence to the act of resorting to the coast, and in particular to the act of bathing in the sea. The strength of the seaside health culture stimulated confidence to invest in the infrastructure of the fledgling seaside resorts, resulting in the creation of new architectural forms such as the bathing machine and bathing room. Although the pursuit of pleasure eventually superseded the pursuit of health, the seaside continued to be advocated as a health-giving environment throughout the 20th century.

for further information on this paper, please visit: www.tourism-culture.com

Chapter 13

Light entertainment
by Steve Hayler

Fairgrounds, penny-arcades
by Anya Chapman

Beach huts
Kathryn Ferry

Light entertainment by Steve Hayler

This brief comment on live entertainment at the seaside provides a context in which to begin to consider its role in coastal regeneration. Live entertainment is not only suggested as an important ingredient in the mix of cultural activities but, at many seaside locations, it is proposed as an essential part of the critical mass required for basic sustainability of the town, let alone its potential role in regeneration. Perhaps controversially, 'basic sustainability' might be more to do with the preservation of any cultural norms that live entertainment represents, as opposed to any economic imperative.

Background data and research confirms that, during the first decade of the twenty-first century, live entertainment continues to be a 'given' in the 'mosaic' of the cultural offer at many seaside locations.[1] It has been changing over the years and has become less focused on traditional seaside entertainment such as variety shows and is now, in many resorts, a somewhat eclectic mix of mostly 'low' but some 'high' (performing) arts that caters for tourists – including long-stay, short-stay and day-trippers but often, increasingly, for residents and patrons within a 45-minute

drive time.[2] Apart from the changing specifics of the live entertainment programmes (which do not materially affect the actual continuation of the live entertainment offer), consideration also needs to be given to the key issues of the ownership, management, control, and preservation of the theatres where live entertainment is performed. This issue is linked to the changing patterns and tastes of patrons but broadens the debate by taking into account the significance of the built structures that provide the live entertainment spaces.

Clearly, there has been a decline in staying visitors at the English seaside that has led to a consequent prioritisation of capital spend for seaside buildings by local councils and others. So, should a theatre be maintained if its original rationale/function for staying visitors (tourists) is reduced? During the last 15 years or more, certain councils have allowed the private sector to manage a number of seaside theatres. Not necessarily as a consequence of this, but certainly out of economic necessity (not enough funding for all the seaside buildings that might be considered worthy of preservation), this has led to many theatres being under threat of demolition or

mothballing – although some, such as Cromer Pier, have been refurbished as public/private initiatives.

Perhaps too often, theatres have been considered a 'given'. It may be the case that councillors and the private companies involved simply believe the opening statements of this brief resume – live entertainment is a cultural norm at the seaside and must be provided albeit in changing formats and, perhaps, in a variety of locations within the resort.

Rather like swimming pools in hotels, these theatres are something visitors and residents alike expect but may not always patronise. Economic necessity and social and cultural change, along with local and national political imperatives, suggests a need to firmly establish the future role for seaside theatres. From an architectural point of view, owing to their construction and development during the 'hey-day' of English seaside holidays, when councils and private investors competed to out-do other resorts, many of England's seaside theatres are fine examples of their genre, superb examples of the Victorian and Edwardian drive towards architectural 'extravagance'. However, many years' exposure to the elements, shifts in the patterns and patronage of audiences, and in councils' and owners' priorities, has meant many of these theatres are in a poor state of repair. Clearly, there is particular architectural merit to be considered – a 'heritage' role. Additionally, crucially, close consideration must be given to the role these buildings (and the content performed in them) will play in the economic, social, but particularly cultural, and sometimes political context, of England's seaside locations during the early part of this century.

There has been no significant research to establish the contemporary relative significance of seaside theatres and identify those 'at risk' – both as physical structures but also as no longer fully performing their original or adapted tasks. A cultural capital taxonomy – that would include in any such list the categorising of seaside theatres and the performances in them – is needed in order to assist planners and strategists in decisions regarding the future use and preservation of these examples of England's seaside heritage. Any such taxonomy needs to take on the contentious issue concerning how far seaside live entertainment is art/culture, and thus how far it might be included in regeneration initiatives noted for their cultural content – be they culture-led regeneration, cultural regeneration, or culture and regeneration.[3]

Certainly, a (new) morphology of cultural capital at English resorts may be usefully postulated, and may be emerging, as seaside live entertainment changes to sit somewhere between the exclusive entertainments provided at the early spa resorts, the traditional live entertainment provided during the period of mass tourism, and the live entertainment provided during the subsequent decline of the traditional visiting tourists. Significantly, these trends may also be part of a broader shift that is seeing some seaside resorts being transformed into 'towns by the sea'. These shifts need to accommodate an emerging description and perhaps a prioritisation of aspects of the cultural capital (yet to be agreed) that might be acquired by people patronising live entertainment performances at seaside resorts. There is a need to establish a much firmer foundation in relation to any theoretical and practical acceptance of a cultural capital taxonomy as applied to English seaside resorts and the live entertainment therein. This may lead to certain resorts acquiring a particular, and possibly unique, widely understood level of cultural standing/capital – including the position of (the town's) live entertainment in all of this. In turn, this branding/marketing (cultural) perspective might then be more closely incorporated into any regeneration initiatives that suggest cultural activities are either fundamental, or tangential via any of the three (Dryburgh) regeneration models, mentioned above.

Fairground culture: part of our seaside heritage, or something the resorts would rather forget? by Anya Chapman

Think of the British seaside fairground. Do your thoughts turn to images of candy floss and sticks of rock, hooplas and hook-a-ducks, adrenaline rides overlooking the beach and the fun house? Or do you think of a very different environment; one where gangs of youths dominate the scene, where the rides have seen better days, the paint is peeling, the burgers are undercooked, and the staff look like they have been in a fight? This contribution

to the *Handbook* looks at the contrasting images of the British seaside fairground, drawing on interview data with employees and customers at a former fairground/amusement park in Southport as this attraction struggled to distance itself from its past image of 'fairground'

and progress to a 'theme park' associated with safety, technology, and modernity.

Southport is currently aspiring for 'Classic Resort' status. Sefton Council defines classic resorts as having quality as their main focus and 'of being

attractive for their sense of quiet sophistication and their contemporary preservation of their spirit of the traditional seaside resort'. In 2008 it was announced that Southport would not be replacing its fairground, but instead developers Urban Splash would be regenerating the site into a 'Marine Park' featuring a winter garden, a lido-style pool, accommodation and a marine lake. This development is considered by the developers, Sefton Council, and other tourism organisations within Southport to be representative of a 'classic resort' rather than a fairground.

Penny arcades: trading on nostalgia, but still the future?

by Anya Chapman

Amusement arcades have been a fundamental component of the British seaside resort offer since the early 1900s, when the first 'sports arcades' began to open at the resorts' fairgrounds. Since then almost every town that lays claim to the title of 'seaside resort' has at least one amusement arcade in order to entertain visitors. Indeed, at the start of the twenty-first century, many smaller resorts featured few other indoor activities with which to occupy their guests (for example New Brighton or Barmouth).

However, in recent years the

seaside family amusement arcade has been bombarded by a range of issues, leaving these attractions struggling to survive. The arcades' heyday of the late 1970s was fuelled by the new developments in video games, but many arcades today cannot compete with the home games consoles that provide better graphics, interactive game play, and online gaming and downloads.

As the seaside arcades moved away from the videos and simulators in the 1990s they became more dependent on the gambling and gaming offers

of Amusement With Prizes ('fruit machines'), 'penny falls', and 'cranes' or 'grabbers' (teddy bear machines). In 2005 the Gambling Act was passed, making legislation on these gambling and gaming machines much tighter. The arcade industry claimed that the Act made their operations much less competitive as gambling establishments, meaning that the seaside arcades sought to diversify their product offering. In recent times a new type of amusement arcade began to open in Britain's seaside resorts – the arcade that traded on nostalgia, or the 'penny' arcade.

These arcades represented a move away from the gambling and gaming products and a return to 'harmless' or 'innocent' fun and amusement with fortune telling, test your strength, and old-style pinball games on offer – all for one old penny! Are the penny arcades the acceptable, gentrified and 'heritagised' face of the amusement arcade industry in changing times – not only for the arcades, but for the resorts themselves? Is this just a repositioning of the seaside arcade product, or just a niche market within the arcade industry?

From bathing machines to beach huts: evolution of a seaside icon by Kathryn Ferry

Interest in the humble beach hut has reached new heights, with prices climbing to unprecedented levels as a reflection of demand. The beach hut has become a tangible symbol of coastal regeneration, but behind its brightly painted silhouette is a history that stretches back to the earliest days of the seaside.

Its wheeled predecessor, the bathing machine, emerged as an aid to fashionable sea bathing in the early eighteenth century, offering a private changing room with direct access to the waves. The Victorians subsequently relied on bathing machines as a necessary intermediary between sea and shore, employing them to separate rich from poor,

men from women. But bylaws only ever enjoyed partial success. As support grew for mixed bathing in the 1890s, the need for mobile changing accommodation diminished. Tents, bungalows and early beach huts appeared on the sands; and as the craze for sun worship took hold during the inter-war years modesty was off the agenda. On the beach or at the vast modern lidos, Bright Young Things wore tight-fitting costumes and stretched out in the sun.

Bathing machines continued to cater for an older generation until at least the Second World War, but by this time the beach hut had already defined its role as a 'home-from-home', a place to hide from summer showers and to brew a reviving cup of tea. Indeed it is these simple pleasures that still attract people in the twenty-first century.

Despite a heritage of nearly 300 years, beach hut design has change little. An international architectural competition in 2006 (www.bathingbeauties. org.uk) proved that this need not be the case in the future, and that these diminutive structures can be not only icons of the seaside but also icons of design.

Gentrification and family migration in Old Town, Hastings -

Jenna Truder, University of Brighton, UK

Focusing on the regeneration of Hastings, South-east of England, this paper argues for a more encompassing perspective of long-distance migrants as potential gentrifiers, and as key actors in the regeneration of seaside spaces. Key here is the need to more fully acknowledge the diverse and complex decision-making processes of inmigrants as gentrifiers. This includes the appeals of more family-friendly employment practices, an enhanced quality of life, and an alternative lifestyle 'by the sea'. It is argued that long-distance migrants are placing more emphasis on the meanings of place, and are increasingly motivated by distinctive cultural and historical appeals, the allure of the sea, and the desire for local character. It is argued that by examining the sociocultural impacts of DFL's (Down from London) in Old Town, Hastings, a more robust understanding of how specific appeals and enticements are re-shaping how processes of gentrification unfold, at what rate and with what effects, can be captured. By unravelling the connections between long-distance migration and processes of gentrification, a broader perspective of how the processes and effects of gentrification unfold within the margins of the "seaside' may be adopted.

for further information on this paper, please visit: www.tourism-culture.com

Chapter 14

The planning system and
coastal regeneration
by Christopher Bamber

Planning Brighton
by Martin Taylor

National planning

The spatial planning system operates at three levels – national, regional and local – with the latter being more practically relevant for coastal resorts. We start at the top!

While there is no national spatial plan for England, topic-based Planning Policy Guidance notes (PPGs), and more recent Planning Policy Statements (PPSs), set out the government's planning policy.

PPS25, 'Development and Flood Risk' (2006), includes policy advice for regional and local authorities on appraising and managing coastal flood risk in a spatial policymaking and decision-making context. The government has recently consulted on a draft 'Development and Coastal Change' PPS (July 2009) that focuses on coastal protection. There is no specific policy guidance on coastal regeneration. This is included in generic regeneration policy such as PPS3 'Housing' and the emerging PPS4 'Planning for Prosperous Communities'.

Planning policy for the coast is evolving into a framework that dovetails with planning policy on flood protection, along with the emerging river basin management plans and updated Shoreline Management Plans.

Planning policy focuses on long-term adaptation, and how spatial planning should provide for the reshaping of settlements vulnerable to managed coastal change or sea level rise and associated flooding.

Most coastal communities are protected under the 'hold the line' regime in Shoreline Management Plans (SMPs), and physically at least, regarded by national planning policy much the same as inland towns. However, SMPs are increasingly considering managed realignment in the longer term (50–100 years) given the impacts of climate change and sea level rise.

Regional planning

The key planning policy vehicle in the last ten years has been the Regional Spatial Strategy (RSS, formerly 'Regional Planning Guidance' or RPG). This is part of a tripartite approach. The Regional Economic Strategy, essentially prepared by the Regional Development Agency as an expression of its priorities for spending, but by extension for the economic development of the region, is an important input. The Regional Transport Strategy is incorporated in the RSS, as are the priorities of the Regional Housing Strategy and other key documents, such as the Regional Environmental Strategy.

RSSs have been prepared by Regional Planning Bodies (RPBs), their powers being vested in Regional Assemblies, which are federations dominated by local authority representatives but also involve the private and voluntary sector bodies, universities and others.

The RSS is also the document which allocates housing numbers to be delivered at a local authority level. These figures are usually 'annualised' (the total figure is divided by the number of years the plan covers), and this gives a general indication of the scale of development expected each year. Each local authority will have to distribute that housing development through the Local Development Framework, and this may have a particular impact on coastal towns where ew housing can be a significant contributor to the local economy.

rom 2010 it is expected that here will be a single regional rategy prepared by the egional Development Agency, s the Regional Planning Board RPB). Regional Assemblies are eing replaced by 'leadership oards' representing local overment, and the Regional trategy will be endorsed y the new boards. In some egions the Regional Strategy is ready under preparation, in nticipation of the legislation. he nature of the strategy nd its 'ownership' will nange, buy for the purposes f local planning and coastal egeneration this 'higher level' lanning context will remain nuch the same.

arly Regional Strategies ended to include 'coastal' vith 'rural' areas. This remains nderstandable in some egions, where the coast predominantly rural; but others areas the coast is xtensively built up. In the te 1990s, the emergence

of Integrated Coastal Zone Management (ICZM) led to a better appreciation among regional planners of the need to take a holistic look at the onshore coastal zone, the economy and at coastal communities. In the North West of England, for example, a quarter of the regional population can be regarded as coastal.

Additionally, the Regional Strategy can be a vehicle for taking forward development concepts which otherwise might founder on lack of will among local authorities to work together. One example is the concept of the 'regional park', which is not a less grand version of a National Park but a means of developing concepts of linked attractions or developments that can be marketed and enjoyed as a larger whole.

The Mersey waterfront regional park, for instance, includes the urban waterfront of Liverpool, plus country parks on the Wirral and around the estuary, and other visitor destinations such as parks, museums and stately

homes. A North West regional coastal trail, with individual stretches linking towns on the coast and connecting into residential neighbourhoods in those towns, is similarly being promoted using the Regional Park policy in the Regional Spatial Strategy.

The ongoing Partial Review of the East Midlands Regional Plan will be informed by the Lincolnshire Coastal Study, mandated by the Secretary of State. This will consider long-term spatial planning options for the Lincolnshire coastal districts of East Lindsey, South Holland and Boston, which include extensive areas and settlements within the coastal flood plain. The study considers the environmental, social and economic consequences of sea level rise and climate change and is a partnership between local authorities, the Environment Agency, Government Office East Midlands, East Midlands Regional Assembly and Natural England.

Local Development Frameworks

is in the Local Development ramework (LDF) of every ocal planning authority, with its onstituent Local Development Documents, that the planning ystem will develop locally istinctive responses to the

issues affecting individual coastal resorts.

The key component of the LDF is the Core Strategy and, unlike an 'old style' Local or Unitary Development Plan, the Core

Strategy does not have to be comprehensive, but should focus on issues critical to the district's development strategy. Its objectives should flow from the Sustainable Community Strategy (SCS) for the area, and

the Local Strategic Partnership (LSP) should be involved in its preparation.

The Core Strategy is an opportunity for coastal authorities to develop positive planning strategies that are 'bought into' by other bodies such as development agencies, health authorities, further education and infrastructure providers. Further than that, there is the freedom to develop plans which speak with a distinctive voice in 'selling' the town to investors as well as acting as lobbying documents for external funding from central government or Regional Development Agencies.

The Core Strategy of the LDF should:

- provide for enough housing to meet the needs of the community over the next 15 years;
  In resort towns, providing affordable housing for a low-income community may be a particular challenge, not least where there is significant flood risk.

- ensure that there is land to provide enough jobs over the next 15 years;
  This may be an issue for resorts that are hemmed in by AONB, cliffs, and/or valuable agricultural lands. However, for many resorts the real issue is attracting new business sectors to the area and to the available sites and premises. A few larger resort towns have grown and diversified – Bournemouth, Brighton, Scarborough – but many resorts will require creativity and external funding to stimulate economic diversification.

- establish how much investment in retail and other relevant development is needed in town centres (not to mention other parts of the town such as resort or port areas);
  A healthy town centre will provide a 'wet weather' draw involving our most prevalent leisure activity, shopping, as well as making the town more appealing to the wider coastal hinterland for leisure and entertainment purposes

– the coastal resorts USP! Resorts can lend themselves to additional town centre developments, such as creative quarters or public administration – for example the existence of thousands of public sector jobs in Lancashire resort towns.

- demonstrate that the community can take the level of development envisaged (traffic, water supply, drainage, broadband);
  Flood risk in many areas, utility capacity in others and poor infrastructure can all combine to influence the capacity of a community to effectively accommodate needed development.

- protect and enhance the built environment, both heritage 'assets' and the local character of streets, neighbourhoods and open spaces;
  The built environment and the 'heritage assets' of resorts determine their popularity and attractiveness that require robust protection and visionary enhancement in order to maintain and maximise the expectation and satisfaction for residents and visitors alike.

- make sure the natural environment is looked after – particularly, protected areas, which are much more likely to be very close to coastal settlements than is usually the case inland –

and these are tourism assets;

The natural coast clearly contextualises seaside resorts in historic, aesthetic and liminal contexts and, as with heritage assets, combine to make areas unique, evocative and desirable. As with the coastal build-up areas, deterioration of the natural environment can deter visitors and reduce the quality of life for residents.

- keep housing, community and key infrastructure development away from areas vulnerable to flooding.

Sitting 'beneath' the Core Strategy may be a number of more detailed documents, including, where necessary, site allocations documents, setting out the specific sites that will help deliver the strategy.

Many authorities are producing *Area Action Plans* (AAPs), or, where they may want to provide additional clarity to existing policies or sites, *Supplementary Planning Documents* (SPDs)) for particular areas of significant change, or conservation, within their districts. A resort town might produce an AAP promoting the regeneration of an area dominated by B&Bs, for instance; or a port might do so to guide the evolution or redevelopment of parts of its

port for tourism or housing-led mixed-use development. And of course, any coastal town is likely to want to develop a planning framework for its town centre, or a residential or industrial area undergoing change, just as an inland town would, albeit perhaps with particular attention being given to characteristics of the community, the economy or the built environment which derive from its coastal location.

- Planning implementation.

Policies have to be put into effect, and it is important that 'development management' is operated both sensitively and proactively. Modern tourists are much less tolerant of 'tat' than their forebears; for too many years, too many resorts took a laissez-faire approach to (for example) hotel frontages and roofscapes, and paid scant respect to their architectural and public realm heritage. The result is that most British resorts became very unattractive compared to the places people could afford to go to in Greece or Portugal. This trend has been reversed, of course, Llandudno being a noted pioneer. We see a stark contrast in Southport between the striking new bridge over the boating lake, and the 1990s retail sheds which turn their back on it. Planners need to be vigilant

and combat any tendency for elected members or chief executives to look for low-grade 'easy win' development.

The same also goes for the *enforcement* of planning conditions and against unauthorised development – though admittedly there is a line, very indistinct perhaps, to be drawn between what is off-puttingly tawdry and what captures the 'cheap and cheerful' spirit that makes the British resort so distinctive.

With regard to the role of *compulsory purchase* in regeneration, the 2004 Act was intended to revamp CPO powers to make them less cumbersome. Unfortunately, the decline of positive, comprehensive planning in the 1980s and 90s has left many local authorities short of expertise in negotiating the pitfalls that can stymie redevelopment needing compulsory purchase. The use of consultants is one option, but Regional Development Agencies have increasingly stepped in to undertake that phase of regeneration schemes.

If you wish to contribute to the debate on the role of planning in coastal regeneration, please contact Patrick.Browne@lincolnshire.gov.uk .

Brighton: Regeneration of a major resort

by Martin Taylor MRTPI, MIED, MTS, Director – Planning and Consulting, HLL Humberts Leisure

In the 1970s, Brighton Council was one of the first to respond to the threat to British resorts from cheap overseas package holidays to the Mediterranean by successfully diversifying its tourism economy through the opening of Brighton Conference Centre in 1974. At the same time, the council supported the growth of Brighton's office sector as a base for the financial services industry.

When I arrived in Brighton to take up my new post as a Senior Planning Officer in 1988, the town was booming with a terrific buzz, and sky-high property prices. That boom quickly turned to bust in the late 1980s and early 90s, and by 1992 the city's unemployment had risen to 15 per cent with rates as high as 30 per cent in some parts of the inner city and outlying council estates. With a large private rented sector, central Brighton became a focus for people living on breadline benefits and with the recession particularly hitting the financial services and retail sectors Brighton quickly resembled a ghost town of empty shops and offices. The closeness of London made it easy for journalists to travel to Brighton and print articles featuring the

resort in all its 'faded glory'.

By 1992, I was working in the newly formed Economic Development Unit. Meetings with local business leaders revealed that the city's major hotels were advising their guests to avoid Brighton seafront as a dangerous place occupied by drunks, beggars and drug users. Clearly, with the seafront being Brighton's 'shop window', something had to be done. Following meetings with the then South East of England Tourist Board, a small pool of funding was identified to support a Strategic Development Initiative (SDI) to regenerate the seafront.

Consultants were commissioned to take a fresh look at the seafront. Their report found little support for investment in the resort from major multiple players, and recommended that little could be done to regenerate the seafront without first restoring the West Pier – which had been closed since 1976. Unfortunately the council did not own the West Pier, nor did they have the £30 million needed to restore it. Undeterred, the council set up a corporate team with officers from departments across the

council led by the Director of Arts and Leisure. This team managed to find a more modest but not insignificant sum of £1 million from a budget that would otherwise have been used simply to maintain the seafront in its then soulless state.

This money was not itself sufficient to regenerate the whole of the seafront, so the project was split up into phases. The first phase took place between the main pier and the main road leading from Brighton station. This stretch, which was fronted by deep arches, had the most opportunity to attract private sector investment. A young in-house landscape architect was recruited to the team who drew up innovative designs for the landscaping of the lower promenade area. This new landscaping was implemented while at the same time marketing the arches for private sector investment. The fact that the council had shown its faith in the seafront by implementing new landscaping proposals meant that local private investors and entrepreneurs placed their own faith in the seafront. A number of exciting enterprises began to prosper on the seafront.

The first phase of the regeneration coincided with a national crackdown on 'raves', so people were seeking new legal locations in which to cater for dance music. The seafront represented an ideal location and was given a market edge with the granting of entertainment licences until 5 o'clock in the morning. This meant a great deal of the investment was in nightclubs, extending Brighton's 'club scene' along the seafront. It was also time for the 'chameleon bar' concept, and operators were encouraged to develop the arches as bar–restaurants by day, nightclubs by night. This meant that the seafront was just as vibrant by day as it became at night.

Later phases of the SDI successfully sourced funding from the Single Regeneration Budget as Brighton had demonstrated a track record in both project and matched funding delivery during the first phase. These later phases addressed different resort markets, including an artists' quarter, sports such as basketball and beach volleyball, and more family-orientated areas with children's play.

Some £14 million of funding was sourced for the regeneration of the West Pier from the Heritage Lottery Fund. However, protracted negotiations with matched funding developers failed to deliver a scheme acceptable to English Heritage before the pier burnt down, and subsequently partly fell down, and the funding was withdrawn. A new proposal for an elevated viewing platform called the i360 by Marks Byfield (the architects behind the London Eye) has now been approved, but this has been delayed by funding difficulties in the current recession. The important point, however, is that the regeneration of the seafront was not allowed to become dependent on restoration of the West Pier which was, and still is, largely outside the control of the council.

Of course, regeneration of Brighton's seafront did not happen in splendid isolation. It was part of an overall corporate and city-wide regeneration strategy. People visit Brighton as much for its historic core and independent shopping areas as they do for its vibrant seafront. A Town Centre Strategy and Action Plan was drawn up which resulted in the appointment of one of the country's first Town Centre Managers, replacement of Churchill Square (the city's ailing 1960s concrete shopping centre) with a new £90 million covered shopping centre, and reinvestment in the independent shopping quarters of the Lanes and the North Laines

Culture was a key theme in the regeneration of the city, with SRB funding used for redevelopment of the Dome arts complex, and funding towards several other fringe theatre and arts centres. An award-winning new library was developed through an innovative PFI scheme. A 'Percent for Art' programme is applied to all new developments across the city and many examples have been showcased on the seafront.

Tourism, culture and the arts provide a buzzing city life attractive to young innovative entrepreneurs in the media sector. Therefore, with further enabling from the council, Brighton town centre also became a location for new media professionals and businesses. Small amounts of public sector funding were used to support the development of a first, and then a second, Brighton Media Centre, while the private sector followed suit in dividing redundant industrial and office spaces into flexible high-tech office suites for budding media and IT professionals.

Brighton was already a major centre for education, with two universities, technical and sixth-form colleges, and a large number of language schools. The council worked proactively with the education sector through the 'Academic

Corridor' initiative, resulting in one of the first Innovation Centres outside of Cambridge and in the growth of the city's education businesses. There are some 30,000 students in the city, who add to its vibrancy, supporting pubs, nightclubs, theatres and independent shopping districts, and provide a pool of graduate employment for local businesses. Compared to most university cities, many more students from Brighton's universities seek to stay in the city after graduation.

The regeneration of Brighton provides important lessons for other resorts. While part of the effort was concentrated on key features of the resort, especially the seafront, this was just a part of a city-wide and cross-sectoral programme. All resorts, big and small, need to try to avoid reliance on one (tourism) business sector alone. However, they can use tourism – and the vibrancy it can bring to a place – to attract other business sectors. The other key lesson was that regeneration was a corporate responsibility. Regeneration was not confined to one small team within a larger department; rather it was led by the Chief Executive and Corporate Management Team with the support of the Leader of the Council with key projects targeted, and achieved through corporate teams working across the council and involving different groups of business leaders from across the city.

So here we are now, during a recession that is reportedly deeper and worse than that of the early 1990s. Yet, I look out of my window and Brighton is still thriving. Sure, businesses are still finding it hard, and there are a few shop vacancies. However, without exception these vacancies have been caused by the closure of national multiple chains, whereas the independent sector has remained more resilient. In this recession, Brighton has been less reliant on the decisions of major national and international companies with most business decisions being undertaken by local entrepreneurs based here in the city. The resort looks well set for a prosperous future.

Resorts of the world: From Cap Saint-Jacques to Vung Tau, the spatial path of a Vietnamese seaside resort by Emmanuelle Peyvel, University of Lyon, France

Using an approach of cultural geography, I have been studying the seaside resort of Vung Tau (South Vietnam), from its colonial inception to today, and so put into perspective the longstanding but ever-changing relationship between humans and the oceans.

During the colonial period, Vung Tau used to be called Cap Saint-Jacques and was created for the benefit of French colonials, especially for those who lived in Saigon. Its primary function was to provide them with rest during their holidays, often linked with medical infrastructures such as – but not limited to – sanatoriums. In order to compensate for the blandness of the mother country, Cap Saint-Jacques – like all colonial resorts of Indochina – was spatially modelled on French seaside resorts of the Riviera, as can be seen from its urban morphology and the French-style architecture of the large residential houses.

Following the end of the war period (1954–75), Vung Tau remained one of the major seaside resorts of Vietnam. Currently, however, he majority of tourists are Vietnamese. The practices of domestic tourists differ from those of the former French colonials because Vietnamese tourists have different conceptions of 'beauty' and rest'. In consequence, their tourist territories and the meaning ascribed to the place have profoundly changed even though its location and functions remain identical.

Vung Tau thus provides a good opportunity to analyse the patterns and trends in how tourists mobilise the resources of sea, sand and shore in the specific framework of a developing Asian country like Vietnam – especially as this former French colony, currently under a socialist government, has seen the successive development of two different tourist cultures.

further information on this paper, please visit: www.tourism-culture.com

Chapter 15

In their own words…
services for coastal
regeneration
by National and regional players

In researching this book we requested information from national, regional and local organisations on the services they provide to coastal communities. If you are not here, you can be on the website www.coastalcommunities.co.uk

Government departments and coastal regeneration

Department for Business, Innovation and Skills (BIS)

The BIS is currently working with city regions to develop Multi Area Agreements (MAAs). These provide local partners with the opportunity to secure specific flexibilities in the national skills arrangements in order to meet local needs. For example, MAAs offer city region partnerships the opportunity to establish an employer-led Employment and Skills Board (ESB) with formal strategy-setting powers. These powers will allow ESBs to develop an 'employment and skills strategy' that will guide the Skills Funding Agency's (SFA) delivery. In areas where there are no MAA partnerships, the SFA Regional Director will work with local and regional partners to determine the skills priorities for the area.

In addition the BIS, through the Learning and Skills Council, delivers skills to support local economies, including coastal towns. These are delivered to employers through apprenticeships and Train to Gain, and to individuals through further education. In order to do this the Learning and Skills Council works with key partners such as:

- local authorities – to deliver provision for 16 to 18 year-olds;
- Regional Development Agencies (RDAs), the Department for Work and Pensions and Jobcentre Plus – for those aged 19 and over.

The Council also focuses on meeting individuals' and employers' needs and the identified needs of the local economy. It works to:

- secure greater integration of employment and skills;
- prepare young people for the world of work;
- strengthen links between skills and regeneration;
- improve the flexibility and responsiveness of the skills system.

In this way the Council covers many of the coastal issues identified, especially those concerned with low employment levels, skills for local tourism, economic diversification and regeneration.

Its activity impacts on infrastructure, educational attainment and recruitment in coastal towns.

Looking to the future, planned changes to the machinery of government will result in the Council's responsibilities being taken over by a new Skills Funding Agency and a new learning agency for young people, alongside an increased role for local authorities.

Department for Culture, Media and Sport (DCMS)

The government invests almost £50 million a year in tourism marketing through VisitBritain. Each of VisitBritain's campaigns features a different location, but it aims to achieve a balanced regional spread overall and recognises the continuing importance of the seaside within British tourism.

Seaside destinations are promoted through VisitBritain's international offices, campaigns, public relations and websites, and the attractions of the seaside are included in a variety of themed campaigns. At the national Tourism Summit on 8 January 2009 in Liverpool, the prime minister emphasised the importance of taking advantage of the competitive tourism product available in the UK. In response to this, VisitBritain launched a £6.5 million marketing campaign in April, themed around 'value for money', to highlight cultural and historical heritage, landscape and natural heritage, vibrant cities and exciting sports and cultural events. Seaside destinations will benefit from this initiative.

In April, responsibility for marketing England within the UK moved from VisitBritain to VisitEngland. VisitEngland is working with the English Regional Development Agencies (RDAs), which have had responsibility for tourism in the regions since 2003, and which have developed regional tourism strategies and delivery structures based around marketing and branding, product quality assessment and investment, skills development, sustainable tourism frameworks and improved accessibility. There has been significant research into tourism and seaside destinations as part of RDA wider research programmes. The challenges faced by coastal towns are well understood in the context of regional economic strategies, led by the RDAs.

Longer term planning for the development of the visitor economy is contained in 'Winning: a tourism strategy for 2012 and beyond', which was released by the DCMS in October 2007. The strategy looks towards:

- maximising the benefits of the 2012 Olympic and Paralympic Games opportunity;
- providing the best possible visitor welcome and showcasing the UK to the world;
- creating a platform for the longer term development and sustainability of the industry.

The government's SeaChange programme, led by the Commission for Architecture and the Built Environment (CABE) on behalf of DCMS, has also boosted wider economic regeneration in coastal areas through investment in culture and heritage. Funding so far to 35 resorts allocated grants of £38 million to create new performance spaces, improve theatres, restore promenades, enable spectacular beach-front redesigns and provide new exhibition spaces.

Coastal towns have also benefited from other policies and programmes through cultural regeneration and investment in the built and historic environment. In

October 2007, English Heritage published *An Asset and a Challenge; Heritage and Regeneration in Coastal Towns in England* which was accompanied by a conference in Hastings discussing some of the issues. The report brought together a range of case studies from around the coast, looking at drivers for success and the role of the historic environment as a dynamic resource for regeneration in seaside towns as diverse as Whitehaven and Margate. The case studies put an increased emphasis on 'local' bottom-up approaches to addressing longstanding regeneration issues, with many examples of effective partnership working across sectors. They bring out the continuing value and importance of tourism to coastal economies. The report is available on the Historic Environment Local Management website (www.helm.org.uk) along with other guidance on management of coastal heritage issues.

Some museums in coastal towns have benefited from regional museum investment through the Renaissance in the Regions programme, combined with Single Regeneration Budget and European Development cultural funding for deprived areas – including Hull, Plymouth, Bournemouth and Chatham. Hull also has the award-winning The Deep science centre and aquarium, which is a real boost to tourism in the town and was funded by the Millennium Commission. The Deep has continued to win tourism awards in 2008/9. The Heritage Lottery Fund (HLF) supports a wide variety of schemes in coastal towns, ranging from parks and regeneration, to museums and community projects. The main funding stream for this has been the Townscape Heritage Initiative, now in its eleventh year. Funding is allocated through local authorities in partnership with private businesses to improve historic street frontages and other street features. The HLF has given over £234 million to 864 projects in English coastal resorts to support their regeneration since 1997. This funding has included well over £100 million to coastal resorts in deprived areas, including Blackpool, Falmouth, Great Yarmouth, Hastings, North Shields, Penzance, Redcar, Saltburn-by-the Sea and Southport.

Some seaside towns are under threat from climate change and coastal erosion. The DCMS and English Heritage's policy on the historic environment at risk from coastal erosion has been outlined in Defra's consultation on coastal change policy, launched on 15 June 2009.

Tourism is only one of the employment sectors in such towns but remains significant, and has reportedly been boosted by the effects of the economic downturn affecting holiday choices. As the English Heritage report noted, one of the challenges for seaside resorts is to define a unique visitor offer for each town, whether focusing on culinary heritage tourism (e.g. Whitstable, Seahouses), iconic heritage sites or maritime associations (Whitby, Portsmouth, Battle Abbey), museums and art galleries (Margate, Falmouth) or adventure tourism (Hunstanton, Saltburn-by-the-Sea). Each offer should compete on quality as well as price.

Department for the environment, farming and rural areas (Defra)

Coastal change is a natural process that has and will continue to shape and mould our coastline. We know from the latest science on climate change that the risks of coastal erosion and flooding will increase over the next 100 years. We will defend where it is sustainable and affordable to do so, but it will not be possible to protect every piece of coastline.

Communities likely to be affected will need to start preparing for and managing

change. Defra is working with communities and national and local partners to understand the risks associated with climate change and is developing a range of approaches to support community adaptation, particularly in those communities where it will not be possible to defend.

Significant progress has already been made with a programme of activities designed to support adaptation. These include the provision of better planning information through shoreline management plans, and support for households to protect against flood risk through a £5 million grants scheme. The government published a new Coastal Change policy consultation on 15 June 2009, including the launch of a pathfinder programme to pilot a new coastal change fund of up to £11 million. Local authorities were able to bid to become pathfinders and use money from this fund to run their own adaptation schemes, working in partnership with their local communities. Money could be spent, for example, on restoring coastal footpaths, maintaining public car parks and beach access points at risk from erosion, or supporting re-routing of coastal roads. The three-month consultation sought views on the way forward on providing financial help for demolition and moving costs to the few homeowners

who in the next 20 years will lose their homes to erosion.

The consultation also included details of how communities can plan for change as well as looking at what managing change might mean for properties, businesses, local infrastructure and our historic and natural environment.

There is an important link between the Coastal Change policy and Communities and Local Government's (forthcoming) consultation on new planning policy for the coast. This aims to ensure that the impact of coastal change is taken into account at all stages of the planning process so that the government strikes the right balance between economic prosperity and reducing the consequences of coastal change on communities.

- *Marine planning from Defra*

The Marine and Coastal Access Act 2009 introduces a marine planning system in UK waters for the first time in order to contribute to the achievement of sustainable development of the marine area. Marine planning will be one of the major functions of the new Marine Management Organisation (MMO), which will have responsibility for preparing marine plans for the English inshore and offshore regions in accordance with the policies and objectives set out by the government in the Marine Policy Statement.

The Marine Policy Statement will provide a clear framework for managing our seas, clarifying objectives and priorities, and directing decision-makers, users and stakeholders to a more strategic and efficient approach towards the sustainable development of marine resources. The marine plans that will be developed by the MMO are in accordance with the Marine Policy Statement.

The MMO and other public authorities will then have a duty to take licensing and enforcement decisions in accordance with the Marine Policy Statement and the marine plans. The marine plans

will extend to the mean high-water mark, with local authority boundaries going down to low water – this means that there will be an overlap between planning systems. This overlap will mean that the MMO and local authorities will need to work very closely. Indeed, the government is considering how best to enable local authorities to be fully involved in the development of marine plans.

- For more information on the Marine and Coastal Access Act, see www.defra. gov.uk/environment/marine/ legislation/index.htm.
- For more information on the MMO, see www.mfa. gov.uk/mmo/planning.htm.

Department for Works and Pensions (DWP)

The DWP provides a national welfare system, and the support available to people who are out of work largely depends on the type of benefit they claim and their individual characteristics. As a department, the DWP provides part of the overall help and support that people receive when they are out of work. Principally the policies cover the national offer – those elements that people expect should be the same regardless of where they live, such as access to benefits on a fair and consistent basis and minimum levels of help and support at different stages of unemployment or worklessness.

However, although it is a national offer it is delivered locally. Since benefit payments and labour market programmes are delivered direct to the individual, areas that have higher rates of worklessness and benefit dependency automatically receive a greater level of support from Jobcentre Plus (JCP) and through contracted provision such as the New Deal.

On top of the national system, there are a number of area-based initiatives supported by the DWP that target additional resource at the most deprived areas. These include the City Strategy Pathfinders, Local Area Agreements and Multi Area Agreements, and the Working Neighbourhoods Fund. Partly as a result of the success of this approach, there is evidence that over the last decade the biggest improvements in employment and unemployment have been in areas that started in the worst position, leading to some narrowing in labour market disparities across the country. The Sub-National Review of Economic Development and Regeneration (SNR) recommended that, to maximise the impact of area funding, the government should focus on a smaller number of areas where deprivation is most acute. In pursuit of this recommendation, the government has targeted areas with the highest concentrations of worklessness – this includes some, but not all, coastal towns.

Data from the Annual Population Survey suggests that around 7 per cent of the UK population live in coastal towns, and 1 in 10 of those people live in wards that receive Working Neighbourhoods Funds.

Claimants of incapacity benefit (IB) or employment and support allowance (ESA) in coastal towns will benefit from the national Pathways to Work programme which is available to everyone in Great Britain receiving IB or ESA.

Regional Development Agencies and coastal regeneration

RDAs were established in 1999 and are the responsibility of the Department for Business, Innovation and Skills. The primary role of the RDAs is to act as the strategic drivers of regional economic development.

In 2007 the government, in response to the Select Committee Inquiry into coastal towns, established the RDA Coastal Towns Network which aims to:

- improve coordination of interventions in coastal towns between central, regional and local government;
- provide a focus on good practice dissemination;
- identify barriers to policy implementation.

The network brings together representatives from all the coastal RDAs, and includes central government departments, agencies and local authorities with an interest in the costal towns' agenda.

What follows are samples of RDA activities with coastal communities in their areas. Fuller details are available on RDA websites.

East of England Development Agency (www.eeda.org.uk)

The RDA contributed £6 million in Kings Lynn to a £23 million programme to support the redevelopment of 50 hectares of brownfield land for a mixed-use development scheme. The project enabled the major inward investment by Palm Paper to be located in Kings Lynn, plus associated infrastructure, new homes and integration with the town. OrbisEnergy is a regional centre of excellence in Lowestoft, which has created a business environment that promotes and fosters the development of the offshore wind sector.

The new £7.9 million Jerwood DanceHouse on Ipswich Waterfront was provided with £1 million of EEDA funding to create a performance space and a headquarters for dance agency DanceEast.

EEDA has contributed over £10 million for regeneration schemes, including public realm and tourism enhancements in Great Yarmouth and Lowestoft including OrbisEnergy.

East Midlands Development Agency (www.emda.org.uk)

EMDA allocated £2 million, under the LEADER approach element of the Rural Development Programme for England (RDPE), to the East Lindsay coastal action zone, and is working with Boston Borough Council and South Holland District Council to develop their RDPE programmes.

EMDA provided capital funding to public realm work in Mablethorpe, and is working with the owners of Fantasy Island theme park at Skegness on their development plans.

One North East (www.onenortheast.com)

In Blyth, the RDA has invested significantly in an internationally recognised centre of new and renewable energy research (NaREC) and has stimulated a cluster of innovative manufacturing around this critical new economic sector.

In other areas, such as Seaham, a former colliery town with significant economic challenges, the RDA has invested in place-based regeneration and supported the attraction of businesses through business accommodation projects and public realm investment.

North West Development Agency (www.nwde.co.uk)

In Southport, completion of the Lord Street area improvement initiative benefited from a contribution of £2.6 million in total from the RDA. There was refurbishment of Southport Floral Hall and Theatre 2009 with a total RDA contribution of £4.4 million, and support for the acquisition of Pleasureland amusement park by Sefton Metropolitan Borough Council with a total RDA contribution of £2.7 million.

In Morecambe, NWDA has signed a Resort Action Plan with the local authority to provide the framework for Morecambe's regeneration, including funding for the restoration of the Midland

Hotel and feasibility work for the refurbishment of Morecambe Winter Gardens.

In Blackpool, NWDA has been providing ongoing support for ReBlackpool, the urban regeneration company and the main delivery mechanism for Blackpool's regeneration.

South East of England Development Agency (www.seeda.co.uk)

SEEDA produced, with partners, a Coastal South East Framework in 2008 that is reflected within both the Regional Economic Strategy and Corporate Plan of the agency. This identifies a number of actions to support regional and local action.

A number of the region's coastal areas are identified as priority places for investment and growth: Hastings, Margate and Dover for major regeneration, whilst Portsmouth and urban South Hampshire is one of the initial MAAs and a Diamond for Investment and Growth.

Brighton and Hove, West and East Sussex and Thames Gateway, Kent are identified as a Diamond and a potential MAA.

SEEDA is supporting new university campuses in Hastings Folkestone and Bognor Regis, and major infrastructure projects in Hastings, Southampton and Chatham Maritime.

South West Development Agency (www.southwestrda. org.uk)

The RDA is currently contributing funding to the region's Market and Coastal Towns Network (MCTN). Each county network receives approximately £70,000 over three years (total funding £450,000). The MCTN's purpose is to maintain and expand a comprehensive network of town partnerships across the region to provide mutual support, advocacy and development of closer links to Local Strategic Partnerships, the Local Area Agreement delivery framework and statutory community planning.

- *Torbay*

The RDA has invested £2.9 million in the Torbay Development Agency which will support the Mayor's Vision setting out the 20 key projects for the future success of the bay by encouraging private sector investment in regeneration and a prosperous economy. Examples of projects for investment in Torbay:
- £8.4 million investment in the completion of the Brixham regeneration

project, new fish market, employment and residential uses on the harbour;
- providing road and other infrastructure for the opening of the 35-acre White Rock Business Park at Paignton, a prime site for 2,000 high-quality jobs;
- development of a new higher education centre at South Devon College, Paignton, to provide higher level skills for graduates entering into business and commerce, subject to confirmation of LSC funding.

There is also an ERDF Competitiveness Programme to fund business start-ups and new enterprise in deprived parts of Torbay. Cockington Court creative industries incubation centre is being considered for funding within this European Union programme.

The RDA is supporting businesses across Devon through its contact with strategic companies, its funding of Business Link, sustained support for the 'Bites Back' campaign, as well as supporting individual events (such as the Mayor's event on the recession). Area Action Forces are established to deal with instances of significant job losses.

- *Dorset*

The RDA's priority investment in Dorset remains the former

Royal Naval air station on Portland where it is investing in excess of £40 million to create a centre for sailing excellence and a magnet for leisure and marine industries. The agency is also making almost £10 million available for the Twin Sails Bridge scheme in Poole Harbour. Both these projects are employment-led regeneration schemes that aim to deliver thousands of new jobs.

Apart from the £30.5 million already invested at Portland, other major RDA investments include £4.73 million to upgrade the Bournemouth International Centre – which helped it generate an estimated £127 million for the local economy last year compared with £70 million before the upgrade. The RDA invested £2.5 million in the Enterprise Pavilion at the Arts Institute at Bournemouth, which now supports 90 jobs; and spent £1.4 million to help free up a site next to Sunseeker in Poole to help the company expand, creating 500 jobs.

Through the Rural Development Programme for England, the RDA is providing almost £6 million to community groups in north, south and west Dorset to support rural regeneration and business support projects. Around £12.8 million of RDPE investment has also been earmarked for sustainable tourism projects across the region, including an off-road cycling hub on the outskirts of Bournemouth, and investment to interpret and conserve 83 heritage sites along the South West Coast Path.

The RDA is also contributing considerable investment to the highly innovative Wave Hub project – to create the world's largest wave energy farm off the north Cornwall coast. The agency is also continuing £7.3 million investment in the Peninsular Research Institute for Marine Renewable Energy (PRIMARE), to make the South West a world leader in marine renewables.

Yorkshire Forward (www.yourshire_forward.com)

Yorkshire Forward has invested £9.5 million in Scarborough's economic development through its Renaissance Programme. This includes a new creative and digital business centre, Woodend, the Rotunda Museum, and developments of the marina and spa theatre. Over £200 million of private sector investment has been secured for the town.

Refurbishment of the Bridlington Spa Complex was completed early in 2008, and discussions are continuing with regard to redevelopment of the

Marina. A major improvement scheme has commenced around the Spa Complex to upgrade the public areas and provide outdoor performance spaces.

In Cleethorpes, under the Renaissance Programme, work has been completed on the Lakeside Arena. Currently there is a process of commissioning a strategic development framework for the whole of Cleethorpes. A 'Town Team' has been formed from interested residents and businesses to steer the process of remaking their town.

Regional Government Offices and coastal regeneration

The Government Office (GO) network brings together central government departments' interests in the regions. The GO's role is to be a key intermediary between local and regional delivery and national policymaking. This includes facilitating the development and implementation of strong local strategies, as well as 'troubleshooting' key issues, and ensuring they reflect the needs of both rural and urban areas. Government Offices are centrally involved in managing existing regional governance structures, working

alongside Regional Assemblies and Regional Development Agencies to implement the Sub-national Review and ensuring a smooth transition.

GOs have locality managers allocated to a local authority area. Their role is to:

- know the area in order to represent it to Whitehall and give the opportunity for the area to influence government policy and activity;
- represent, interpret and explain government

policy and intentions to the area, enabling successful implementation;
- broker agreements between local partners and between the locality and Whitehall;
- manage agreements between government and the local area, in particular Local Area Agreements

GO – East Midlands (GOEM)

GOEM is a member of Defra's Coastal Policy Steering Group. This group works with Defra to advise and support them on the development of coastal change policy – see the earlier section from Defra.

GOEM is a key partner in the Lincolnshire Coastal Study that seeks to assess the future needs of the coastal areas on the Lincolnshire coast, large parts of which are at or below sea level. The study will inform the review of the East Midlands Regional Plan, and will report in March 2010.

GOEM is a member of all even district Local Strategic Partnerships (LSPs), including East Lindsey, Boston and South Holland, which all contain coastal communities.

GOEM responds where possible to specific requests – for example, securing a consultant who offered support to East Lindsey District Council on neighbourhood management with deprived communities along the coast.

GO – East (GOE)

Recognising the coincidence of high-quality assets, deprivation and physical change on the east coast, the East of England Coastal Initiative is an innovative, multi-agency project started by GOE and guided by a number of regional bodies. The initiative responds to a number of long-term challenges facing

the region's coast, including:

- the need to understand the possibilities and tensions created by high-quality natural environments and areas in need of regeneration;
- the additional pressures presented by climate change and the need to identify ways in which the coast and its communities can adapt;
- the need for more consistent approaches to coastal management and for improved policy integration.

GOE has negotiated challenging LAAs with Norfolk, Suffolk, Essex, Southend and Thurrock. Recognising the adaptation challenge that will be faced particularly on the coast, all of these LAAs include National Indicator 188, adapting to climate change.

A number of the region's coastal localities face regeneration challenges. The Government Office is involved in brokering solutions to enable appropriate development in areas at risk

and in supporting these localities in responding to the challenges and opportunities arising from their coastal location.

GO – Yorkshire and Humberside (GOYH)

The national Government Office Coastal Network is led by the GOYH Environment Directorate. Defra has provided support to the network to help regions:

- build up a coalition of engaged partners, work with them to identify future coastal challenges and fill gaps within the coastal evidence and knowledge base;
- ensure that coastal challenges, priorities and evidence are understood by partners and reflected in the Integrated Regional Strategy and other plans;
- support the development, consultation and implementation of Defra's coastal change policy;
- lead and participate in a

GO network of coastal leaders, giving feedback to Defra on the region's views and experiences.

GOYH have had discussions with Scarborough regarding specific housing issues, such as a transitional population, people living in poor-quality rented stock, and high levels of incomers who are elderly and may require modifications to properties. A mini regeneration pathfinder approach to areas of Scarborough will be incorporated into the new North Yorkshire Housing Strategy.

Following a GOYH approach, the Home Office held a national Seaside Violent Crime Conference in April 2009. Seaside towns were targeted owing their relatively high levels of violent crime, which are based on a number of factors: high numbers of visitors and concentrations of confined accommodation; tensions between 'locals' and visitors, the capacity of custody resources, and their distance from larger resources in cities.

GO – North West (GONW)

The Blackpool Task Force was formed in March 2007 following a request from the government to look into the long-term regeneration plans for Blackpool, in the wake of the regional casino reversal. Blackpool had hoped to attract substantial private sector investment to the town.

GONW is negotiating a Multi Area Agreement (MAA) with Lancashire, Blackpool, Wyre and Fylde to cover the three geographic authorities of the Fylde coast and around a third of a million people. The MAA objectives include:

- securing the commitment of government to helping Blackpool to scale the socioeconomic challenges of the resort town;
- improving the transport infrastructure to support economic growth;
- growing, diversifying and enhancing the quality of the Fylde coast business base;
- better developing people's skills and employment prospects;
- tackling fundamental housing issues.

GONW is in regular contact with the Office of Government Commerce (OGC) to discuss opportunities for governmental relocations to Blackpool.

The Victoria & Albert (V&A) trustees made an offer to Blackpool to provide a frequently refreshed V&A exhibition for 10 years in a new building that will be branded V&A@Blackpool on the Tower Headland. GONW will continue to work with the DCMS, Blackpool and the V&A to support this initiative. Capital costs are around £20 million and revenue costs £1.9 million. Blackpool has already committed £1.1 million to revenue.

Big Lottery Fund

The Big Lottery Fund (BIG) is the largest distributor of Lottery money, responsible for giving out half the money raised by the National Lottery for good causes. This money goes to community groups and to projects that improve health, education and the environment. BIG is committed to bringing real improvements to communities, and to the lives of people most in need. BIG has a range of programmes that organisations can apply to. Further details on programmes currently open can be found at www.biglotteryfund.org.uk, or phone 0845 410 20 30.

Reaching Communities is an England-wide programme that gives grants of more than £10,000 and up to £500,000, including a maximum of £50,000 for capital grants. Projects can be funded for up to 5 years. An overall maximum project size has been set at £750,000, with a maximum of £200,000 for the total capital element.

Awards for All is another England-wide programme that provides funding to help improve local communities and the lives of people most in need. Awards for All gives grants of between £300 and £10,000 for new or developed projects. An application form and guidance notes can be downloaded from www.awardsforall.org.uk.

The Big Lottery Fund supports many projects around the coastal areas of England, Wales, Scotland and Northern Ireland. BIG's regional and country teams work with local stakeholders to understand the needs and issues facing each local coastal area. The teams are part of local networks and partnerships that regularly run events for groups looking for funding in these areas.

- *Case study: Brighton*

  Borders and Boundaries, funded by BIG, used photography and film to work with a small group of young vulnerable people aged 13–18 who criminally offended or were at risk of offending, who were referred through youth support agencies. The project enabled the young people to share experiences in a safe environment and learn new skills such as photography and film-making. After four months the group produced a short film that will be used as a teaching resource.

  The 10-minute film is accompanied by a short teaching resource for teachers in the subject areas of art and design, film and media studies, citizenship, health and social care and humanities. The film explores various themes relevant to young people including identity, conflict, isolation, stereotypes, communication and making choices.

- *Case study: Weston-super-Mare*

  Weston-super-Mare & District Credit Union has two service points located in Central and South wards, which are the two most deprived wards in north Somerset. The organisation services a population of approximately 16,000. It offers an outlet in the town centre and at service points throughout the area, offering a service to people disadvantaged through poor credit ratings or other factors restricting their ability to access mainstream banking facilities.

  The Money Advice Centre is a unique partnership between the Credit Union, the local Citizens Advice Bureau and the local registered social landlord North Somerset Housing. Doorstep lenders in the area had been offering £100 loans that required £165 to be paid back, while the Credit Union would charge just £6.50 on top of the initial £100. Since December 2006 when the service started, CAB advisers have helped 1031 people, and the Credit Union has given out 300 loans totalling £72,000. In addition, North Somerset Housing's rent arrears have reduced by 9 per cent and the number of people in more than £1000 worth of debt has fallen.

British Holiday & Home Parks Association

The British Holiday & Home Parks Association (BH&HPA) is the national trade body representing owners and operators of holiday, caravan and chalet parks and residential home parks in the UK. The membership owns and manages around 80 per cent of the 'on-site' pitches on the estimated 3500 licensed holiday parks in the UK – parks are geographically dispersed to the coastal and rural areas that are attractive to holidaymakers. The industry includes well-known brands, however, the majority of the businesses in the sector are SMEs or micro-enterprises, usually independently owned and managed as a family concern.

Holiday parks

Holiday parks in particular are often a significant presence in coastal communities where park owners and operators make an important contribution to their economic, social and environmental sustainability. Accommodation on BH&HPA members' parks includes holiday chalets, caravan holiday homes, lodges, touring caravans, tenting and all types of self-catering accommodation. Parks offer caravan holiday homes, lodges and chalets for letting and caravan holiday homes that are sold as second homes with a pitch that is let for an annual fee.

Over nine hundred BH&HPA member holiday parks were located within two miles of the coast in July 2009, providing 192,061 pitches for caravan holiday homes (privately owned 'second homes' or to let) , touring caravans and tents. Research data leads us to conclude that, around the UK, privately owned caravans and caravans 'to hire' contribute £1507 million annually to coastal economies.

Park facilities (such as a swimming pool or local shop) are often open to the local community, ensuring the provision of local amenities that would not otherwise be available; parks are also users of local goods and services.

Residential parks

The Association's membership also owns or manages residential parks, often known as 'Park Home Estates' or 'Mobile Home Parks' accounting for 60 per cent of residential home park pitches in the UK. There are 304 residential parks near the coast in BH&HPA membership; the 14,742 residential park homes within 5 miles of the coast house approximately 22,000 residents.

Residential parks provide the sole place of residence for park home owners who pay council tax in the usual way and live very much as part of the local community. They are predominately older residents but with some parks providing affordable accommodation for key workers.

Understanding parks' contribution to sustainable communities

The importance of parks to coastal communities is often underestimated. The accommodation provided by holiday parks is of fundamental importance to many local rural coastal economies, providing facilities that allow families drawn from across all socioeconomic groups to enjoy traditional seaside holidays at reasonable prices.

Contact: enquiries@bhhpa.org.uk www.ukparks.com

Chapter 16

The highlights, a checklist, and doing small things better

By Patrick Browne

This final section makes suggestions to improve the national coordination of coastal regeneration activity, highlights some of the main points from our diverse range of contributors and concludes with a facilitation checklist for local authorities designed for you to pepper and season with your own experiences and knowledge.

Despite the range of coastal issues debated here, and particularly: the shortages of appropriate research in many areas; the concerns about political and funding timescales and priorities, and the looming challenge of increased local authority responsibilities with decreasing resources, the dominant messages from the *handbook* are the need and desire to move from analysis to action by employing new thinking, new policy and new leadership in maximising the skills and the resources that are currently available to deliver new futures for our coastal resorts.

To support coastal regeneration practitioners in their work, the following actions are recommended:

- Recognise the problem! National and local government accept the resort "dimension" and lead on better coordination between all organisations involved in coastal regeneration.

- Government departments, GOs and RDAs to nominate and promote their coastal resort specialists.

- Government departments to participate in the workings of the XDWGCT and the RDA Coastal Network.

- Clarifying national research is required into the scale and importance of coastal tourism.

- Research is also required into the barriers, opportunities and support needs for enterprise development in coastal areas.

- Maintenance of the hughly popular SeaChange programme – the morale and partnership boosting coastal regeneration fund.

- The establishment of national topic groups on coastal leadership, management, research, education, housing, enterprise, arts and culture, worklessness, planning and demography.

- Creation of a national funded small coastal intelligence team, such as the CCA, to maintain resort momentum and to support coastal regeneration practitioners and the coastal topic groups.

- Promote the activities and membership of all coastal interest groups and networks to increase their impact and capacity and to disseminate their work.

Review the above proposals in January 2011.

This book began with the affirmation that while coastal resorts are in difficulties, these difficulties are far from being terminal and that they are very much worth preserving. However, there is a recognition that new thinking is now needed on how resorts can be regenerated for the 21C. The new thinking will require national and local leadership and strong facilitation by local government to focus and unite the coastal regeneration "industry". With diminishing resources and increasing service demands, the emphasis will be on creative partnerships, greater cooperation and cultural change.

to revitalise areas and extend effectiveness.

Despite the contribution of the SCI Coastal Towns report, many practitioners believe that greater engagement is still required and that national policy-makers need a better understand of, and engagement with, coastal delivery issues, particularly in education, enterprise, worklessness and health, and to evaluate the additional public sector costs involved in coastal delivery.

Allied to the need for greater national awareness, is the concern, even frustration, at the lack of co-ordination, and the disconnected impacts, of the many organisations with an interest in coastal regeneration. Greater outcomes could be achieved, it is argued, if the skills and resources of disparate forces were united behind agreed coastal visions. The emerging "place-shaping" role of local government creates the framework for greater integration of effort through local leadership and facilitation in coastal regeneration.

Constant themes that emerged throughout the *handbook* were the need for fresh visions on coastal resorts, for better research, for stronger leadership, for innovative partnerships and thinking, and for a more pro-actively energising approach to

established problems. These themes will re-emerge as we review the more specific points raised by our many authors, starting with regeneration.

Coastal regeneration

Conventional regeneration is not working at the seaside, there are issues around regeneration and deprivation, economic growth versus well-being, and about opportunity versus need.

Coastal regeneration based on reviving and revitalising rather than destroying and replacing, should generally be the order of the day at the British seaside. Coastal regeneration needs to be conceived in a holistic way – it is more than an economic concept - it will be successful if it maintains the positive distinctiveness of the area.....

There is the need for 'coastal' to become as established a category as 'rural' for policy purposes.

The challenge of minimising 'leakage' from the local economy and spreading the benefits of regeneration into local pockets, need consideration

Enterprise

There is a need for coastal towns to foster greater levels of innovation in enterprise development.

There is also a need for more innovation in enterprise support in coastal towns.

As elsewhere, there is a limited evidence base around the specific nature of enterprise development in coastal towns.

Without access to such evidence there is a danger that programmes are supply-led rather than demand led. Traditional forms of business support have generally failed in such areas.

Location, lack of critical masses, skills, seasonality and recruitment present a set of distinctive coastal enterprise challenges.

Heritage, Art and Culture

Strong leadership at local political level is required, allied to a specific artistic vision for an area connected with its distinctiveness, and a genuine and broad engagement process.

Regeneration practitioners should explore ways in which less expenditure-intensive approaches might be delivered by increased involvement of cultural and educational bodies.

Cultural organisations should prepare for involvement in the planning and direction of local delivery.

Health

There is a need for coastal towns to foster greater levels of innovation in enterprise development.

There is also a need for more innovation in enterprise support in coastal towns.

As elsewhere, there is a limited evidence base around the specific nature of enterprise development in coastal towns.

Without access to such evidence there is a danger that programmes are supply-led rather than demand-led. Traditional forms of business support have generally failed in such areas.

Location, lack of critical masses, skills, seasonality and recruitment present a set of distinctive coastal enterprise challenges.

Ageing Coast

Coast areas are at the forefront of demographic ageing, a trend that will become more marked in future.

Ageing is seen as a 'pensions and care' issue in the UK, with older people viewed as dependent and a growing burden on society.

Research shows that older people, including those

Local delivery agencies should rethink ways of involving cultural and educational bodies in planning and governance.

Cultural and educational projects should be encouraged to participate in local business networks.

Researching the Coast

There are shortages of appropriate research in many coastal issues, particularly tourism, enterprise and public costs.

Coastal quantitative analysis should start with the smallest units of statistical capture to maximise understanding.

Look critically and analytically at statistics and understand how, when and why they were gathered and classified.

Identify clusters or systems of coastal towns which would benefit from complementary development, and how this might work.

Access information to evidence the distinctiveness and value of

coastal assets and understand the 'informal coast' to underpin the sort of regeneration that will enliven and not sterilise.

Economic Assessment

The Economic Assessment (EA) provides LAs with the opportunity to develop a unique narrative about how their coast works.

The EA has the potential to provide a new impetus to joined-up thinking by the council and its partners,

The EA has the potential to re-energise commitments to coastal regeneration from the national tier downwards.

LAs should seize the opportunity provided by "place-shaping" and the EA to renew and refocus their direction and engage others in the coastal regeneration agenda.

Not for the shelf! This import and timely opportunity will be lost if the EA is allowed to sit on the shelf and gather dust.

approaching or over state pensionable age, want to remain economically and socially active. Demographic ageing represents a tremendous opportunity for coastal areas to develop innovative and cutting-edge products and services to deal with the trend.

Evidence suggests that older people are more successful in starting and sustaining a new business than their younger counterparts.

Planning and the Coast

There is no specific planning policy guidance on coastal regeneration.

Planning policy focuses on adaption and reshaping settlements vulnerable to sea level rises and flooding.

The Local Development Framework is the vehicle for developing locally distinctive responses to the issues affecting individual coastal resorts.

The Planning System faces challenges in providing housing and business sites in areas of flood risk or in resorts hemmed-in by cliffs, agricultural land AONBs.

Protecting and enhancing the built and natural environments are important planning services in resort areas.

These are a snap-shot of some of the issues raised in the *handbook*. To join the debate and share your coastal experiences and knowledge please contact: patrick. browne@lincolnshire.gov.uk

Big Bang! or a hundred small things better?

Much of the energy, funding and public face of regeneration is focused upon the large scale, the "iconic", the transformational. This is understandable given the hoped for outcomes from such projects, the objectives of funders, the professional or political desire to leave a mark, and the attraction of much vaunted media coverage. Yet there are only so many totemic projects, conference/hotels, angels, greenhouses, celebrity chefs and rich paternalists to go round, and not just among coastal resorts.

The less public faces of regeneration are the hundreds of small things that are done well by public and private bodies involved is some aspect of resort development and management. These include providing quality services, sprucing-up existing assets, maximising the available skills, talent and resources, engaging communities, raising local pride, and increasing ambition in small corners. This form of regeneration is probably more

relevant for many seaside resorts given their tourism popularity, their lack of access to resources and their size and location. Facilitating such outcomes is an important role for local government and this section contains a "checklist" to assess how your authority is structured for facilitating "a hundred small thing better!"

The new LA powers of place -shaping and producing an Economic Assessment (EA) can be positively employed in addressing what can be one of the barriers to coastal resort regeneration. As has been illustrated, there are many organisations whose products, services and findings impact to varying degrees on coastal areas and communities. Local authorities that harness the activities of these disparate organisations behind a clearly agreed local vision for the area can maximise diminishing resources and develop more powerful holistic solutions for resort problems. The following checklist for reviewing your facilitation role is based upon the experience of Beacon Councils in the September 2004 IDeA paper: "facilitating the development of the rural economy".

A Coastal Facilitation Checklist

LAs need to structure themselves both internally and

externally to maximise their impact on resort development. This may be more pressing in small coastal District Councils where resources, staff and direct service delivery may be limited.

Self-Assessment Checklist

1: Fit for purpose

Delivering effective facilitation in coastal areas is not an easy option. To be successful requires the necessary drive, ambition and appetite to meet the challenges. The first checklist aims to help Local Authorities consider whether they are able to deliver effective facilitation. Answering the questions will enable you to appreciate the strengths and weaknesses of the authority, and highlight areas for change.

Getting the conditions right is an important first step in being able to demonstrate to other bodies that they should work with you for mutual benefit and to deliver the vision for the area.

Effective Leadership.

The delivery and effectiveness of LAs are maximised when underpinned by focussed political leadership and clear, well understood management objectives. When this leadership approach is coupled with a commitment to supporting coastal regeneration, it empowers and gives confidence to local authority management at all levels. It also provides a strategic direction which can bring partners together and provide a focus for joint working. Relationships rely upon mutual trust built from a commitment to follow through

on promises. Sometimes this may mean accepting a level of calculated risk (both material and perceived) with which local government is often uncomfortable, and that may lead to failure. Progressive coastal LAs highlight the importance of the following:

Political leadership that signals clear priorities and style for the authority.

Political 'management' between elected members from different political parties that was driven by pragmatism and a consensual view about the needs of the area.

Positive relationships between elected members and officers offering a dynamic management interaction.

Self-assessment questions.

How has the Council demonstrated that it is committed to supporting coastal delivery?	*Is the commitment reflected in the Corporate Objectives?*	*Do political leaders and chief officers accept that they will need to take some calculated risks and are they willing to do so?*

2. Enabling management

'Enabling management' is characterised by a management style that gives freedom and responsibility, and fosters

initiative. The management culture within a LA will offer sufficient autonomy to all stakeholders (both within and outside the council) to allow relationships to thrive.

Roles and responsibilities will be allocated based on a clear understanding of objectives and resources. The focus is on achieving successful delivery and using resources flexibly, making changes to traditional structures and practices if it is necessary to do so. An enabling management structure is one which is prepared to back colleagues if things go wrong.

A 'can do' culture gives confidence to local authority management at all levels. Where external partners look for a strategic direction it can bring partners together and provide a focus for joint working.

'Enabling management' can: Clarify operational objectives for the authority and what is expected of its staff in order to achieve them.

Secure sufficient resources to give facilitation an effective critical mass.

Establish management protocols that exemplify the approach to calculated risk taking and decision making.

Have the confidence to step back and let others take the lead.

Achieve a planning process and communication mechanism that is inclusive.

When these conditions come together the capacity to get things done is considerable.

Self-assessment questions.

How many 'business units' in the Local Authority are involved in coastal service delivery?

Is there mutual trust between the 'unit' managers, and lead Members?

Is there a commitment to work together? Are communications between managers and lead Members frequent and open?

Are structural changes necessary to bring the

relevant business units closer together?

Does the management style enable and empower staff to deliver the coastal development objectives?

3. Resource generating

An ability to find the resources, internally or externally.

Leadership and management need to be backed up by the resources necessary to do the job. Effective facilitation requires officer time and other technical resources. These may be available from a variety of departments within the authority e.g. planning,

construction management, finance and IT.

Having the right people in the right places is a key to success. Facilitation has worked well where there has been a strong officer commitment, and this attitude appears to be self-generating as like-minded people are attracted to posts within such organisations.

A 'can do' culture is of significant value when seeking out and securing resources. Proactive councils demonstrate a willingness to approach the resourcing of activity in a creative way. This may be an internal commitment to funding valuable posts, or lateral thinking prompting access to funding programmes that might not immediately seem appropriate.

This commitment is also evident in a council's approach to the management of its own human and technical resources.

Successful facilitators offer access to these resources to local delivery groups in order to get things done, but also to

increase the value of a project and so maximise the cash element in funding.

Self-assessment questions.

Have the corporate objectives led to a prioritisation of council resources for coastal facilitation?

Do the council staff have the skills and knowledge to access external resources?

Is there a willingness to learn from other authorities and partnerships?

4. Oil the wheels of participation

A willingness to develop delivery capacity.

Facilitation of coastal regeneration is all about enabling delivery by the local community (in whatever form that might take). To do this successfully and achieve disproportionate outputs relative to available resources requires a real commitment to engage with external organisations, groups and networks. Engagement and consultation is the first step to identifying those individuals and groups who can play a more substantial role in delivery.

Effective local authorities recognise that constraints on resources, coupled with

responsibility for delivery of core services, mean that often they cannot realistically deliver everything themselves. They must instead identify the most effective delivery vehicle, support its development, build the necessary capacity and then facilitate its delivery activities. Only in this way can local projects be fully sustainable, and enjoy a life span that extends beyond any immediate funding programme.

Councils have developed delivery capacity through:

- Learning about local distinctiveness and understanding the issues from a local and regional perspective.
- Reflecting back local expectations and priorities into local and regional plans.

- Supporting the development of autonomous delivery bodies.
- Aligning expectations with regional strategy, and proposals with policy. Plans developed by local groups need to be consistent with the wider programme context to gain support.
- Supporting and enabling – helping with funding applications, recruitment, administration and personnel management.
- Making connections – for example with the work being done at other local authority levels.
- Sharing resource – using the resources (human, technical and physical) of the council to add value to projects and project delivery.

Self-assessment questions.

*Is there a willingness
to build real working
relationships with local
communities, businesses,
voluntary and community
groups?*

*What evidence is there
that the Authority is*

*focussed on the customer?
Does the ethos of the
Council put customers
at the centre of service
delivery?*

*Are there plans in place
to get feedback from
customers?*

*In two tier areas, do
working partnerships
exist between the County
and District to support
local delivery groups?*

. Make friends

A commitment to break down
barriers to partnership working.

Where resources and
capacity are thinly spread a
commitment to partnership
working has been an essential
pre-requisite to successful
facilitation. Whether through
local Strategic Partnerships/
local Area Agreements or
through specific regeneration
partnerships, good facilitation is
characterised by real working
relationships that extend
beyond the superficial. They
will challenge organisational
boundaries and methods of
working to break down cultural
barriers.

Successful facilitation strikes a
balance between the strategic
and local through pragmatic,
effective partnership. The key
to achieving this is establishing
a representative partnership
and ensuring effective
communications between
partners. Strategic partnerships
should include regional bodies
wherever possible. This
ensures that the coastal agenda
maintains a voice in regional and
national policy making, and that
local strategies remain relevant.

The SNR and the Framework
for Regeneration processes
are focusing regeneration and
economic development on
the local delivery level and it
will therefore be increasingly
important that all 'business
units' of a Council are working
together and moving in the
same direction.

Self-assessment questions.

*Would statutory and
non-statutory partners
agree that the Council is
committed to collaborative
partnership working?
How do you know?*

*Are economic, social and
environmental issues
all taken into account
through one partnership
structure?*

*Do changes need to
be made to current
structures to ensure that
all the key players are
represented?*

If the partnership is not the LSP, does it dovetail with the LSP structures?

What role does the Council play in supporting the partnership?

Is the partnership set up in such a way that it can ensure there is a link between local delivery organisations and the main partnership representatives?

Checklist 2: How to facilitate coastal delivery

Local Authorities can rate their leadership and delivery capacity using the second checklist. Applying 'effective leadership' and 'enabling management' will lead to a focus on the customer, working through partnerships. Delivery can be assessed by examining the resources, skills and quality of provision.

1. Going interactive

Engaging local communities, listening to customers.

If where facilitation has been most successful there has been a commitment to building long-term engagement with coastal communities. A continuing dialogue enables local people to see the decision-making and investment as legitimate. Consulting communities regularly builds confidence and thus the process strengthens effective governance.

Engaging communities can be time consuming and resource hungry and will be quickly seen through if it is in any way token. Nevertheless effective engagement can be done on a relatively modest scale by supporting communities to take the lead.

Listening to customers can be measured by the tangible difference made to the actions that are planned and implemented. The engagement process should take the opportunity to add value to proposals, and develop greater ownership and responsibility.

Self-assessment questions.

How successful are you in building long term engagement? Does the public trust the process?

How effective is your use of consultation to influence the planning and delivery of services? Are there examples of feedback being used to change service delivery?

Are you effective at communicating the results of consultation? Are you really reaching a groups of the population?

2. Policy development and reviewing strategies.

Local Authorities have an important role to play in enabling the partnership to develop a Strategy or Action Plan to guide their work. Local strategies will need to be in line with regional plans, if they are going to attract external resources. There will increasingly be a requirement to ensure that plans are consistent with the sustainable development framework. A broad based partnership will be able to link economic, social and environmental plans and policies.

Successful facilitation strikes the balance between the strategic and local through pragmatic partnership. Establishing the right representation and ensuring effective communications between partners is key to achieving this. Local authorities have the knowledge, drawn in many cases from their statutory responsibilities and dedicated resources, to understand conditions at the local scale. They can use the EA to help all stakeholders build a shared understanding of local issues. Furthermore, the Council can demonstrate its leadership through aligning its own plans and actions with that of the partnership.

Some LAs consider that their entire area is a coastal economy, and have subsequently aligned their Corporate Plan with the Strategy or Action Plan prepared by the local partnership. Others have focused on a set of actions and objectives as the priority and have set out to deliver activity on the ground that will support the core objective (e.g. job creation).

Self-assessment questions.

What is your understanding of and involvement in regional plans, and plans of stakeholders?

What are your skills to facilitate the development of a shared vision, involving partners and the local community?

What is your dedication to the local economy? Are the authority's own functions focused on finding new ways of realising coastal revival?

What is your experience of using local intelligence to develop strategies? Are there examples of innovative solutions to local problems?

3. Servicing the partnership

Partnerships are essential in the activities of many LAs, and not least in resort regeneration where there are extensive internal and external delivery organisations. Delivering coastal regeneration increasingly relies upon the resources of a wide range of organisations operating locally, regionally or nationally. LAs have been responsible for bringing those organisations together into mutually reinforcing partnerships. In so doing, LAs have provided strategic direction without necessarily having to lead, have developed local sensitivity for delivery of mainstream services, and ensured maximum access to competitive funding regimes.

Local Authorities do not have to lead partnerships or be seen to dominate their activities.

Nevertheless it is important to support the organisation through guidance and administration. Membership criteria and the roles of members are often set out in a written constitution or other form of agreement.

Servicing the partnership will include:

- organising meetings and maintaining records,
- enabling members to network and share information
- encouraging all stakeholders to take part
- managing sensitivities between partners
- providing training and development to enable all partners to contribute fully

to the partnership
- communicating activities and successes to the partnership
- creating links with other relevant strategic and community partnerships

Self-assessment questions.

What is your resource availability to guide and administer the partnership?

Can you support the structure long term?

What is your understanding of the responsibilities, history and aspirations of members?

What is your ability to communicate and network

with members on a continuing basis?

Is your support for the partnership through sound procedures and administration? Is accountability clear?

4. Building local voluntary and community capacity.

Successful facilitation organisations achieve greater value for money when projects are delivered jointly with other delivery agencies. These agencies may be official bodies (e.g. GOs, RDAs), a local forum (e.g. town centre partnership, residents group or chamber of trade), or a community group dealing with one issue (e.g. after school club, local charity or trust). The capacity of these partners to deliver will

substantively influence value for money.

A vital pre-requisite is to apply the 'can do' culture and encourage the delivery organisation to do the same. One committed officer spending a few hours a week supporting a specific project can make a great deal of difference. Similarly, investment in developing a local champion can go a long way towards developing the capacity of a community.

Aspects of building delivery capacity include

- initiating new forums and action groups, and supporting local champions
- assisting groups to identify their needs and priorities, and understand options for change
- encourage commitment and involvement
- brokering joint working between groups

What is your commitment to deliver through voluntary and community organisations? Are you ready to work alongside volunteers? Are grants available for administration?

What is your capacity building skills to enable groups to hone their own priorities? Are delivery bodies encouraged to lead?

Have you expertise to work with all target groups, including the least affluent or articulate? Are there examples of connecting with hard-to-reach-groups in your area?

Accessing and managing fund

Local authorities can make a significant contribution to financial management through the facilitation process. Councils have financial procedures and systems in place and valuable expertise, for example, tendering, accountable body. The capacity to run projects through local authority accounts and make use of technical expertise can be essential to a project's success. The authority needs to remember, however, that it is managing the funds on behalf of the project partners. Whilst in some cases it may legally own the assets, in other cases it will not, and in all cases it does not 'own' the project.

Accessing and managing funds will include

- making applications for programme funds which can be distributed locally to projects, including carrying out the administrative role of accountable body
- advising on or carrying out tendering
- bankrolling projects either by managing activities through the Council's financial systems or by loans which are repaid once grants are received
- making use of external funds to employ project staff
- using internal mainstream funds to support projects and develop assets

What is your knowledge of funding programmes and success in making bids? Have external funds been used to support development officers?

What is your finance departments'

preparedness to manage project accounts? Can they produce the right information to meet claim, monitoring and audit requirements?

What is your willingness to take on lease, purchase and tendering tasks? Would the Council do this even if it didn't own the asset?

What is your readiness to bankroll or make loans to community-led projects?

6. Organisation, delivery and project implementation

Extending the delivery capacity of partner organisations ranges from something that can add value to particular projects to being absolutely fundamental to a facilitation organisation's chances of success. Very often the relationship that emerges between council officers and local groups is one of mutual respect and moral commitment. This is especially true in rural coastal areas, and where elected members take an active part and support the officers within the Council.

Developing community groups can be a substantial commitment, and is by nature a long-term investment. However, it is very often directly aligned with the council's obligations to deliver core services, and is necessary to inform the development of a valid Community Strategy.

Facilitating project delivery will ensure that the local group understand that the responsibility for action and delivery lies with them. Continuing guidance and support may be required on:

- administration and financial management
- grant claims and how to collect monitoring information
- sharing knowledge of exemplar projects
- training and development
- building or project management

Practical assistance may be given through grants for administration, arranging training, enabling groups to make use of external funding streams, and commitment of officer time to carry out specific tasks. Facilitating LAs have understood that the better equipped their delivery partners, the greater and more sustainable the outputs and return on investment.

Self-assessment questions.

How does the council deals with setbacks and finds solutions when problems arise with project implementation?

What is staff availability and expertise to work with communities?

What is your experience of development training for the voluntary and community sector? Are you aware of national and regional bodies or local experts with this capability?

What is in two-tier areas your willingness to work in partnership to maximise the strength of both?

What is Member understanding and enthusiasm for facilitating coastal delivery?

Is there partnership commitment in all the business units of the authority?

7. Local planning and resource management

Councils will need to keep an overview of projects, internal resources and funding to ensure that expectations can be fulfilled. It is inevitable when a local authority formally engages with a local community that expectations can be raised. It is therefore important that capacity is extended in a manner that scopes and manages expectations. Failure to grasp this nettle will lead to a mutual lack of respect and can materially prejudice local capacity to deliver.

Authorities may need to reallocate resources if the regional or local partnership strategies change. Delivery bodies may need specific support through transition periods. Exit strategies need to be in place to manage time-limited external funding. Similarly, authorities can keep a lookout for new funding opportunities which will help to meet identified needs. Councils can bring them to the attention of the local partnership and delivery bodies and make speculative applications on their behalf.

Self-assessment questions.

What resources available to continue to support existing and planned activities? What are the risks associated with the availability of staff time, technical support and money?

What is your reliance upon time limited external funding? What measures are in place to ensure a smooth transition to sustainability?

What are your abilities to spot and take advantage of new funding or other resource opportunities exist? What examples are there in the authority?

8. Monitoring and evaluation frameworks, maintaining an evidence base

Effective evaluation and monitoring is a key part of successful facilitation. It informs policy and prioritisation, and demonstrates what has been achieved. An effective monitoring framework

measures progress against objectives and outcomes
measures the impact of actions

- assesses how efficient service delivery has been
- demonstrates what has changed to external bodies, funders and the local community
- benchmarks activities against other areas and initiatives.

The consistent use of accessible and relevant indicators, rather than reliance on 'high-level' themes which may be more appropriate to an urban area, provides a clearer picture of the outcomes of activity. Even when recorded at ward level,

'traditional' indicators can give a distorted picture; negligible unemployment rates can mask a very low wage and seasonal economy, high property values and levels of car ownership might obscure a local problem of access to affordable homes and limited public transport. Local measures provide a hard currency to inform partners and stakeholders.

Self-assessment questions.

What is your understanding of the local economy? Is there a set of local indicators that are relevant to the Strategy or Action Plan of the partnership?

What are your processes to monitor the outcomes of individual projects?

What are your skills in interpreting and presenting the information to local partners and the community?

What is your experience of sharing information and benchmarking with similar organisations? Can you access expert advice from a local

Research Observatory? Are they part of the partnership?

What are your processes to provide feedback and measurement of the experience and perceptions of customers and stakeholders?

Perceptions of the host community in respect of the socio-cultural effects of Casino Gambling in a Mediterranean coastal setting: the Case of Kyrenia, Turkish Republic of North Cyprus (TRNC).

Habib Alipour and Edwin M. Vughaingmeh Eastern Mediterranean University, Turkey

This study is an investigation of the perception of a host community in respect of the social and cultural impacts of casino gambling in the major tourist destination of Northern Cyprus, and which represents a vital source of income and employment for the area. The study is also an evaluation of this perception within the context of 'tourism-host community' interaction in respect of the general theory of community participation in the decisionmaking process. To achieve this aim, a survey questionnaire was applied to collect data from the Kyrenia district (the main venue for casino gambling activities) in Northern Cyprus (TRNC). The questionnaires were analyzed in order to access: (1) the general attitude towards casino gambling, (2) to identify the social and cultural impacts of casino gambling on local residents, (3) to identify community concerns about the presence of casinos in their community, and (4) to develop a profile of respondents in respect of their attitude towards gambling behavior. Findings indicated that the respondents had a negative attitude towards casino gambling. The socio-cultural impacts that were cited most frequently were crime and domestic violence, prostitution, threat to the traditional way of life, social values, diminishing the historic, aesthetic value of Kyrenia town, and threatening the basis of family structure and life. Findings also revealed that tourism planners and developers need to be aware of the perceptions of the community and of actively encouraging their involvement in the any decision-making processes, connected to exposing and subjecting their environment to specific types of tourismparticularly e.g. gambling. In respect of the city's coastal zones, many casinos have been planted on the coastal environment where numerous ecological issues can be raised regarding the impact of the casinos on the health and sustainability of the coastal areas. Study revealed that there is no integrated coastal zone management (ICZM) in place which 'emphasizes the integration of systems, co-ordination of policies and institutions, management concerns, development objectives and stakeholder interests across the different landscapes of the coastal zone' (Hope and Lekorwe, 1999 : 853). The community's concern in this respect was, at best, the lack of awareness regarding this issue.

further information on this paper, please visit: www.tourism-culture.com

The sharing of indicators and performance information between coastal resort councils can provide both benchmarking and performance data for the purposes of continuous improvement. Intelligence is shared through partnerships, member and officer networking and attendance at national and regional training and conference events. Also, coastal experience shows that speaking to the customer and getting a first-hand view of delivery at regular intervals can

be a more powerful form of evaluation than hard statistics.

While still scouring the horizon of hope for the Big Bang solution, much can be achieved in coastal resort regeneration by doing a hundred small things better. You can start that process now by joining our virtual topic groups and sharing your expertise, concerns and ideas with you fellow coastal regeneration practitioners.

Not THE END

This is the end of the *handbook* but not the end of the coastal regeneration debate which will continue on the CCA website where an electronic version of this publication now resides. If you wish to share your facilitation checklist (above) and/or the earlier "Barriers, opportunities and priorities" questionnaire (page 49) with other coastal areas via the website, please send to: patrick. browne@lincolnshire.gov.uk

Notes to the
chapters

Notes to the Introduction

1. Helen Carter and Steven Morris, 'Home and away in "staycation" UK', *The Guardian*, 18 July 2009, p. 11.

2. Peter Walker, 'Better off at home – era of the "staycation" dawns as Britons abandon foreign holidays', *The Guardian*, 14 August 2009, p. 3.

3. Laura Barton, 'Barton's Britain: Skegness', *Guardian G2*, 7 April 2009, p. 5.

4. Mary O'Hara, 'Weathering the storm', *The Guardian*, 12 September 2007.

5. '"When it's sunny it's glorious": the reality of holidays in Britain', *Guardian G2*, 18 August 2008.

6. John K. Walton, *The British Seaside: Holidays and Resorts in the Twentieth Century* (Manchester University Press, 2000), ch. 1.

7. BBC2: *Coast*, series 4, programme 5, 'Anglesey to Blackpool', first broadcast 11 August 2009.

8. John K. Walton and Jason Wood, 'Reputation and regeneration: history and the heritage of the recent past in the re-making of Blackpool', in L. Gibson and J. Pendlebury (eds), *Valuing Historic Environments* (Aldershot: Ashgate, 2009), pp. 115–37.

9. J. Demetriadi, 'The Golden Years', in A. Williams and G. Shaw (eds), *The Rise and Fall of British Coastal Resorts* (London: Cassell, 1997), ch. 5.

10. C. Beatty and S. Fothergill, *The Seaside Economy: the Final Report of the Seaside Towns Research Project* (Sheffield Hallam University: CRESC, 2003).

11. John K. Walton, 'Whitby: une station balnéaire, du XVIIIe au XXe siecle' [Whitby: a seaside resort from the eighteenth to the twentieth century], in Y. Perret-Gentil, A. Lottin and J.-P. Poussu (eds), *Les villes balnéaires d'Europe occidentale du XVIIIe siecle a nos jours* (Paris: Presses de l'Université Paris-Sorbonne, 2008), pp. 233–59. English language text available from the author.

12. John K. Walton, 'Seaside resorts and maritime history', *International Journal of Maritime History 9* (1997), pp. 125–47.

13. Select Committee of the Office of the Deputy Prime Minister: Housing, Local Government, Planning and the Regions, *Coastal Towns*, Minutes of Evidence, Annexe 1, memorandum by David Lloyd, 18 April 2006.

14. *Report of the Select Committee on ... Coastal Towns* (London: The Stationery Office, March 2007).

15. Lincolnshire Coastal Action Zone: *National Coastal Futures*, Report of Symposium at the Royal Renaissance Hotel, Skegness, 18–19 July 2006.

16. *Government Response to the Communities and Local Government Committee Report on Coastal Towns* (London: The Stationery Office, May 2007).

17. House of Commons, Communities and Local Government Select Committee on Coastal Towns: the Government's Second Response. First Report of Session 2007–8 (London: The Stationery Office, November 2007).

18. M. Parkinson et al., *The Credit Crunch and Regeneration* (Department for Communities and Local Government, 30 January 2009).

19. A. Brodie and G. Winter, *England's Seaside Resorts* (Swindon: English Heritage, 2007).

20. Fred Gray, *Designing the Seaside* (London: Reaktion, 2006). For more work in this vein, see John K. Walton, 'Architecture, history, heritage, and identity: built environment, urban form and historical

context at the seaside', *International Journal of Regional and Local Studies*, Series 2, 3 (2007), pp. 65–79.

21. Tom Dyckhoff, 'Let's move to ... Eastbourne', *Guardian Weekend*, 25 July 2008, p. 63.

22. Report of the Casino Advisory Panel, 30 January 2007, p. 31. For a historical perspective on 'redevelopment' and 'urban renewal' from the vantage point of the early 1980s, see M. S. Gibson and M.J. Langstaff, *An Introduction to Urban Renewal* (London: Hutchinson, 1982).

23. David R. Green to Lincolnshire County Council, 11 August 2009.

24. European Parliament, A6-0442/2008, *Report on the Regional Development Aspects of the Impact of Tourism on Coastal Regions* (2008/2132 INI), 12 November 2008.

25. See also European Parliament, Policy Department B: Structural and Cohesion Policies, *The Impact of Tourism on Coastal Areas: Regional Development Aspects*, PE.397.260, IP/B/REGI?IC/2006-166-Lot 01-C03-SC01, 15 April 2008.

Notes to Chapter 1

1. For 'Fordism', see for example Waleed Hazbun, Beaches, Ruins, Resorts (Minneapolis: Minnesota University Press, 2008), ch. 1 and p. 243, note 7. For a case study of the individuality of a 'Fordist' resort, see Charles Wilson, *Benidorm: the Truth* (Comunitat de Valencia, 1999).

2. J. Urry, 'Cultural change and the seaside resort', in G. Shaw and A. Williams (eds), The Rise and Fall of British Coastal Resorts (London: Cassell, 1997), pp. 102–13.

3. John K. Walton, *The English Seaside Resort: a Social History 1750–1914* (Leicester University Press, 1983); also The British Seaside: *Holidays and Resorts in the Twentieth Century* (Manchester University Press, 2000).

4. Xing Ruan and Paul Hogben (eds), *Topophilia and Topophobia: Reflections on Twentieth Century Human Habitat* (London: Routledge, 2007).

5. See also C. Beatty, S. Fothergill and I. Wilson (for DCLG), *England's Seaside Towns: a Benchmarking Study*, Department of Communities and Local Government, 3 November 2008.

6. Fred Gray, 'Folkestone in context: a briefing paper on seaside towns, for the Creative Foundation, Folkestone', University of Sussex, April 2008, pp. 14–17.

7. *Ibid.*, p. 11.

8. Colin Ward and Dennis Hardy, *Arcadia for All* (London: Mansell, 1984).

9. Fred Gray, *Designing the Seaside* (London: Reaktion, 2006).

10. John K. Walton, *The English Seaside Resort* (note 3), pp. 54–69. See also J. K. Walton, 'The seaside resorts of England and Wales, 1900–1950: growth, diffusion and the emergence of new forms of coastal tourism', in A. Williams and G. Shaw (eds), The Rise and Fall of British Coastal Resorts (London: Cassell, 1997), pp. 21–48.

11. *Seaside Watering Places* (London: L. Upcott Gill, 5th edn, 1885).

12. Maurice Hope, *Castles in the Sand: the Story of New Brighton* (Ormskirk: Hesketh, 1982). Harry Cameron is working on the fate of post-war New Brighton for a PhD thesis at Leeds Metropolitan University.

13. For 'rurban', see (e.g.) M. Pacione, *Urban Geography: a Global Perspective* (London: Routledge, 2001), ch. 30. See also Colin Pooley, 'Mobility in the twentieth century: substituting commuting for migration?',

in D. Gilbert, D. Matless and B. Short (eds), *Geographies of British Modernity* (Oxford: Blackwell, 2003), ch. 4.

14. Office of National Statistics, *A Review of Urban and Rural Area Definitions: Project Report*, August 2001, pp. 14–15 and Table 2.1.

15. For what follows, see especially C. Beatty *et al.* (note 5).

16. Torquay and Ilfracombe are compared historically in N. Morgan and A. Pritchard, *Power and Politics at the Seaside* (University of Exeter Press, 1999).

17. John K. Walton, *Blackpool* (Edinburgh University Press, 1998).

18. C. Beatty and S. Fothergill, *The Seaside Economy: the Final Report of the Seaside Towns Research Project* (Sheffield Hallam University: CRESC, 2003), p. 16.

19. For a historical context, see Laura Chase, *The Creation of Place Image in Inter-war Clacton and Frinton*, PhD thesis, University of Essex, 1999.

20. Ian Carter, *Railways and Culture in Britain* (Manchester University Press, 2001); Alastair J. Durie, *Scotland for the Holidays: a History of Tourism in Scotland, 1780–1939* (East Linton: Tuckwell Press, 2003).

21. Kathryn Ferry, *Beach Huts and Bathing Machines* (Oxford: Shire Publications, 2009); Laura Chase, 'Public beaches and private beach huts: a case study of inter-war Clacton and Frinton, Essex', in John K. Walton (ed.), *Histories of Tourism: Representation, Identity and Conflict* (Clevedon: Channel View, 2005), pp. 211–27.

22. John K. Walton, *The British Seaside: Holidays and Resorts in the Twentieth Century* (Manchester University Press, 2000), pp. 1–3; Bill Bryson, Notes from a Small Island (London, 1995), pp. 124–5.

23. See above, notes 5 and 11; also Steve Fothergill, *England's Coastal Towns*, report for NCRA panel, 2008.

24. John K. Walton, 'Marketing the imagined past: Captain Cook and cultural tourism in North Yorkshire', in Rhodri Thomas (ed.), *Managing Regional Tourism: a Case Study of Yorkshire, England* (Ilkley: Great Northern Books, 2009), pp. 220–32.

25. *Whitby Gazette*, 12 May 2006, 12 June 2007 and 24 April 2008; Catherine Mack, 'Checking in: La Rosa Hotel, Whitby', *The Observer*, 11 January 2009.

26. Steve Fothergill, *England's Coastal Towns*, report for NCRA panel, 2008.

27. John K. Walton, 'Whitby: une station balnéaire, du XVIIIe au XXe siecle' [Whitby: a seaside resort from the eighteenth to the twentieth century], in Y. Perret-Gentil, A. Lottin and J.-P. Poussu (eds), *Les villes balnéaires d'Europe occidentale du XVIIIe siecle a nos jours* (Paris: Presses de l'Université Paris-Sorbonne, 2008), pp. 233–59. An English language version is available from the author.

28. John K. Walton and Jason Wood, 'Reputation and regeneration: history and the heritage of the recent past in the re-making of Blackpool', in L. Gibson and J. Pendlebury (eds), *Valuing Historic Environments* (Aldershot: Ashgate, 2009), pp. 115–37.

29. Lynn F. Pearson, *The People's Palaces: Seaside Pleasure Buildings 1870–1914* (Barracuda, 1991); also *Piers and Other Seaside Architecture* (Oxford: Shire Publications, 2nd edn, 2008).

30. Janet L. Smith, *Liquid Assets: the Lidos and Swimming Pools of Britain* (Swindon: English Heritage, 2005).

31. Anna Minton, Ground Control: *Fear and Happiness in the Twenty-first Century City* (Penguin, 2009); Jonathan Glancey, 'Cities of the damned', *Guardian Review*, 1 August 2009, p. 7.

32. John K. Walton, *Tourism, Fishing and Redevelopment: Post-war Whitby, 1945–*

1970 (Cambridge: Wolfson Lectures, 2005).

33. J. Urry, 'Cultural change and contemporary holiday-making', *Theory, Culture and Society* 5 (1988), p. 44; J. Bale, *Landscapes of Modern Sport* (Leicester University Press, 1994).

34. John K. Walton, 'Tourism and architectural heritage in context: Whitby, North Yorkshire', *The Georgian*, autumn/winter 2004.

35. K. Lindley, *Seaside Architecture* (London: Hugh Evelyn, 1973), p. 19; R. Shields, *Places on the Margin* (London: Routledge, 1991).

36. Fred Gray, 'Folkestone in context' (note 6), p. 18.

37. K. Lindley, *Seaside Architecture* (note 35), pp. 23–6; J. K. Walton, 'Blackpool and the varieties of Britishness', in S. A. Caunce, E. Mazierska, S. E. Sydney-Smith and J. K. Walton (eds), *Relocating Britishness* (Manchester University Press, 2004).

38. R. Butler (ed.), *The Tourism Area Life Cycle* (Clevedon: Channel View, 2006), 2 vols.

39. John K. Walton, *The Blackpool Landlady: a Social History* (Manchester University Press, 1978); also *The English Seaside Resort* (note 3), ch. 4; *The British Seaside* (note 3), chs 5 and 6.

40. John A. Hassan, The Seaside, *Health and Environment in Britain since 1800* (Aldershot: Ashgate, 2003).

Notes to Chapter 4

1. This chapter is in broad agreement with the recent English Heritage report on *Regeneration in Historic Coastal Towns*, which should ideally be read in conjunction with it: www.helm.org.uk/upload/pdf/Coastal-Regeneration.pdf (accessed 13 December 2009).

2. Andrew Tallon, *Urban Regeneration in the United Kingdom* (London: Routledge, 2009).

3. T. Edmans and G. Tarifa, *The Regeneration Maze* (London: King's Fund, 2001).

4. L. Porter and K. Shaw (eds), *Whose Urban Renaissance? An International Comparison of Urban Regeneration Strategies* (Abingdon: Routledge, 2009).

5. See (e.g.) Y. Perret-Gentil, A. Lottin and J.-P. Poussu (eds), *Les villes balnéaires d'Europe occidentale du XVIIIe siecle a nos jours* (Paris: Presses de l'Université Paris-Sorbonne, 2008); B. Simon, *Boardwalk of Dreams: Atlantic City and the Fate of Urban America* (New York: Oxford University Press, 2004); C. Wilson, *Benidorm: the Truth* (Valencia: Comunitat de Valencia, 1999); V. Balducci and S. Bica, *Architecture and Society of the Holiday Camps: History and Perspectives* (Timisoara: Editura Orizonturi Universitare, 2007); V. Orioli, *Cesenatico: Turismo Balneare tra Otto e Novecento* (Firenze: Alinea, 2008); M. B. Stofik, *Saving South Beach* (Gainesville: University of Florida Press, 2005).

6. Neil Lee, *Distinctiveness and Cities: Beyond 'Find and Replace' Economic Development* (The Work Foundation, October 2007).

7. J. Karn, *Narratives of Neglect: Community, Regeneration and the Governance of Security* (Cullompton: Willan, 2007).

8. The practical, continuing importance of seasonality in coastal economies, which is emphasised elsewhere, is underlined by Ray Drury of the Prince's Trust, who points out the difficulties it generates for start-up businesses, which need to do well enough in their first summer to survive the lean months that follow: Ray Drury to Patrick Browne, 29 October 2009.

9. R. Paddison and S. Miles (eds), *Culture-led Urban Regeneration* (London: Routledge, 2006), especially chapters by Miles and García.

10. John K. Walton, *The British Seaside: Holidays and Resorts in the Twentieth Century* (Manchester University Press, 2000), ch. 7; also *The English Seaside Resort: a Social History 1750–1914* (Leicester University Press, 1983), ch. 6; N. Morgan and A. Pritchard, *Power and Politics at the Seaside* (University of Exeter Press, 1983).

11. M. Gottdiener, *The Decline of Urban Politics: Political Theory and the Crisis of the Local State* (London: Sage, 1987).

12. M. Loughlin, M. D. Gelfand and K. Young (eds), *Half a Century of Municipal Decline, 1935–1985* (London: George Allen & Unwin, 1985); Tony Travers, *The Decline and Fall of Local Democracy: a History of Local Government Finance* (London: Policy Exchange, 2003).

13. Tom Symons and Chris Leslie, *Capital Contingencies: Local Capital Finance in an Era of High Public Debt* (New Local Government Network, 2009).

14. Mark Smulian, 'The future of funding: regeneration and renewal', 12 September 2009.

15. www.blackpoolgazette.co.uk/blackpoolnews/Council-to-buy-Tower-and.5880226.jp (accessed 13 December 2009); and www.dailymail.co.uk/news/article-1232990/Blackpool-Tower-nationalised (accessed 13 December 2009).

16. John K. Walton, 'Municipal government and the holiday industry in Blackpool, 1876–1914', and R. Roberts, 'The corporation as impresario: the municipal provision of entertainment in Victorian and Edwardian Bournemouth', in J. K. Walton and J. Walvin (eds), *Leisure in Britain, 1780–1939* (Manchester University Press, 1983), pp. 158–85 and 137–57.

17. *Reinvent Europe through Innovation*, Report of the Business Panel on Future European Union Innovation Policy.

18. Cahal Milmo, 'How the battle of Whitstable became a struggle for the soul of seaside resorts', *The Independent*, 15 October 2007; also see www.handsoffourharbour.co.uk (accessed 5 November 2009).

19. Richard Samuel, chapter 5 in this *Handbook*.

20. 'Screening will show how much Thanet has lost', *Thanet Star*, 30 October 2009 (http://thanetstar.com, accessed 31 October 2009).

21. Jason Wood, 'From port to resort: art, heritage and identity in the regeneration of Margate', in P. Borsay and J. K. Walton (eds), *Resorts and Ports: European Seaside Towns since 1700* (Bristol: Channel View, forthcoming 2010).

22. Nick Evans, *Dreamland Remembered* (Whitstable, 2003).

23. J. F. Porter, 'Arlington House: eyesore or icon', *Margate Civic Society Newsletter* 342, spring 2006, p. 2.

24. V. Orioli, *Cesenatico: Turismo Balneare tra Otto e Novecento* (Florence: Alinea, 2008).

25. Gibson and Pendlebury (eds), *Valuing Historic Environments*.

26. Ann E. Murphy, *Strategic Management for Tourism Communities* (Clevedon: Channel View, 2004), p. 149.

27. *Exmouth Journal*, 30 March 2005; also visit www.exmouthtownmanagement.co.uk (accessed 5 November 2009). Thanet's Westwood Cross shopping mall also illustrates some relevant problems: http://thanetstar.com/article/thanet-s-reaction-to-westwood-cross (accessed 31 October 2009).

28. Hastings, article in Chapter 5 in this *Handbook*.

29. Rachel Cooke, 'Bugger Broadstars for another holiday', and 'Can art put new heart into our seaside towns?', *The Observer*, 9 and 16 August 2009.

Notes to Chapter 6

1. Regeneris Consulting, *LEGI: National Baseline and Evaluation Feasibility – Scoping Report* (Regeneris Consulting, London and Manchester, 2007).
2. S. Fothergill, 'England's coastal towns: a short review of the issues, evidence base and research needs', paper for the NCRA Panel, CRESR, Sheffield Hallam University, 2008.
3. R. J. Bennett, 'Government and small business', in S. Carter and D. J. Jones-Evans (eds), *Enterprise and Small Business: Principles, Policy and Practice* (Harlow: FT/ Prentice–Hall, 2006).
4. See note 1.
5. S. Fothergill, *England's Seaside Towns: a Benchmarking Study* (CRESR, Sheffield Hallam University, 2009).
6. F. J. Greene, K. Mole and D. J. Storey, *Three Decades of Enterprise Culture? Entrepreneurship, Economic Regeneration and Public Policy* (London: Palgrave Macmillan, 2007).
7. Shared Intelligence. *What Future for England's Struggling Seaside Towns?* Si Policy Roundtable (London: Shared Intelligence, 2008).
8. Chitty; see also www.enterprisegrowth. co.uk.
9. Scarborough Renaissance Partnership, European Enterprise Awards – Entry Form (London: BERR, 2008).
10. F. J. Greene, K. Mole and D. J. Storey, 'Does more mean worse? Three decades of enterprise policy in the Tees Valley', Urban Studies 41 (2004), pp. 1207–28.
11. HM Treasury (with the Small Business Service and Office for the Deputy Minister), *Enterprise and Economic Opportunity in Deprived Areas: a Consultation on Proposal for a Local Economic Growth Initiative* (London: HMSO, 2005).
12. Doward, 'Wealthy elderly turn backs on seaside havens', *The Observer*, 26 July 2009.
13. S. Bridge, K. O'Neil and S. Cromie, *Understanding Enterprise, Entrepreneurship and Small Business* (Basingstoke: Palgrave Macmillan, 2003), ch. 4.
14. A. Clegg and S. Essex, 'Restructuring in tourism: the accommodation sector in a major British coastal resort', *International Journal of Tourism Research* 2(2) (2000), pp. 77–95.
15. A. A. Gibb, 'Small firms training and industrial competitiveness: building on the small firm as a learning organisation', *International Small Business Journal* 15(3) (1997), pp. 13–29.
16. W. Archer and J. Davison, *Graduate Employability: What Do Employers Think and Want?* (London: Council for Industry and Higher Education, 2008).
17. C. Hartshorn and L. Sear, 'Employability and enterprise: evidence from the North East', *Urban Studies* 42 (2005), pp. 271–83.
18. L. Lloyd-Reason and L. Sear, *Trading Places: SMEs in the Global Economy* (Cheltenham: Edward Elgar, 2008), ch. 12.
19. See note 3.
20. M. Parkinson, T. Hutchins, T. Champion et al. *State of the English Cities* (London: Office of the Deputy Prime Minister, 2006).
21. J. Seddon, *Systems Thinking in the Public Sector: the Future of the Reform Regime ... and a Manifesto for a Better Way* (Axminster: Triarchy Press, 2008).
22. SeaChange Initiative: see www. whitehallpages.net/modules.php?op=mod load&name=News&file=article&sid= 182828&mode=thread&order=0&tho ld=0 (accessed 18 December 2009).
23. See note 11.
24. See note 8.
25. See note 3.

26. G. Allinson, P. Braidford, M. Houston and I. Stone, *Myths Surrounding Starting and Running a Business* (Sheffield: Small Business Service, 2005).
27. See note 3.
28. See note 7.
29. A. Atherton, 'Unbundling enterprise and entrepreneurship: from perceptions and preconceptions to concept and practice', *International Journal of Entrepeneurship and Innovation*, May 2004, pp. 121–7; see also note 8.
30 See note 7.

Notes to Chapter 7

1. This précis is based on an essay 'What can arts and culture contribute in the regeneration of traditional English seaside resorts?' © Lesa Dryburgh. For the Clore Leadership Programme with support from the Arts and Humanities Research Council, supervised by staff at Leeds Metropolitan University. The full essay is available at www.cloreleadership.org/fellows_profile.php?name=lesa_dryburgh. Lesa Dryburgh is a communications consultant for the cultural industries and led the international communications for the Bathing Beauties® project conceived by artist Michael Trainor. She can be contacted at post@stopthepigeon.co.uk.
2. *The Contribution of Culture to Regeneration in the UK*. Report compiled for the Department for Culture, Media and Sport (DCMS).
3. Antony Gormley, *Another Place* (cast iron, 100 elements), situated at Crosby Beach, Merseyside, 1997.
4. Folkestone Triennial: see www.folkestonetriennial.org.uk.
5. Creative Foundation, Folkestone: see www.creativefoundation.org.uk.
6. Turner Contemporary, Margate: see www.turnercontemporary.org.
7. BBC1 South East, *The Politics Show*, 'Time for Turner', 23 November 2008.
8. The Great Promenade Show, Blackpool: see www.greatpromenadeshow.co.uk.
9. Michael Trainor, *They Shoot Horses, Don't They?* (mirrored glass, GRP, galvanised steel, 47,000 mirrors), situated at Blackpool South Shore Promenade, 2002.
10. Art Car Parade: see www.artcarparade.co.uk.
11. Lincolnshire Bathing Beauties®: see www.bathingbeauties.org.uk.

Notes to Chapter 8

1. See (e.g.) D. Throsby, Economics and Culture (Cambridge University Press, 2001); National Economic Research Associates, *The Value of the Built Heritage* (2003), ch. 2; www.english-heritage.org.uk/heritage.counts.old/newpdfs/DATA2.pdf (accessed 18 December 2009; 'eftec', *Valuation of the Historic Environment* (London: eftec, 2005).
2. This is, for example, a live issue in the politics of regeneration in Blackpool. For some recent historical examples, see: John K. Walton, 'Seaside politics', in *The British Seaside: Holidays and Resorts in the Twentieth Century* (Manchester University Press, 2000), ch. 7; and Riding on

Rainbows: *Blackpool Pleasure Beach and its Place in British Popular Culture* (St Albans: Skelter, 2007), pp. 71–3.

3. Alastair Fairley, *Bucking the Trend: the Life and Times of the Ninth Earl De La Warr* (Bexhill: Pavilion Trust, 2001), pp. 33–42.

4. Fred Gray, *Walking on Water: the West Pier Story* (Brighton: West Pier Trust, 1998); also *Designing the Seaside* (London: Reaktion, 2006); also see a letter from G. Lockwood to S. Johnson at www.westpier. co.uk/pdfs/letter16Feb04.pdf (accessed 18 December 2009).

5. Nigel Morgan and Annette Pritchard, *Power and Politics at the Seaside* (University of Exeter Press, 1999).

6. List of MPs, All-Parliamentary Group on Coastal Issues, Patrick Browne to John Walton, 16 July 2009; Leadership Centre for Local Government, Joe Simpson, 'Living on the edge: marginal and competitive coastal communities', Bournemouth, 2009; North-West Coastal Forum and 4NW, 'Understanding the Coastal Communities of the North-West', June 2009.

7. John K. Walton and C. F. O'Neill, 'Numbering the holidaymakers: the problems and possibilities of the June census of 1921 for historians of resorts', *Local Historian 23* (1993), pp. 205–16.

8. John K. Walton and David Tidswell, "Classified at random by veritable illiterates": the taking of the Spanish census of 1920 in Guipúzcoa province', *Continuity and Change* 20 (2005), pp. 287–313.

9. Edward Higgs, *A Clearer Sense of the Census* (London: HMSO, 1996); Joan Scott, *Gender and the Politics of History* (New York: Columbia University Press, 1988), ch. 6; L. Goldman, 'Statistics and the science of society in early Victorian Britain', *Social History of Medicine 4* (1991), pp. 415–34.

10. Gareth Stedman Jones, Outcast London (Oxford University Press, 1970); Stephen Reynolds, *A Poor Man's House* (London: London Magazine Edns, 1980, first published 1908); George Meek, George Meek, Bath Chair-man: By Himself (London: Constable, 1910); John K. Walton, 'Seaside economies', in *The British Seaside: Holidays and Resorts in the Twentieth Century* (Manchester University Press, 2000), ch. 6.

11. T. H. MacDonald, *Basic Concepts in Statistics and Epidemiology* (Abingdon: Radcliffe, 2007); Allyson Pollock et al., NHS plc (London: Verso, 2005).

12. Shalini Singh (ed.), 'Introduction', in *Domestic Tourism in Asia: Diversity and Divergence* (London: Earthscan, 2009).

13. David J. James, 'Overview of STEAM', GTS (UK) Ltd, 24 March 2003.

14. See Casino Advisory Panel: www.culture. gov.uk/Cap/proposals.htm (accessed 18 December 2009).

15. See note 13.

16. Articulated in the Allnutt Report in 2004'.

17. Memorandum of Professors John E. Fletcher and Victor Middleton to the Select Committee on Culture, Media and Sport, January 2008.

18. This report can be found at www. partnersforengland.com (accessed 26 August 2009).

19. See (e.g.) www.local.communities.gov.uk/ finance/1011/swg/SWG-09-15.pdf (accessed 25 August 2009).

20. John K. Walton, 'Municipal government and the holiday industry in Blackpool, 1876–1914', in J. K. Walton and J. Walvin (eds), *Leisure in Britain, 1780–1939* (Manchester University Press, 1983), pp. 158–85; John K. Walton, Blackpool (Edinburgh University Press, 1998).

21. This can be suspected, but not demonstrated: see (e.g.) J. Simmons, *The Railway in Town and Country, 1830–1914* (Newton Abbot: David & Charles,

1986); and T. R. Gourvish, *British Railways 1948–73: a Business History* (Cambridge University Press, 1986), ch. 10.

22. S. Billi et al., 'Coastal tourism in Italy: best practices, trends and models', abstract submitted to international conference 'Resorting to the Coast', in *Conference Handbook*, Centre for Tourism and Cultural Change and Institute of Northern Studies, Leeds Metropolitan University, at the Winter Gardens, Blackpool, 25–29 June 2009, p. 20.

23. Chris Bull and Steve Hayler, 'The changing role of live entertainment at English seaside resorts at the beginning of the twentieth century', *Tourism Geographies* 11 (2009), pp. 281–307.

24. See www.admissionallclasses.com.

25. John K. Walton and Jason Wood, 'World heritage seaside', *British Archaeology* 90 (Sept/Oct 2006), pp. 10–15.

26. See especially Allan Brodie and Gary Winter, *England's Seaside Resorts* (Swindon: English Heritage, 2007).

27. L. Gibson and J. Pendlebury (eds), *Valuing Historic Environments* (Aldershot: Ashgate, 2009).

28. See (e.g.) Tony Ray-Jones, *A Day Off: an English Journal* (London: Thames & Hudson, 1974); also Russell Roberts, *Tony Ray-Jones* (London: Chris Boot, 2004); Martin Parr, *The Last Resort*, 2nd edn (Stockport: Dewi Lewis, 1998); P. Garner, *A Seaside Album: Photographs and Memory* (London: Royal Pavilion Association, 2003); Val Williams, *Martin Parr* (London: Phaidon, 2002); and recent exhibitions at the National Media Museum, Bradford, the Museum of Childhood, Victoria and Albert Museum, London, and the National Maritime Museum, Greenwich.

29. Most recently 'Once Upon a Time in Revoe', 2009.

30. C. Ward and D. Hardy, *Arcadia for All* (London: Mansell, 1984); A. Dowling, *Humberston Fitties* (Cleethorpes: A. Dowling, 2001).

31. See www.bbc.co.uk/photography/genius/gallery/jones.phtml (accessed 29 August 2009).

32. Report of the Casino Advisory Panel, 30 January 2007.

Notes to Chapter 9

1. David Powell Associates with Fred Gray, *South East Coastal Towns: Economic Challenges and Cultural Regeneration* (August 2009), a report funded by SEEDA and commissioned through the Creative Foundation on behalf of Arun District Council, Creative Foundation, Margate Renewal Partnership, Portsmouth City Council, Shepway District Council, SEEDA, University of Chichester and the University of Portsmouth. The research reviewed 30 indicators of local economic performance and deprivation/prosperity over the period 2000 to 2008. Contact details: f.g.gray@sussex.ac.uk and david.powell@dpa-ltd.co.uk.

Notes to Chapter 10

1. [Sub-National Review of Economic Development and Regeneration.] – Sub-National Review of Economic Development and Regeneration – HM Treasury July 2007
2. [The new proposals for Planning Policy Statement (PPS) 4 point to a positive and more integrated way forward in this context.] - Draft Planning Policy Statement 4 – "Planning for Prosperous Economies" – Department of Communities and Local Government - May 2009
3. Matthew Taylor's recent review of rural economies and housing ... about what makes a settlement sustainable.] – "Living Working Countryside – The Taylor Review of Rural Economy and Affordable Housing" Department of Communities and Local Government July 2008
4. Globe Regeneration (www.globelimited.co.uk) and Rocket Science (www.rocketsciencelab.co.uk). It can be viewed on-line at www.communities.gov.uk. DCLG guidance can be found at: http://www.communities.gov.uk/publications/localgovernment/localeconomicassessments
5. [Transforming Place, Changing Lives: a Framework for Regeneration, CLG July 2008.] – Nothing to add!!
6. [Houghton Review.] – "Tackling Worklessness: A Review of the contribution and role of local authorities and partnerships - Final Report" Department for Communities and Local Government March 2009.
7. The Nomenclature of Territorial Units for Statistics (NUTS, for the French *nomenclature d'unités territoriales statistiques*) is a geocode standard for referencing the administrative divisions of countries for statistical purposes. The standard was developed by the European Union.
8. [This work was prepared for evidence I gave to an All Party Parliamentary Inquiry into rural coastal deprivation.] All Party Parliamentary Group Coastal and Marine – Inquiry into deprivation and disadvantage in coastal rural areas – 3rd session 8 July 2009 House of Commons – Chaired by Norman Lamb MP supported by Coastnet as the secretariat.
9. [rural–urban definitions developed by Professor John Shepherd for the 2004 Rural Strategy.] – "Rural Strategy 2004. Department for Environment, Food and Rural Affairs" July 2004

Notes to Chapter 11

1. The Improvement and Development Agency (IDeA) have funded this chapter as part of their work within the Healthy Communities Programme (see www.idea.gov.uk/idk/core). The programme aims to build the capacity of local authorities to tackle health inequalities, provide leadership to promote wellbeing, foster a joined-up approach to health improvement across local government itself, and through partnership working improve the impact of LAAs and LSPs on the health and wellbeing of the local community. Thanks are due to Julia Sherfield and Liam Hughes (IDeA) and to Patrick Browne for comments on the draft text. Thanks to Paul Iggulden

for comments on the survey design. Thanks to the Association of Directors of Public Health for assistance with the survey. Finally, thanks to all survey respondents and all those who contributed to the case studies.

2. World Health Organization, *Constitution*, available at www.who.int/governance/eb/who_constitution_en.pdf (accessed 18 December 2009).

3. Comment of a respondent to the IDeA survey.

4. HM Treasury and Department of Health, Tackling Health Inequalities: Summary of the 2002 Cross-cutting Review (London, 2002); available at www.hm-treasury.gov.uk.

5. Further information on, and results from, this survey can be found at www.idea.gov.uk.

6. C. Beatty and S. Fothergill, *The Seaside Economy,* final report of the seaside town project, Sheffield Hallam University, 2003; available at www.shu.ac.uk.

7. Personal communication, D. Harrison, Deputy Regional Director of Public Health, Department of Health North West, 2009.

8. Communities and Local Government Committee, *Coastal Towns: Second Report of Session 2006–7*, HC 351.2007 House of Commons; available at www.publications.parliament.uk.

9. C. Bambra, K. Joyce and A. Maryon-Davis, *Priority Public Health Conditions*, final report prepared on behalf of Task Group 8, 2009: Strategic Review of Health Inequalities in England post-2010 (Marmot Review); available at www.ucl.ac.uk/gheg/marmotreview.

10. A. Costello, M. Abbas, A. Allen et al., Managing the health effects of climate change, *The Lancet* 373 (2009), pp. 1693–733; available at www.thelancet.com/journals/lancet/issue/current?tab=pastwww.thelancet.com.

11. Personal communication, Patrick Browne,

'Definition of a coastal resort', 2009.

12. HM Treasury, Department for Business, Enterprise and Regulatory Reform, and Department for Communities and Local Government, *Review of Sub-national Economic Development and Regeneration*, 2007. Available at www.hm-treasury.gov.uk.

13. Communities and Local Government Committee. Coastal Towns: *First Report of Session 2007–8*, HC 69.2007 House of Commons; available at www.publications.parliament.uk. See also notes 5 and 7.

14. John Walton, in his foreword to the coastal futures symposium report (2006), argues that while traditional tourism has declined since its heyday in the 1950s and 60s, it continues to be a vital and important industry that should not be overlooked.

15. R. G. Wilkinson and M. Marmot, *Social Determinants of Health: the Solid Facts*, 2nd edn (Denmark: World Health Organization, 2003). Available at www.euro.who.int/InformationSources/Publications/Catalogue/20020808_2 (accesed 18 December 2009).

16. Department of Health, 'New Horizons: Government consults on mental health and well-being', DH website, 2009. Available at www.dh.gov.uk/en/News/Recentstories/DH_103186.

17. H. Barton, 'A health map for urban planners: towards a conceptual model for healthy sustainable settlements', *Built Environment* 31 (2005), pp. 339–55.

18. G. Dahlgren and M. Whitehead, *Policies and Strategies to Promote Social Equity in Health* (Stockholm: Institute for Future Studies, 1991).

19. Commission on the Social Determinants of Health, *Closing the Gap in a Generation: Health Equity through Action on the Social Determinants of Health* (World Health Organization, 2008); available at

www.who.int/social_determinants/final_
report/en/index.html. Also see:
Department of Health (available at
www.dh.gov.uk), Tackling Health
Inequalities: a Programme for Action, 2003;
*Tackling Health Inequalities 10 Years On:
a Review of Developments in Tackling Health
Inequalities in England, 2009; Health
Inequalities: Progress and Next Steps*, 2008.

20. Health Select Committee report on health
inequalities; available at www.publications.
parliament.uk/pa/cm200809/cmselect/
cmhealth/286/28610.htm#a80 (accessed
18 December 2009).

21. Communities and Local Government
Committee, Coastal Towns: *First
Report of Session 2007–8*, HC 69.2007
House of Commons; available at www.
publications.parliament.uk.

22. Association of Public Health Observatories,
Welcome to Health Profiles: available at
www.apho.org.uk/defaultaspx?RID=49802.

23. H. Walford and S. Brodhurst, 'What makes
coastal areas different? The facts and
figures', PowerPoint presentation, 2007.

24. M. Whitehead, 'A typology of actions to
tackle social inequalities in health', *Journal of
Epidemiology and Community Health* 61
(2007), pp. 473–8.

25. See www.idea.gov.uk.

26. Case study: with thanks to Jonathan Sexton,
Consultant in Public Health, NHS Eastern &
Coastal Kent.

27. Canterbury City Council, *Connecting Herne
Bay Area Action Plan: Preferred Options*,
CCCI Local Development Framework,
2008; available at www.canterbury.gov.uk.

28. L. Hovard, D. West, A. Cooke and
D. Haywood, *Health Impact Assessment:
Connecting Herne Bay* (Herne Bay Area
Action Plan Preferred Options Document)
2009, Public Health Resource Unit for NHS
Eastern and Coastal Kent.

29. Case study: with thanks to Janet Goult,
Practice Manager, Mablethorpe Health

Centre. Information on the Mablethorpe
Health Centre can be found at www.
Marisco.GPsurgery.net.

30. East Lindsey District Council, *Council and
Democracy*: www.e-lindsey.gov.uk/council.

31. Mablethorpe Imagineering Workshop press
release: www.e-lindsey.gov.uk/News/
media/media_releases/mabworkshop-
16022009.cfm.

32. Case study: with thanks to Tim Allison,
Director of Public Health, NHS East Riding
of Yorkshire and East Riding of Yorkshire
Council. *Sources*: D. Zenner and T. Allison,
'Health of caravan park residents: a cross-
sectional study in the East Riding of
Yorkshire', 2006; T. Allison, L. Gowland,
N. Belt and T. Hall, 'Improving health on
the coast', PowerPoint presentation to
East Riding Local Strategic Partnership,
2009; D. Zenner and T. Allison, 'Health
in caravan park communities: a cross-
sectional study in the East Riding of
Yorkshire', PowerPoint presentation, 2006.

33. Case study: with thanks to Tom Scanlon,
Director of Public Health, NHS Brighton
and Hove, and Tim Nichols, Head of
Environmental Health and Licensing,
Brighton and Hove City Council.

34. 2020 Community Partnership, *Reducing
Crime and Improving Safety: Alcohol*, 2007;
available at www.brighton-hove.gov.uk/
index.cfm?request=c1165405 (accessed
18 December 2009).

35. Local Alcohol Profiles for England, 'Profile
of alcohol related harm – Brighton and
Hove', 2008; available at www.nwph.net/
alcohol/lape.

36. P. Iggulden, E. Ison and B. Cave, 'Health
Impact Assessment of the introduction of
flexible alcohol hours in Brighton and
Hove', Ben Cave Associates Ltd for
Brighton and Hove City Council and NHS
Brighton and Hove, 2009.

37. Home Office, *Explanatory Notes to
Licensing Act 2003*; available at www.opsi.

gov.uk/acts/acts2003/en/
ukpgaen_20030017_en_1 (accessed 18
December 2009).

38. Case study: with thanks to Steve Weaver,
Tim Coglan and Karen Smith at Blackpool
Council and Steve Morton at NHS
Blackpool.

39. Visit Blackpool, *Blackpool – Feel the Buzz*:
www.visitblackpool.com/site/things-to-do.

40. Department of Health and Association
of Public Health Observatories, *Health
Profile: Blackpool*, 2009; available at www.
apho.org.uk.

41. NHS Blackpool, 'ALTN8: campaign to
crack town's drinking culture', available at
www.blackpool.nhs.uk/index.php/
blackpool-life/altn8.

42. Health Select Committee, 'Memorandum
of the Local Government Association
(AL 33)', 2009: available at www.
publications.parliament.uk/pa/cm200809/
cmselect/cmhealth/368/368we34.htm
(accessed 18 December 2009).

43. Chartered Institute of Public Finance and
Accountancy, *Trading Standards Statistics*,
2008; available at www.cipfastats.net.

44. Case study: with thanks to Mike Studden,
Regional Head of Environmental Hazards,
Health Protection Agency. Information on
the 'Our coast and public health'
conference can be found at www.hpa-
events.org.uk/hpa/frontend/reg/thome.cs
p?pageID=17107&CSPCHDx=00000000
00000&CSPIHN=108058-108058:80&CS
PSCN=CSPSESSIONID&eventID=54
(accessed 18 December 2009).

45. Office of National Statistics, *Regional Profile
South West*, 2009; available at www.
statistics.gov.uk/cci/nugget.asp?id=1134
(accessed 18 December 2009).

46. Adrian Roper, SW Coast Path Team,
'Our coast and public health' conference
2006. Environment Workshop: key points.

47. Office of the Deputy Prime Minister,
Local Government Act 2000 (London:

HMSO); available at www.opsi.gov.uk.

48. Royal Town Planning Institute, *Delivering
Healthy Communities*, RTPI Good Practice
Note 5, 2009; available at www.rtpi.org.uk.
See also NHS Healthy Urban Development
Unit, *Health and Urban Planning Toolkit*,
2007; available at www.
healthyurbandevelopment.nhs.uk.

49. N. Cavill, Building Health: *Creating and
Enhancing Places for Healthy, Active Lives.
What needs to be done?* (National Heart
Forum, 2007); available at www.
heartforum.org.uk. See also National
Institute for Health and Clinical Excellence,
Physical Activity and the Environment,
2008; available at www.nice.org.uk/PH008
(accessed 18 December 2009).

50. Department of Health, Draft advice on
assessing population and human health
within Strategic Environmental Assessment
European Directive 2001/42/EC.
Consultation document, 2007; available at
www.dh.gov.uk.

51. See note 23.

52 S. Curtis, B. Cave and A. Coutts, 'Is urban
regeneration good for health? Perceptions
and theories of the health impacts of urban
change'. *Environment and Planning C:
Government and Policy* 20 (2002), pp.
517–34. See also H. Thomson, R.
Atkinson, M. Petticrew and A. Kearns, 'Do
urban regeneration programmes improve
public health and reduce health inequalities?
A synthesis of the evidence from UK
policy and practice (1980–2004)', *Journal of
Epidemiology and Community Health* 60
(2006), pp. 108–15. See also C. Bambra,
M. Gibson, M. Petticrew et al., 'Tackling
the wider social determinants of health
and health inequalities: evidence from
systematic reviews', Short Report 5 (Public
Health Research Consortium, 2008,
available at www.york.ac.uk).

53. H. Thomson, 'A dose of realism for healthy
urban policy: lessons from area-based

initiatives in the UK', Journal of Epidemiology and Community Health 62 (2008), pp. 932–6.

Notes to Chapter 12

1. Economic and Social Research Council, *Mapping the Public Policy Landscape: Demographic Aspects of Population Ageing* (Swindon: ESRC, 2006).
2. BBC News, 'Population growth at 47-year high', 2009; available at http://news.bbc.co.uk/1/hi/uk/8224520.stm (accessed 18 December 2009).
3. R. Baker, 'Age discrimination and bio-medicine', Speech to Council of Europe Ethics Committee Conference, Dubrovnik, April 2005.
4. Commission for Rural Communities, *The State of the Countryside* (Cheltenham: CRC, 2008).
5. *Ibid.*
6. Commission for Rural Communities, *The State of the Countryside* (Cheltenham: CRC, 2007).
7. *Ibid.*
8. Countryside Agency, *The State of the Countryside* (Cheltenham: Countryside Agency, 2004).
9. J. Atterton, Ageing and Coastal Communities: *Final Report for Lincolnshire Coastal Action Zone* (Centre for Rural Economy Research, 2006); available online at www.ncl.ac.uk/cre/publish/researchreports. See also note 6.
10. For further information, see D. Vickers, P. Rees and M. Birkin, 'A New classification of UK local authorities using 2001 Census key statistics', University of Leeds working paper 03/03, October 2003.
11. C. Beatty and S. Fothergill, 'Economic change and the labour market in Britain's seaside towns', *Regional Studies* 38 (2004),

54. IDeA, *Join Our Health Community of Practice*, 2008; available at www.idea.gov.uk/idk/core/page.do?pageId=8988247 (accessed 18 December 2009).

pp. 461–80.
12. J. Shepherd, *A Typology of the Smaller Rural Towns of England*, 2009; available online at www.rerc.ac.uk.
13. S. Baines, M. Lie and J. Wheelock, 'Volunteering, self-help and citizenship in later life: a collaborative research project by Age Concern Newcastle and the University of Newcastle upon Tyne', 2004
14. European Policies Research Centre, *Regions for All Ages: the Implications of Demographic Ageing for Regional Policy*, final report prepared by the European Policies Research Centre, University of Strathclyde to the Regions for All Ages Research Programme (supported by the European Older People's Platform [AGE], Age Concern England, Northern Ireland Executive Office, North West Regional Assembly and Scottish Enterprise, January 2006.
15. 'How Britain is coming to terms with growing old', *The Guardian*, 17 May 2009; available at www.guardian.co.uk/uk/2009/may/17/ageing-population-retirement-saga-housing (accessed 18 December 2009).
16. R. C. Cressy and D. J. Storey, 'Small business risk: a firm and bank perspective', SME Centre working paper 39, 1995. See also A. Green, 'Employment and the older person in the countryside', in P. Lowe and L. Speakman (eds), *The Ageing Countryside: the Growing Older Population of Rural England* (London: Age Concern, 2006), pp. 94–118. See also R. Moreton, E, Malhomme, L. South and P.

Taylor, *Rural Lifelines: Older People and Rural Social Enterprises* (London: Plunkett Foundation, PRIME, Countryside Agency and Age Concern, 2004).

17. A. Atherton and K. Frith, *Lincolnshire's Future Entrepreneurial Economy: a Study of the Significance and Potential of Business Start-ups to the County's Development*, final report on behalf of Lincolnshire Enterprise and Lincolnshire Development, December 2005.

18. See note 11.

19. R. Baker and L. Speakman, 'The older rural consumer', in P. Lowe and L. Speakman (eds), *The Ageing Countryside: the Growing Older Population of Rural England* (London: Age Concern, 2006), pp. 119–32.

20. M. Godfrey, J. Townsend and T. Denby, *Building a Good Life for Older People in Local Communities* (York: Joseph Rowntree Foundation, 2004). See also A. Green, 'Employment and the older person in the countryside', in P. Lowe and L. Speakman (eds), *The Ageing Countryside: The Growing Older Population of Rural England* (London: Age Concern, 2006), pp. 94–118. See also N. Le Mesurier, 'The contributions of older people to rural community and citizenship', loc. cit., pp. 133–46. See also R. Moreton, E. Malhomme, L. South and P. Taylor, *Rural Lifelines: Older People and Rural Social Enterprises* (Plunkett Foundation, PRIME, Countryside Agency and Age Concern, 2004). See also Office for National Statistics, *National Survey of Voluntary Activity 1997.*

21. G. C. Wenger, 'Help in old age: facing up to a change', a Longitudinal Network Study, Institute of Human Ageing, occasional paper 5 (Liverpool University Press, 1992).

22. K. Croucher, *Making the Case for Retirement Villages* (York: Joseph Rowntree Foundation, 2006).

23. J. McLaren and M. Hakim, *A Better Life: Private Sheltered Housing and Independent Living for Older People* (London: McCarthy Stone/HMSO, 2004); available at www.mccarthyandstone.co.uk/pdf/McCarthyStone_Final.pdf. See also K. Croucher, Making the Case for Retirement Villages (York: Joseph Rowntree Foundation, 2006).

24. D. Brown and N. Glasgow, *Rural Retirement Migration* (New York: Springer, 2008); N. Glasgow and R. Reeder, 'Economic and fiscal implications of nonmetropolitan retirement migration', *Journal of Applied Gerontology* 9 (1990), pp. 433–51.

25. D. Brown and N. Glasgow, *Rural Retirement Migration* (New York: Springer, 2008).

26. Retirement Special, *The Sunday Times*, 30 April 2006.

27. 'How Britain is coming to terms with growing old', *The Guardian*, 17 May 2009; available at www.guardian.co.uk/uk/2009/may/17/ageing-population-retirement-saga-housing (accessed 18 December 2009).

28. BBC News (2009), 'Sunny side down' (http://news.bbc.co.uk/1/hi/magazine/7937086.stm); also 'Weak sterling income sends ex-pats packing' (http://news.bbc.co.uk/1/hi/business/7918723.stm). See also The Times Online (2009), 'The pain in Spain proves too much as expat Britons pack their bags' (http://www.timesonline.co.uk/tol/money/pensions/article6297037.ece). Sites accesed 18 December 2009.

29. K. O'Reilly, *The British on the Costa del Sol* (London: Routledge, 2000); C. Oliver, *Retirement Migration: Paradoxes of Ageing* (London: Routledge, 2008).

Notes to Chapter 13

1. S. M. Hayler, 'Live entertainment at the seaside', *Cultural Trends* 13 (2004), pp. 41–75; see also S. M. Hayler and C. J. Bull, 'The changing role of live entertainment at seaside resorts at the beginning of the 21st century', *Tourism Geographies* 11 (Aug 2009).
2. S. M. Hayler, 'Live entertainment at the seaside: how far a part of the cultural offer?', *Leisure Societies Association* (2008), pp. 135–42.
3. L. Dryburgh, 'What can arts and culture contribute in the regeneration of traditional English seaside resorts?', School of Cultural Studies, Leeds Metropolitan University, 2009.

Index

A

Action for Employment - 103

Admission All Classes - 127

Ageing - 175ff

ageing population - 43, 87, 176

negative perceptions - 97, 181

pyramid - 25

structures - 177

Alcohol – 25, 51, 61, 62, 160ff

Allnutt Report 2004 - 125

Antisocial behaviour – 66, 89, 123, 162, 169

Area Action Plans (AAPs) - 50, 194

Audit Commission – 86, 88, 102

B

Baby boom – 176, 177

Barriers to regeneration – 43,

Bathing Beauties® - 115

Bathing machines - 188

Bathing water quality - 120

Beach huts - 2, 19, 115, 116 188

Beatty, see Fothergill

Benefit claimants – 32, 35, 42, 43, 51, 53, 157

Big Lottery Fund – 209, 210

Birkenhead - 14

Black economy - 123

British Resorts and Destinations Association (BRADA) - 3, 6, 14, 34, 55, 115

British Urban Regeneration Association (BURA) - 6, 55

Broadband access - 86

Business

development - 98

incubation - 102

support - 98

Business Link - 103, 106, 206

Butlins – 133, 135

C

Cambridge Economic Impact model - 119

Caravans - 38, 41, 42 , 87, 157, 159, 167

Care in the community – 25

Casino Advisory Panel – 123, 127, 129

CCA – 36, 48, 49, 54, 56, 57, 61, 98

Centre for Regional Economic and Social Research (CRESR) – 29

Checklists:

coastal facilitation – 216, 219

self-assessment – 217-227

Climate change – 33, 43, 44, 46, 50, 55, 59, 60, 91, 139, 153, 161, 16, 191, 192, 202, 208

CoaST - 60

Coastal

authorities (map) - 31

erosion – 38, 91, 139, 153, 202